new york

a **Virgin** pocket guide

First published in 2001
Virgin Publishing Ltd, London w6 9HA

contents

Written by 20 contributors in-the-know, this guide gives the inside take on New York. The focus is on having fun; where to hang out, shop, eat, relax, enjoy and spoil yourself. And there's a selection of the top cultural hot spots...

area lowdown

Mayor Giuliani's citywide clean up may have turned NY into a kind of sanitized theme park, but it's one hell of a theme park: chichi, edgy, boho, society – the Big Apple comes in many flavours.

bronx
♀off map

A few major attractions (Bronx Zoo, Botanical Gardens, Yankee Stadium) and recent investment mean the Bronx is no longer a no-go zone. The elevated subway lines go through NY's most ethnically diverse communities and provide a safe view of the erstwhile battlegrounds of the South Bronx.

brooklyn
♀off map

Manhattan's skyrocketing rents have turned Brooklyn into an appealing alternative. Over the last 150 years generations of immigrants have settled here, their diversity contributing to the wild variety of neighbourhoods, from up-and-coming Fort Greene, artsy Williamsburg, and elegant Brooklyn Heights, to the irresistibly tacky Coney Island and the Russian enclave of Brighton Beach. Gentrified areas provide the requisite cool cafés, boutiques, and restaurants to meet the needs of the fashionable bohos who now call this borough home.

chelsea & the meatpacking district
♀maps 9–10

Following the defection of Manhattan's gay scene from West Village, and the relocation of influential art dealers from Soho, Chelsea has recently exploded with a variety of venues (fab boutiques, hip bars and eateries, big-deal nightclubs, and major contemporary art spaces) drawing the city's cool and queer crowd. More white-hot art galleries and hang-outs can be found in the Meatpacking District on Chelsea's southernmost edge. But Chelsea's new image still has a place for the enduring Chelsea Hotel – where Sid Vicious killed girlfriend Nancy Spungen in 1978 – which adds to the area's somewhat seedy fascination.

east village
♀maps 11–12

The refuge of choice for the dispossessed: over the last century the East Village has attracted Eastern European immigrants (early 1900s), Allen Ginsberg and the Beats (1950s), hippies and free thinkers (1960s), punk rockers (1970s), and experimental artists and performers (1980s). These days, this area still boasts a vibrant energy all of its own. Alphabet City's Hispanic joints and downhome Eastern European restaurants sit next to trendy boutiques and funky bistros. In spite of the influx of young professionals and bridge-and-tunnel crowd, street culture is really what counts and it's easy to spend a good few hours ogling the non-stop parade of colourful folk and free spirits who call East Village home.

gramercy park & the flatiron district ✎maps 9–10

The area encompassing Gramercy Park, Union Square, the Flatiron District, and Madison Square Park was the height of fashion in the 19th century, when it was home to the likes of Edith Wharton and the Roosevelts. Then the rich migrated uptown, leaving this neighbourhood's lovely buildings to fall into disrepair and its pretty parks to become squalid. Now, city clean-ups, renovations, and the arrival of publishing, advertising, and new media companies have rejuvenated the area, which is a haven for those in search of fine dining (especially around Union Square and Gramercy Park) and historic architecture. Shoppers also fare well, particularly for home furnishings around the Flatiron building.

harlem & the heights ✎maps 1–2

Harlem holds an vital place in African-American history: the great jazz musicians lived here in the 20s; in the 60s this was the centre for black activism; and in the 80s rap burst onto its mean streets. Although still predominantly black in population, more and more young New Yorkers of all ethnic origins are moving in. You can still see the signs of urban decay which gave Harlem a bad rap, but there are also rows of beautiful brownstones, cheap eateries, and the colourful chaos of 125th Street. Just south, in Morningside Heights, home to Columbia University, the streets are flooded with students and lined with bookstores and cafés.

lower east side & chinatown ✎maps 11–12

Nowadays, the tenement buildings of the Lower East Side (LES), Manhattan's one-time Jewish ghetto, are more likely to be occupied by Hispanics and Koreans than Hassidim. However, evidence of the district's ancestry can still be found in its die-hard delis and crumbling synagogues. Recently, a new generation of dream-seekers – boutique keepers, bar owners, trust-fund anarchists, and latter-day bohos – has migrated here in search of lower rents. As a result, real estate prices have rocketed, and the LES has been reborn as Hipster Central. Chinatown, meanwhile, remains irrepressibly Oriental. Bolstered by a steady stream of Chinese immigration, it teems with authentic markets, restaurants, and teahouses. In spite of its proximity to ritzier, more gentrified areas, Chinatown's booming, energetic stronghold will probably never be fully repressed.

lower manhattan ✎maps 13–14

Bustling by day, ghost town by night, the tapered end of the island of Manhattan is home to City Hall, Wall Street, and the NY Stock Exchange. New residential developments in Battery Park City house the movers and shakers living in the shadow of the World Trade Center.

area lowdown

midtown & hell's kitchen   ⊘maps 7–8

For many, New Yorkers office-heavy Midtown means only one thing: work. But with its vertigo-inducing skycrapers, world-famous hotels, fancy stores, and expensive restaurants, Manhattan's central segment is as exciting for the visitor as any place on earth. Its hub is Times Square, a dazzling neon morass cut through by *the* Broadway, with its slew of legendary theatres, and 42nd Street – once the city's red light district, now a haven of theme stores and renovated theatres. To the west, Hell's Kitchen – formerly the stamping ground of Irish and Hispanic immigrants – is a fully gentrified neighbourhood. Directly south is the busy Garment District, home to clothing manufacturers and textile wholesalers. And the vista of Fifth Avenue's historic skyscrapers to the east, can take the breath away.

nolita & noho   ⊘maps 11–12

Nolita (north of Little Italy) is yet another acronym created by the city's sharp real estators. It is not just the name that has changed, however. Over the last few years, Italian delis and restaurants have mostly been driven out and the area has become so gentrified that it's hard to imagine these were once the mean streets on which Scorsese grew up and Coppola filmed The Godfather. The neighbourhood's characteristic red brick buildings hung with fire escapes are now home to some of the coolest boutiques, cafés, and bars. Next door Noho (north of Houston) is a tiny, laid-back enclave which holds a smattering of chic attractions, including a few of NY's hottest names in both fashion and food.

queens   ⊘off map

Visitors to the Big Apple (and most New Yorkers) will probably only see Queens when journeying to or from its two airports. But the borough's multicultural make-up has lots to offer, including Long Island City's PS1 – the super-cool studio space and gallery, the Greek 'hood of Astoria, Irish Woodside, and Indian and South American Jackson Heights. The huge steel 'Unisphere' globe (as seen in Men in Black) is a leftover from the 1964 world fair in Corona Park.

soho   ⊘maps 11–12

The big-name designer stores, elegant restaurants, and exclusive bars clustered in tiny Soho could only act as a magnet for fashion and media types. Even if you don't run into Gwyneth Paltrow in Miu Miu, catching sight of some impossibly thin beauty dashing to a shoot at one of the many local photo studios is a regular occurrence. Despite so many manifest distractions, Soho's magnificent architecture, largely comprising 19th-century monumental cast-iron buildings, is hard to ignore. While there are still plenty of highbrow art galleries, the cutting-edge art scene has shifted to Chelsea, causing many to observe that Soho's reign as the coolest neighbourhood in NYC could well almost be over.

With its availability of cavernous factory and warehouse space, Tribeca (the Triangle Below Canal Street) has emerged as the Hollywood of the East Coast – both Robert De Niro's Tribeca Films and Miramax are based here. In spite of its chic eateries and bars and a smattering of interesting stores, the area feels positively residential. Starry residents include Bobby himself and Harvey Keitel, who, if you believe the gossip pages, can be seen regularly chowing down in the local diners. In reality, you're more likely to encounter bankers and brokers who have made Tribeca their home for its proximity to the neighbouring Financial District.

upper east side   *maps 3–4 & 5–6*

The UES is the domain of New York's financial aristocracy. From Fifth Avenue's exclusive clubs and 19th-century mansion houses built by some of America's legendary millionaires to Madison Avenue's flagship designer stores and commercial art galleries where the fake-tan-and-fur-coat brigade flock, to the magnificent museums along the edge of Central Park, every inch of this privileged enclave screams big money. East of Lexington Avenue, the prevailing atmosphere becomes more neighbourly and family-oriented, but it's still far from edgy.

upper west side   *maps 3–4 & 5–6*

Characterized by its spacious avenues, landmark apartment buildings, and closeness to Central Park, the UWS feels like a residential neighbourhood, albeit a very rarefied one. Celebrity sightings are plentiful and you might even run into famous locals like Woody Allen at Zabar's deli or Jerry Seinfeld at the Reebok gym. Without the distraction of happening nightspots or cutting-edge stores, residents (including lots of well-to-do families) take pride in two of the city's most important cultural institutions – the Lincoln Center and the American Museum of Natural History – plus a healthy sprinkling of dining options.

west village   *maps 11–12*

In the heady 60s, when Bob Dylan and Joan Baez busked in Washington Square, Greenwich Village was the centre of the bohemian universe. While associations still persist, the image of this neighbourhood as a haven for artistic types became outdated a good 20 years ago. Today the term West Village denotes the blocks of tacky, tourist-geared shops and bars in the area's eastern reaches as well as the pretty tree-lined streets and beautiful brownstones further west. Needless to say, this part of town is now home to those who can afford to live in such elegant abodes. The area's strong gay identity is still key, though the edgier gay scene has moved to Chelsea. For some residual bohemia, Washington Square Park, in the shadow of the NYU buildings, is still a hang-out for students, skate kids and, to this day, busking Dylan wannabes.

Village Idiot (neighbourhood bar) 143

CLUBS
Baktun 156
Hell (club) 161
Limelight 156
Tunnel 158
Twilo (club) 161

RESTAURANTS & CAFÉS
A Different Light (café) 160
Alley's End (American) 82
Big Cup (cafés) 159
Bottino (Italian) 115
Bright Food Shop (global & fusion) 111
Cafeteria (American) 83
El Cid (Spanish) 132
El Rey del Sol (Mexican) 126
Empire Diner (diner) 105
F&B (Scandinavian) 130
Joe Jr's (diner) 105
La Lunchonette (French) 110
Le Gamin (cafés & coffee shops) 100
Markt (Belgian) 93
Negril (African & Caribbean) 82
O Padeiro (Portuguese) 129
Petite Abeille (Belgian) 93
Red Cat (American) 90
Restaurant 147 (American) 90
Rocking Horse Café Mexicano (Mexican) 127
The Tonic (American) 91

SHOPPING
Annex Flea Market (market) 67
Apartment 48 (interiors & furniture) 62
Auto (interiors & furniture) 62
Barney's Co-Op (streetwear) 74
Bed Bath and Beyond (interiors & furniture) 62
Chelsea Garden Store (gifts & stationery) 59
Chelsea Market (food store) 56
Comme des Garçons (designer clothes) 40
Dave's New York (streetwear) 75
Eclectic Home (interiors & furniture) 63
Garden of Eden (food store) 57

Hold Everything (interiors & furniture) 63
Works Thrift Shop (thrift store) 77
Jazz Record Center (CDs, records & tapes) 32
Jeffrey (department stores) 37
La Maison Moderne (interiors & furniture) 64
Lee's Mardi Gras (menswear) 69
Loehmann's (discount stores) 53
Mxyplyzyk (interiors & furniture) 64
Old Navy (chain stores) 35
Raymond Dragon (menswear) 69
Tom of Finland (menswear) 70
Williams-Sonoma (interiors & furniture) 65

SIGHTS, MUSEUMS & GALLERIES
Barbara Gladstone (commercial gallery) 191
Dia Center for the Arts (art museum/gallery) 185—6
John Weber (commercial gallery) 192
Matthew Marks Gallery (commercial gallery) 192
Metro Pictures (commercial gallery) 192
Pat Hearn (commercial gallery) 192
Paula Cooper (commercial gallery) 192
303 Gallery (commercial gallery) 193

East Village

BARS
Alphabet Lounge (DJ bar) 137
Angel's Share (quiet retreat) 153
Baraza (DJ bar) 137
Black & White (cocktail & champagne bar) 139
The Cock (bar) 159
Dick's (bar) 159
Decibel (theme bar) 149
Drinkland (DJ bar) 138
Guernica (DJ bar) 138
Joe's Bar (theme bar) 149
KGB (theme bar) 149

Flatiron District

Gramercy Park

Harlem

BARS
Café Largo (bar with live music) 143
Coogan's (sports bar) 154
Lenox Lounge (bar with live music) 145
Londel's (bar with live music) 145
St Nick's Pub (bar with live music) 145
Zapatas Manoletas (neighbourhood bar) 143

RESTAURANTS & CAFÉS
Africa (African & Caribbean) 81
Bayou (American) 82
Copeland's (American) 84
Hungarian Pastry Shop (teas & patisseries) 133
Krispy Kreme's (cafés & coffee shops) 100
Obaa Koryoe (African & Caribbean) 82
Slice of Harlem (Italian) 119
Sugar Shack (American) 91
Sylvia's (American) 91
The Terrace (French) 111
Tom's Restaurant (diner) 106

SHOPPING
African Paradise (interiors & furniture) 61
Bamboozle Studio (jewellery) 66
The Harlem Collective (designer clothes) 43
Home Boy of Harlem (jewellery) 66
Kaarta Imports (fabrics) 56
Malcolm Shabazz Harlem Market (market) 68
Mart 125 (market) 68
Scheme (designer clothes) 50
Studio Museum Gift Shop (museum store) 71

SIGHTS, MUSEUMS & GALLERIES
Morris-Jumel Mansion Museum (historic house) 180-1
St John the Divine (landmark) 174
Schomburg Center for Research in Black Culture (art museum/gallery) 189—90
Studio Museum of Harlem (art museum/gallery) 190-91

Inwood

SIGHTS, MUSEUMS & GALLERIES
The Cloisters (one-off) 182

Lower East Side & Chinatown

BARS
Baby Jupiter (DJ bar) 137
Good World Bar & Grill (theme bar) 149 ***
Idlewild (theme bar) 149
Kush (theme bar) 150
Max Fish (great dive) 151
Meow Mix (bar) 160
169 Bar (great dive) 152
Orchard Bar (DJ bar) 138
Slipper Room (bar with live music) 145
Tonic (bar with live music) 146
Welcome to the Johnsons' (theme bar) 151
Winnie's (bar with live music) 146

CLUBS
Angel 156
Fun 156

RESTAURANTS & CAFÉS
Bereket (Turkish) 134
Casa Mexicana (Mexican) 126
Chinatown Ice Cream Factory (ice cream) 113
El Sombrero (Mexican) 127
Grand Sichuan (Chinese) 102
Great Shanghai (Chinese) 102
Hong Kong Egg Cake Co (Chinese) 102
Jing Fong (Chinese) 102
Joe's Shanghai (Chinese) 103
Katz's Deli (Chinese) 104
Lotus Club (cafés & coffee shops) 100
New Wonton Garden (Chinese) 103

Lower Manhattan

Meatpacking District

BARS

Bellevue Bar (neighbourhood bar) 140
Blue Bar (quiet retreat) 153
Chase (bar) 159
ESPN Zone (sports bar) 154
Japas 55 (bar with live music) 144
Jimmy's Corner (sports bar) 155
Metrazur (cocktail & champagne bar) 140
One 51 (DJ bar) 138
O'Reilley's Pub (neighbourhood bar) 142
Regents (bar) 160
(great dive) 152
The Russian Samovar (theme bar) 150
Siberia (great dive) 152
Swine on Nine (theme bar) 150
Top of the Tower (big-deal bar) 148
Wet Bar (big-deal bar) 148
Whiskey Blue (big-deal bar) 148
Whiskey Park (big-deal bar) 148
Xth Ave Lounge (neighbourhood bar) 143

RESTAURANTS & CAFÉS

Aquavit (Scandinavian) 129
Asia de Cuba (global & fusion) 111
The Brasserie (bistro) 94
Bryant Park Grill & Café (American) 83
Cho Dang Gol (Korean) 122
Don Giovanni (Italian) 116
Ellen's Stardust Diner (diner) 105
Esca (Italian) 116
Ess-A-Bagel (bagels) 93
Guastavino (bistro) 94
Hangawi (vegetarian) 134
Island Burgers & Shakes (burgers) 97
Keens Steakhouse (steaks & grills) 132
La Bonne Soupe (bistro) 95
Lakruwana (Sri Lankan) 132
Le Bernardin (seafood) 130
Lespinasse (French) 110
Los Dos Rancheros Mexicanos (Mexican) 127
Mezze (cafés & coffee shops) 100
Michael Jordan's The Steakhouse (steaks & grills) 132
Oyster Bar (seafood) 131
Russian Tea Room (East European) 106
Soup Kitchen International (soup) 131
The Tea Box (cafés & coffee shops) 101
Trattoria dell'Arte (Italian) 119
Tuscan Square (cafés & coffee shops) 102
'21' Club (American) 92
UN Delegates' Dining Room (global & fusion) 113
Virgil's Real BBQ (steaks & grills) 133
Vynl Diner (diner) 106

SHOPPING

B & H Photo-Video (electronics) 54
Bergdorf Goodman (department stores) 36
Burberry (designer clothes) 39
Cartier (jewellery) 66
Chanel (designer clothes) 40
Christian Dior (designer clothes) 40
Coliseum Books (books) 29
Colony Records (CDs, records & tapes) 31
Columbus Circle Market (market) 68
Crate & Barrel (interiors & furniture) 62
Disney Store (theme store) 76
Express (chain stores) 34
FAO Schwarz (toys) 77
Felissimo (department stores) 36
Fendi (designer clothes) 43
Foot Locker (sports gear) 73
French Connection (chain stores) 34
Gap (chain stores) 34
Godiva Chocolatier (food store) 57
Gotham Book Mart (books) 29
Gucci (designer clothes) 43
H&M (chain stores) 34
Henri Bendel (department stores) 37
HMV (CDs, records & tapes) 32
Jimmy Choo (shoes) 71

Morningside Heights

Noho

M&R (neighbourhood bar) 141
Milano's (great dive) 151
Spring Lounge (aka The Shark Bar) (neighbourhood bar) 143
Sweet & Vicious (DJ bar) 139
288 (great dive) 152
Velvet (quiet retreat) 153
Von (quiet retreat) 153
Ñ (theme bar) 150

RESTAURANTS & CAFÉS
Acquario (Mediterranean) 125
Astor Restaurant & Lounge (American) 82
B-Bar & Grill (American) 82
Bond St (Japanese) 120
Buffa's Delicatessen (Chinese) 104
Café Gitane (cafés & coffee shops) 98
Café Habana (Latin American) 123
Clay (Korean) 123
Eight Mile Creek (Australian) 93
Five Points (American) 85
Great Jones Café (diner) 105
Il Buco (Mediterranean) 126
Indochine (Vietnamese) 135
Jones Diner (diner) 105
Kitchen Club (global & fusion) 112
Mekong (Vietnamese) 135
Mexican Radio (Mexican) 127
Nyonya (Malaysian) 125
Peasant (Italian) 118
Rialto (burgers) 97
Rice (global & fusion) 112
Savoy (American) 90
Va Tutto! (Italian) 12

SHOPPING
À Détacher (designer clothes) 38
Bond 07 (accessories) 24
Built By Wendy (designer clothes) 39
Creed (beauty supplies) 26
Each and Them (vintage clothes) 78
Firefighter's Friend (theme store) 76
Hedra Prue (designer clothes) 44
Hotel of the Rising Star (menswear) 69
Katayone Adeli (designer clothes) 45

Language (designer clothes) 46
Malia Mills (sports gear) 73
Margie Tsai (designer clothes) 46
Mayle (designer clothes) 47
Nylon Squid (designer clothes) 48
Pop Shop (accessories) 25
Screaming Mimi's (vintage clothes) 79
Shi (interiors & furniture) 65
Steinberg & Sons (menswear) 70
Supreme (streetwear) 75
Urban Outfitters (chain stores) 35
X-Large (streetwear) 76
Zero (designer clothes) 53

Nolita

BARS
Mare Chiaro (great dive) 151

RESTAURANTS & CAFÉS
Balthazar (bistro) 94
Le Jardin Bistrot (bistro) 95
Lombardi's (Italian) 117

SHOPPING
Antique Boutique (designer clothes) 38
Calypso St Barths (designer clothes) 40
Find Outlet (discount stores) 53
Ina (vintage clothes) 79
Jamin Puech (accessories) 24
Janet Russo (designer clothes) 45
Kelly Christie (hats) 60
Mark Schwartz (shoes) 72
Me & Ro (jewellery) 67
Other Music (CDs, records & tapes) 32
Pottery Barn (interiors & furniture) 65
Resurrection (vintage clothes) 79
Shakespeare & Co (books) 30
SHI (gifts & stationery) 60
Sigerson Morrison (shoes) 73
Tower Books (books) 30
Tower Flea Market (market) 68
Tracey Feith (designer clothes) 51

Morgane Le Fay (designer clothes) 47
Moss (interiors & furniture) 64
Nicole Miller (designer clothes) 48
Nine West (shoes) 72
Otto Tootsi Plohound (shoes) 72
Philosophy di Alberta Ferretti (designer clothes) 49
Portico Bed & Bath (interiors & furniture) 65
Prada Sport (designer clothes) 49
Ricky's (beauty supplies) 27
Rockport (shoes) 73
Scoop (designer clothes) 50
Sean (menswear) 70
Selima Optique (eyewear) 56
Sephora (beauty supplies) 28
Shabby Chic (interiors & furniture) 65
Shu Uemura (beauty supplies) 28
Soho Antiques Fair Collectibles Market (antiques) 26
Spring Street Market (market) 68
Steve Madden (shoes) 73
Steven Alan (designer clothes) 51
Stussy (streetwear) 75
Tocca (designer clothes) 51
Troy (gifts & stationery) 60
Trufaux (streetwear) 75
Vivienne Tam (designer clothes) 52
Vivienne Westwood (designer clothes) 52
Xoxo (chain stores) 35
Yohji Yamamoto (designer clothes) 52
Yves Saint Laurent Rive Gauche (menswear) 70
Zara (chain stores) 35
Zona (interiors & furniture) 66

SIGHTS, MUSEUMS & GALLERIES

Ace Gallery (commercial gallery) 191
American Fine Arts (commercial gallery) 191
Deitch Projects (commercial gallery) 192
Guggenheim Museum Soho (art museum/gallery) 186
Janet Borden (commercial gallery) 192
Larry Gagosian (commercial gallery) 192
Museum for African Art (art museum/gallery) 187–8
Phyllis Kind (commercial gallery) 193
Tony Shafrazi Gallery (commercial gallery) 193

Spanish Harlem

SHOPPING
Kitchen Arts & Letters (books) 29

SIGHTS, MUSEUMS & GALLERIES
El Museo del Barrio (one-off) 183

Tribeca

BARS
Bubble Lounge (cocktail & champagne bar) 139
Dylan Prime (cocktail & champagne bar) 139
Ice Bar (DJ bar) 138
Knitting Factory's Tap Bar (bar with live music) 144
Liquor Store (neighbourhood bar) 141
Lush (big-deal bar) 147
Nancy Whiskey Pub (great dive) 151

CLUBS
Shine 157
Tribeca Blues 157
Vinyl 158

RESTAURANTS & CAFÉS
Bouley Bakery (American) 83
Bubby's (diner) 104
Capsouto Frères (French) 108
Chanterelle (French) 108
Danube (Italian) 116
Flor de Sol (Mediterranean) 126
Grace (American) 86
The Independent (American) 87
Kitchenette (diner) 106

Upper East Side

clothes) 49
Polo Sport (designer clothes) 49
PS 183 Market (market) 68
Robert Marc (eyewear) 55
Roberto Cavalli (designer clothes) 50
Searle (designer clothes) 50
Shanghai Tang (designer clothes) 50
Stéphane Kélian (shoes) 73
Tod's (shoes) 73
TSE (designer clothes) 51
Valentino (designer clothes) 52

SIGHTS, MUSEUMS & GALLERIES
C & M Gallery (commercial gallery) 193
Central Park (park) 196–7
Central Park Wildlife Center (kids) 195
Cooper-Hewitt, National Design Museum (historic house) 179
Frick Collection (historic house) 179–80
Gagosian Gallery (commercial gallery) 193
Hirschl & Adler (commercial gallery) 193
International Center of Photography (art museum/ gallery) 186
Jewish Museum (one-off) 182-3
Knoedler & Co (commercial gallery) 193
Metropolitan Museum of Art (art museum/gallery) 187
Museum of American Folk Art (art museum/gallery) 188
Roosevelt Island Tramway (viewpoint) 176
Salander-O'Reilly (commercial gallery) 194
Solomon R Guggenheim Museum (art museum/gallery) 190
Whitney Museum of American Art (art museum/gallery) 191
Wildenstein & Co (commercial gallery) 194

BARS
Dive Bar (great dive) 151
Evelyn Lounge (lounge bar) 153
Malachy's Donegal Inn (sports bar) 155
Night Café (neighbourhood bar) 142
Potion Lounge (cocktail & champagne bar) 140
Saints (bar) 160
Smoke (great dive) 152

RESTAURANTS & CAFÉS
Artie's New York Delicatessen (Chinese) 103
Avenue (French) 107
Barney Greengrass (Chinese) 103
Big Nick's Burger (burgers) 97
Café con Leche (Latin American) 123
Café des Artistes (French) 108
Café Lalo (cafés & coffee shops) 98
Calle Ocho (Latin American) 123
Drip (cafés & coffee shops) 99
Gabriela's (Mexican) 127
Jean Georges (French) 110
Josie's (vegetarian) 135
Nougatine (cafés & coffee shops) 100
Pampa (Latin American) 125
Rain (Oriental) 129

SHOPPING
Allan & Suzi (vintage clothes) 78
Columbus Flea Market (market) 68
Eddie Bauer (chain stores) 34
Face Stockholm (beauty supplies) 27
Fairways (food store) 57
Maxilla & Mandible (gifts & stationery) 59
Murder Ink (books) 29
Naughty & Nice (erotic boutique) 55
9 & Co (shoes) 72
Olive & Bette (designer clothes) 48
Only Hearts (lingerie) 67
Penny Whistle Toys (toys) 78

West Village

NEW JERSEY

Jersey City

SIGHTS, MUSEUMS & GALLERIES

QUEENS

Long Island City

RESTAURANTS & CAFÉS

SIGHTS, MUSEUMS & GALLERIES

shops

NYC, the epicentre of the shopping universe, has everything from couture to sneakers. If you can't find it here, you won't find it anywhere...

accessories

Bond 07 *♧A12*
Owned by Selima (of Selima Optique fame), this store is filled with divine, desirable accessories (hats, glasses, shoes, and trinkets), including lots of unique and beautiful jewellery. All irresistible.
7 Bond Street, Noho ☎ 677-8487 Ⓜ 6 to Bleeker St

Casio Baby G-Shock *♧D11*
To pull the whole outfit together, get yourself a watch from the store devoted to the eponymous timepieces.
458 W Broadway, Soho ☎ 260-4570 Ⓜ B•D•F•Q to Broadway-Lafayette St

Chrome Hearts *♧F6*
A mecca for leather fans is hidden away in an unmarked brownstone. The look here is biker-chic-meets-rock-star.
159 E 64th Street, UES ☎ 327-0707 Ⓜ B•Q to Lexington Ave

☆ JAMIN PUECH *♧C12*
Entirely precious bags by this Parisian designer in jewel-like colours are housed in a gorgeous, teeny boutique.
252 Mott Street, Nolita ☎ 334-9730 Ⓜ B•D•F•Q to Broadway-Lafayette St

☆ JUTTA NEUMANN *♧B12*
Her artful leather designs are favoured by designers like Marc Jacobs and Anna Sui (who use her handmade bags and shoes in their catwalk shows). Her sandals are a bit of a bargain, considering the work that's gone into them.
317 E 9th Street, East Village ☎ 982-7048 Ⓜ 6 to Astor Pl; N•R 8th St NYU

☆ KATE SPADE *♧D11*
It's impossible to go anywhere these days without spotting one of Kate Spade's adorable bags on somebody's arm. She makes them saucy, serious, sublime, and for evening, glam. Her store also carries cute accessories, like her date books or very fem stationery.
454 Broome Street, Soho ☎ 274-1991 Ⓜ N•R to Prince St; C•E to Spring St

Louis Vuitton
$D11

Everything in this store is a heart-stopper, especially the price tags! The traditional LV accessories and luggage are still covetable classics.

116 Greene Street, Soho ☎ 274-9090 Ⓜ N•R to Prince St

Lucky Wang
$D12

Satisfy your need for *tchotchkes* and fun accessories here.

100 Stanton Street, LES ☎ 353-2850 Ⓜ F•J•M•Z to Delancey St-Essex St

☆ MANHATTAN PORTAGE
$A12

The bag brand that's been so popular in Europe is finally making an impact at home. Backpacks and DJ bags in the strongest canvas and lots of colours.

333 E 9th Street, East Village ☎ 995-5490 Ⓜ 6 to Astor Pl

Pop Shop
$A12

With more of a graphic spin, novelty items, from T-shirts to key chains, are decorated with the vibrant work of the late, great artist, Keith Haring.

292 Lafayette Street, Noho ☎ 219-2784 Ⓜ 6 to Bleeker St

Refinery
$off map

Stylish, one-off bags made of vintage and recycled materials.

254 Smith Street, Carroll Gardens ☎ 1-718-643-7861 Ⓜ F•G to Bergen St

Suarez
$A8

For a bag on the cheap, this store makes look-alike Hermès, Chanel and more.

450 Park Avenue, Midtown ☎ 753-3758 Ⓜ B•Q to 57th St; N•R to 5th St

Ugly Luggage
$off map

This interesting shop is crammed with trading cards, ashtrays, lunch-boxes, and assorted memorabilia.

214 Bedford Avenue, Williamsburg ☎ 1-718-384-0724 Ⓜ L to Bedford Ave

Vinnie's Tampon Case
$C12

Oozing oestrogen, this store is devoted to selling the consummate carry-all. Vinnie is so immersed in his products, he's even created a performance piece about them.

245 Eldridge Street, LES ☎ 228-2273 Ⓜ F to 2nd Ave; J•M to Bowery

antiques

Howard Kaplan Antiques
$F10

Specializes in 18th- and 19th-century furniture.

827 Broadway, West Village ☎ 674-1000 Ⓜ N•R 8th St

Pall Mall Antiques   ⚲B11
Also deals mainly in 18th-and 19th-century furniture.
99 University Place, West Village ☎ **677-5544** Ⓜ **N•R 8th St NYU**

☆ **SOHO ANTIQUES FAIR COLLECTIBLES MARKET**   ⚲D11
A good bet for vintage clothing, old cameras, and crafts, this popular
market is held every Saturday and Sunday from 7am to 5pm.
Broadway & Grand Street, Soho ☎ **682-2000** Ⓜ **J•M•N•R•Z•6 to Canal St**

beauty supplies

☆ **AVEDA**   ⚲D11
This elegant space is easily the best smelling store in the world. If you're
not going for Aveda's amazing hair care, aromatherapy, or bath and body
collection, pop in for, at the very least, the soothing environment. The hair
salon is upstairs, the spa is nearby on Spring Street.
456 W Broadway, Soho ☎ **473-0280** Ⓜ **C•E to Spring St;
N•R to Prince St; 1•9 to Houston St**

☆ **BIGELOW PHARMACY**   ⚲A11
Founded in 1838, Bigelow's boasts a thoroughly modern variety of beauty
products (hair accessories, essential oils, homeopathic remedies, and lots
of make-up). Spot the celebs at this quintessential West Village pharmacy.
414 Sixth Avenue, West Village ☎ **533-2700** Ⓜ **A•B•C•D•E•F•Q to W 4th
St-Washington Sq**

☆ **BLISS SPA**   ⚲D11
While the who's who is making a bee-line to Bliss for spa treatments, the
real treat at this chichi oasis is the boutique. The products are hand-picked
by the spa's owner, skin-guru Marcia Kilgore. In addition to lines like
Decleor and Yonka, Bliss sells everything you ever wanted beauty-wise, like
upscale tooth-whitening paste and an at-home paraffin manicure kit.
2nd flr, 568 Broadway, Soho ☎ **219-8970** Ⓜ **N•R to Prince St; B•D•F•Q to
Broadway-Lafayette St; 6 to Spring St**

☆ **CREED**   ⚲B11
To see how well you really know your nose, stop by Creed where you can
browse their scent library or join in a smelling seminar. To make you feel
special, they also offer custom fragrance blending ($400–$1000)
guaranteed to be yours and yours only for the next five years.
9 Bond Street, Noho ☎ **228-1940** Ⓜ **6 to Bleecker St**

Demeter *♭A12*
The products here will revive body and soul, and some of the scents available are pretty unique. Dab on some Grass, Holy Water or Dirt, or banish the blues with the Sugar Cookie 'attitude adjustment' lotion.
83 Second Avenue, East Village ☎ 505-1535 Ⓜ 6 to Astor Pl

☆ FACE STOCKHOLM *♭C5*
Face products have become a favourite amongst top make-up artists and the glitterati. You can choose from a bevy of all-natural beauty supplies – from make-up and utensils to bath gels and lotions. Check out the lip gloss – it's the best.
226 Columbus Avenue, UWS ☎ 769-1420 Ⓜ 1•9 to 72nd St

Frédéric Fekkai *♭E6*
This hair stylist has seen his fair share of famous clients. Drop by his in-salon boutique to pick up polished hair accessories and treatment products as well as bags and purses.
874 Madison Avenue, UES ☎ 583-3300 Ⓜ 6 to 68th St-Hunter College

Fresh *♭A6*
A welcome addition to the NY beauty scene. Imported cosmetics, as well as the store's own line, are displayed in an all-white setting.
1061 Madison Avenue, UES ☎ 396-0344 Ⓜ 4•5•6 to 86th St

☆ KIEHL'S *♭F10*
Kiehl's is more than a beauty supply store – it's an American institution. This pharmacy-turned-beauty-brand's natural approach to products, and informative staff, make it a pleasure for you to financially submit (cost accumulates quite easily). Best known for their lip balm and unisex appeal.
109 Third Avenue, East Village ☎ 677-3171 Ⓜ N•R•4•5•6 to 14th St-Union Sq; L to 3rd Ave

☆ M.A.C. *♭D11*
If you want the trendiest new colour then M.A.C. is the place to be. This make-up collection, which was created by a professional make-up artist, is known for its cutting-edge palette and sleek packaging.
113 Spring Street, Soho ☎ 334-4641 Ⓜ N•R to Prince St

☆ RICKY'S *♭D11*
This chain is a magnet for girlies who like their beauty products cheap and cheerful. The Soho branch has everything from fun-coloured wigs and nail polish to discounted high-end products.
590 Broadway, Soho ☎ 226-5552 Ⓜ N•R to Prince St; 6 to Spring St

shops

☆ SEPHORA   ♫*D11*
Product princesses will feel as if they've died and gone to heaven here. It's like a major department store, but just for cosmetics. Bath goods, make-up, perfume, skincare, and everything in between from big-name brands (Chanel, Lancôme, Dior) to more eclectic labels.
555 Broadway, Soho ☎ 625-1309 Ⓜ 6 to Spring St

☆ SHU UEMURA   ♫*D11*
The Armani of make-up, but from Japan. The store – and merchandise – has a Zen-like appeal in that less is more. Shu Uemura is not all about the moment's most fashionable colours, but minimalist beauty and quality.
121 Greene Street, Soho ☎ 979-5500 Ⓜ N•R to Prince St; 6 to Spring St

books

☆ A PHOTOGRAPHER'S PLACE   ♫*D11*
This store is more like a museum dedicated to the best photographs and photographers in the world and is crammed with secondhand photo books to stack up on the coffee table.
133 Mercer Street, Soho ☎ 966-2356 Ⓜ C•E•6 to Spring St; N•R to Prince St

☆ BARNES & NOBLE   ♫*E10*
With convenient locations throughout NYC (including Brooklyn), this store carries selected hardcover new releases at 30% off. Author readings occur nightly and their cafés have a reputation as an interesting singles scene.
105 Fifth Avenue, Gramercy Park ☎ 807-0099 Ⓜ L•N•R•4•5•6 to 14th St-Union Sq

Books of Wonder   ♫*E10*
This store claims to be the oldest and biggest independent children's bookstore in New York and a real Aladdin's cave it is too. The vast stock of children's literature even includes a foreign language section, and while kids check out their favourites, parents can take a nostalgia trip and peruse the selection of rare and collectible children's books. The store also regularly hosts readings.
16 W 18th Street, Flatiron District ☎ 989-3270 Ⓜ 1•9 to 18th St; 4•5•6•L•N•R to Union Square

☆ BORDERS BOOKS AND MUSIC   ♫*B13*
In a similar vein as Barnes & Noble but with fewer locations, Borders offers a wide range of titles at reasonable prices.
5 World Trade Center, Lower Manhattan ☎ 839-8049 Ⓜ C•E to World Trade Center

Coliseum Books ♯B7
The enormous selection and the many, interesting discounts make this large store a must. It's especially well-stocked for paperbacks and reference books.
1771 Broadway, Midtown ☎ 757-8381 Ⓜ N•R to 57th St

☆ FORBIDDEN PLANET ♯E10
Sci-fi, comic, and graphic novel fans make tracks to this store where the selection of new and used collectibles is vast.
840 Broadway, East Village ☎ 473-1576 Ⓜ L•N•R•4•5•6• to 14th St-Union Sq

☆ GOTHAM BOOK MART ♯C8
For used books in a relaxed environment, visit this 80-year-old literary landmark. Replete with used books on all subjects, its walls are lined with photos of folk who have read and met here over the years.
41 W 47th Street, Midtown ☎ 719-4448 Ⓜ B•D•F•Q to 47th–50th Sts-Rockefeller Center

☆ KITCHEN ARTS & LETTERS ♯off map
If your idea of adventure is the rise and fall of a soufflé, then this store is home sweet home.
1435 Lexington Avenue, Spanish Harlem ☎ 876-5550 Ⓜ 6 to 96th St

☆ MURDER INK ♯A3
Judging by the number of mystery bookstores in town, New Yorkers have a voracious appetite for intrigue. Murder Ink is among the best of the bunch.
2486 Broadway, UWS ☎ 362-8905 Ⓜ 1•2•3•9 to 96th St

Oscar Wilde Memorial Bookstore ♯A11
America's first gay bookshop, has an excellent if small selection of tomes dedicated to alternative lifestyles.
15 Christopher Street, West Village ☎ 255-8097 Ⓜ 1•9 Christopher St

☆ RIZZOLI ♯A8
The choice here is impressive but the store made its name as one of the city's best bookstores for art, architecture and design.
31 W 57th Street, Midtown ☎ 759-2424 Ⓜ B•N•Q•R to 57th St

☆ ST MARK'S BOOKSHOP ♯A12
East Village subversives adore their local St Mark's Bookshop, which puts the emphasis on politics, theory and the cutting-edge.
31 Third Avenue, East Village ☎ 260-7853 Ⓜ 6 to Astor Pl

☆ **SHAKESPEARE & CO** ♫*B11*
Strong on fiction, drama, film titles and British imports.
716 Broadway, Nolita ☎ 529-1330 Ⓜ 6 to Astor Pl

Tompkins Square Books ♫*A12*
A local favourite thanks to its cozy, chaotic feel and late opening hours –
there's a good selection of vinyl here too.
111 E 7th Street, East Village ☎ 979-8958 Ⓜ 6 to Astor Pl

☆ **THE STRAND** ♫*E10*
With a purported 8 miles of used books to choose from, The Strand has
enough dusty tomes to keep the most avid bibliophile busy for days. Look
out for new hardcovers at significant discounts too.
828 Broadway, East Village ☎ 473-1452 Ⓜ L•N•R•4•5•6 to 14th St-Union Sq

☆ **THREE LIVES & COMPANY** ♫*B11*
The West Village literary set go for New York's prettiest bookstore, with its
large fiction section.
**154 W 10th Street, West Village ☎ 741-2069 Ⓜ A•B•C•D•E•F•Q to W 4th
St-Washington Sq**

☆ **TOWER BOOKS** ♫*A12*
Although this store focuses on music titles, it also stocks all kind of books.
Readings and signings are often held here.
**383 Lafayette Street, Nolita ☎ 228-5100 Ⓜ 6 to Astor Pl; B•D•F•Q to
Broadway-Lafayette St**

cds, records & tapes

☆ **ACADEMY CDS & RECORDS** ♫*E10*
Those seeking bargains on CDs and vinyl should head for this store that
sells mainly used classical and jazz sounds.
**10 w 18th Street, Gramercy Park ☎ 242-3000
Ⓜ L•N•R• 4•5•6 to Union Sq**

☆ **BLEECKER BOB'S GOLDEN OLDIES** ♫*B11*
Vintage and collectible vinyl and the tour T-shirts to match.
**118 W 3rd Street, West Village ☎ 475-9677 Ⓜ A•B•C• D•E•F•Q to W 4th
St-Washington Sq**
Bleecker Street Records ♫*A11*
Vast selection of vinyl spanning jazz to rock.
239 Bleecker Street, West Village ☎ 255-7899 Ⓜ 6 to Bleecker St

shops

☆ **COLONY RECORDS**   ♫D7
An extensive collection of show tunes – and the sheet music too.
1619 Broadway, Midtown ☎ 265-2050 Ⓜ N•R to 49th St; 1•9 to 50th St

☆ **DANCETRACKS**   ♫A12
DJs make their way to this neighbourhood institution where all the latest
dance music is carried on vinyl.
91 E 3rd Street, East Village ☎ 260-8729
Ⓜ F to 2nd Ave

☆ **DISCO RAMA**   ♫A11
For used CDs including fairly new pop hits, this store is hard to surpass.
**186 W 4th Street, West Village ☎ 206-8417 Ⓜ A•B•C• D•E•F•Q to W 4th
St-Washington Sq**

Ear Wax   ♫off map
An eclectic mix of CDs and some LPs.
204 Bedford Avenue, Williamsburg ☎ 1-718-218-9608
Ⓜ L to Bedford Ave

☆ **8 BALL RECORDS**   ♫A12
The record label's own store is excellent for house and other dance music.
105 E 9th Street, East Village ☎ 473-6343 Ⓜ 6 to Astor Pl; N•R to 8th St

Etherea   ♫A12
A great selection of alternative, indie and experimental sounds.
66 Avenue A, East Village ☎ 358-1126 Ⓜ L to 1st Ave

☆ **FAT BEATS**   ♫A11
Push your way past the DJs for the newest in hip-hop at New York's
premier hip-hop record outlet, which also has a fine selection of reggae
and jazz.
**406 Sixth Avenue, West Village ☎ 673-3883 Ⓜ A•B•C•D• E•F•Q to W 4th
St-Washington Sq**

Finyl Vinyl   ♫A12
An endearing place that still refuses to carry CDs.
204 E 6th Street, East Village ☎ 533-8007
Ⓜ 6 to Astor Pl

☆ **FOOTLIGHT RECORDS**   ♪F10

Musical lovers will browse with relish the extensive collection of rare-to-find CDs and vinyls. Especially strong on soundtracks, jazz and cabaret.

113 E 12th Street, East Village ☎ 533-1572 Ⓜ L•N•R•4• 5•6 to 14th St-Union Sq

☆ **GENERATION RECORDS**   ♪B11

To pick up tour posters and recordings of your favourite live show, this store is a gold mine.

210 Thompson Street, West Village ☎ 254-1100 Ⓜ A•B•C•D•E•F•Q to W 4th St-Washington Sq

☆ **HMV**   ♪B9

A giant store with very helpful and knowledgeable staff and thousands of titles to browse as an in-store DJ entertains you.

57 W 34th Street, Midtown ☎ 629-0900 Ⓜ B•D•F•N•R•Q to 34th St-Herald Sq

☆ **J & R MUSIC & COMPUTER WORLD**   ♪B13

The best place for music bargains, this large store carries all new releases at discount. There are separate departments for jazz and classical CDs.

23 Park Row, Lower Manhattan ☎ 238-9000 Ⓜ J•M•Z•2•3•4•5 to Fulton St-Broadway Nassau; N•R•4•5•6 to City Hall

☆ **JAZZ RECORD CENTER**   ♪D9

Jazz aficionados regularly make pilgrimages here to get their fix. Their collection (including Blue Note label treats) just can't be beat.

8th flr, 236 W 26th Street, Chelsea ☎ 675-4480 Ⓜ C•E•1•9 to 23rd St

☆ **KIM'S VIDEO & MUSIC**   ♪A12

Although St Mark's Place is overrun with decent music stores selling new and used CDs at fair price, this is the biggest and brightest, with a great range and helpful staff. This massive, yellow-painted shop also sells and rents a huge range of videos.

6 St Mark's Place, East Village ☎ 598-9985 Ⓜ 6 to Astor Pl

☆ **OTHER MUSIC**   ♪B11

Hard-to-find titles are tracked down by this store. The knowledge of their staff alone might make it the best record store in the city.

15 E 4th Street, Nolita ☎ 477-8150 Ⓜ 6 to Bleeker St; B•D•F•Q to Broadway-Lafayette St

☆ RECORD EXPLOSION
♫B9
Frequented by DJs looking for bargains.
142 W 34th Street, Midtown ☎ 714-0450 Ⓜ B•D•F•N• Q•R to 34th St-Herald Sq

Temple Records
♫F10
Good for the latest techno, house and electronica.
29a Avenue B, East Village ☎ 475-7552 Ⓜ L to 3rd Ave

Throb
♫F10
More techno, house and electronica.
211 E 14th Street, East Village ☎ 533-2328 Ⓜ L to 3rd Ave

☆ TOWER RECORDS
♫B11
A virtual music supermarket, its three floors of merchandise making a good starting point for any mainstream release.
692 Broadway, Midtown ☎ 505-1500 Ⓜ 6 to Bleecker St

Vinylmania
♫A11
Broad ranging collection of techno and electronica
60 Carmine Street, West Village ☎ 924-7223 Ⓜ 1•9 to Houston St

☆ VIRGIN MEGASTORE
♫D7
Right on Times Square, the giant Virgin Megastore must surely have the biggest and most comprehensive selection of music in town, plus great quantities of videos and books, which compensates for the slightly higher prices.
1540 Broadway, Midtown ☎ 921-1020 Ⓜ A•C•E•N•R•1•2•3•7•9 42nd St-Times Sq

chain stores (fashion)

☆ BANANA REPUBLIC
♫A10
A good bet for timeless casualwear, with separate stores for men and women. Their home furnishings (in the women's store) follow suit.
89 & 122 Fifth Avenue, Gramercy Park ☎ 366-4630/366-4691 Ⓜ F•L to 6th Ave

Bebe
♫A10
Bringing high fashion to the younger crowd. You can find lots of suits, dresses, separates and coats here in current styles and hues: the accent is always on sexy.
100 Fifth Avenue, Gramercy Park ☎ 675-2323 Ⓜ F•L to 6th Ave

☆ **BROOKS BROS** *¢D13*

Conservative tailored suits for the more buttoned-down. This store's Wall Street style goes a long way with men, and the line of preppy womenswear is building momentum.

1 Liberty Plaza, Lower Manhattan ☎ 267-2400 Ⓜ 1•9 to Cortlandt St

☆ **CLUB MONACO** *¢A10*

Upscale and interesting wardrobe essentials, but still reasonably-priced.

160 5th Avenue, Gramercy Park ☎ 352-0936 Ⓜ N•R to 23rd St

☆ **EDDIE BAUER** *¢E5*

Rugged outdoorwear for men and women.

1960 Broadway, UWS ☎ 877-7629 Ⓜ 1•9 to 66th St-Lincoln Center

☆ **EXPRESS** *¢F8*

Mid-priced, mainstream fashion for women

733 Third Avenue, Midtown ☎ 949-9784 Ⓜ 4•5•6•7 to Grand Central-42nd St

☆ **FRENCH CONNECTION** *¢D7*

Upscale and interesting, but still reasonably-priced.

1270 Sixth Avenue, Midtown ☎ 262-6623 Ⓜ B•D•F•Q to 47th-50th Sts-Rockefeller Center

☆ **GAP** *¢F7*

For all ages, this ubiquitous unisex store features reasonably priced understated basics like chinos and white T-shirts. There are also a few upscale surprises, like the luxury baby boutique.

60 34th Street, Midtown ☎ 643-8960 Ⓜ N•R•1•2•3•7•9 to Times Square-42nd St

☆ **GUESS?** *¢D11*

Features the same sexy look as XOXO, at a higher price point.

537 Broadway, Soho ☎ 226-9545 Ⓜ N•R to Prince St

☆ **H&M** *¢A11*

This Swedish store has caused such a big stir with their cheap, chic, or streetwear styles that on day one queues formed around the block. It still continues to attract the crowds, who are drawn here by seemingly endless supplies of super-cheap, fashion knock offs.

640 Fifth Avenue, Midtown ☎ 480-8777 Ⓜ A•B•C•E•F•Q to W 4th St-Washington Sq

☆ J CREW ♯E10

This more expensive and conservative version of Gap remains the perfect outpost for locating just the right T-shirt, sweater or plain chinos.

91 Fifth Avenue, Gramercy Park ☎ 255-4848 Ⓜ L•N•R•4•5•6 to 14th St-Union Sq

☆ K-MART ♯B9

An all-American department store, and one of the best-priced, with rock bottom bargains for the entire family.

250 W 34th Street, Midtown ☎ 760-1188 Ⓜ B•D•F•N•Q•R to 34th St-Herald Sq

☆ OLD NAVY ♯F9

The prime store is on Herald Square, this is in the same vein as Gap with even cheaper prices.

610 Sixth Avenue, Chelsea ☎ 645-0663 Ⓜ F to 14th St

☆ STRUCTURE ♯B9

Mid-price, mainstream fashion for men.

7 W 34th Street, Midtown ☎ 967-5090 Ⓜ B•D•F•N•Q•R to 34th St-Herald Sq

☆ URBAN OUTFITTERS ♯B11

A temple to everything cool, which offers the latest youth-oriented, streetwear fashions for men and women.

628 Broadway, Noho ☎ 475-0009 Ⓜ 6 to Bleecker St

☆ XOXO ♯D11

This upbeat store carries sexy clothing for female style vixens.

426 W Broadway, Soho ☎ 334-9450 Ⓜ N•R to Prince St

☆ ZARA ♯D11

This branch of the Spanish chain is worth investigating for European flair with sleek, reasonably priced separates, casualwear and shoes.

580 W Broadway, Soho ☎ 343-1725 Ⓜ N•R to Prince St

consignment stores

☆ TOKIO 7 ♯A12

Offers a broad spectrum of carefully worn designer clothes (Gaultier, Karan) with an avant-garde edge at reduced prices.

64 E 7th Street, East Village ☎ 353-8443 Ⓜ 6 to Astor Pl

Tokyo Joe ♫F10
Another good consignment store offering up barely-worn, designer labels.
334 E 11th Street, East Village ☎ 473-0724 Ⓜ 6 to Astor Pl

department stores

☆ BARNEY'S NEW YORK ♫A8
Working for one of NY's premier style bastions, Barney's brilliant buyers
seek out the very best in modern design. Fashion-forward clothing by
such luminaries as McQueen and Margiela line the racks upstairs. On the
ground floor the collection of accessories is breathtaking, and the two
shoe departments hold some of the most interesting footwear around.
The annual warehouse sale is as anticipated by New Yorkers as fireworks
on the Fourth of July.
660 Madison Avenue, UES ☎ 826-8900 Ⓜ E•F•N•R to 5th Ave

☆ BERGDORF GOODMAN ♫A8
For pure elegance, the one and only Bergdorf's is hard to top. Exclusives by
designers such as Philip Treacy and Jo Malone attract fashionistas here
like bees to a honey pot. But don't be intimidated by the big names, there
are inspiring lines of casualwear and accessories too. The men's version is
across the street.
754 Fifth Avenue, Midtown ☎ 753-7300 Ⓜ N•R to 5th Ave

☆ BLOOMINGDALE'S ♫B8
Bloomie's has seen better days, but it's making an effort to catch up
fashion-wise by including some high-end urbanwear by the likes of Sean
John, aka Puff Daddy. It is still also a key destination for New Yorkers
looking for home furnishings. Make sure you check out the Barbie
Boutique on the fifth floor, and the in-store chocolate factory on the sixth.
**1000 Third Avenue, UES ☎ 355-5900 Ⓜ N•R to Lexington Ave;
4•5•6 to 59th St**

☆ FELISSIMO ♫B7
New York's most unusual department store appeals to the rich hippy set.
Brimful of amazing gift ideas, from wooden carvings to coloured candles,
and beautiful stationery to indoor fountains, the products here are
gathered from all over the world. Home furnishings, books and divine
accessories are upstairs, as well as an elegant tearoom.
10 W 56th Street, Midtown ☎ 247-5656 Ⓜ B•Q to 57th St

Henri Bendel ♂C8

This jewel of a store was founded in 1896 and recreates the ambience of 1920s Paris. Inside, the store is filled with good things, especially if you're after a sweater (with a myriad colour options), or fabulous make-up brands with staff on hand to give you some top tips.

712 Fifth Avenue, Midtown ☎ 247-1100 Ⓜ E•F to 5th Ave

☆ JEFFREY ♂E9

Jeffrey Kalinsky, the former shoe-buyer at Barneys, has built up a huge following, with this 18,000 sq-ft repository of designer clothes, shoes, accessories, and home products. Alexander McQueen, Helmut Lang, and Jil Sander are all on board. The store also carries its very own private unisex label: KR. The prices may be high, but can you put a cost on style?

449 W 14th Street, Chelsea ☎ 206-1272 Ⓜ A•C•E•L to 14th St

☆ MACY'S ♂B9

Famous for its sponsorship of the annual Thanksgiving Day parade, Macy's also claims to be the world's largest department store. There's virtually nothing you can't buy here. With brand names ranging from Armani to Zenith, as well as cheaper, casual lines, Macy's covers all the bases. The Cellar, in the basement, carries home furnishings and there's also Eatzi's, an excellent deli. Don't miss Macy's notorious one-day sales.

151 W 34th Street, Midtown ☎ 695-4400 Ⓜ B•D•F•N•Q•R to 34th St-Herald Sq

☆ SAKS FIFTH AVENUE ♂C8

Historic Saks should be visited as much for its famed Fifth Avenue setting as anything else. Best for top-of-the-line custom menswear and the exhaustive (and exhausting) bridal section, but the shoe and lingerie departments are loaded with treasures too. Also worth discovering is the surprisingly cutting-edge women's fashion on the fifth floor.

611 Fifth Avenue, Midtown ☎ 753-4000 Ⓜ B•D•F•Q to 47–50th Sts-Rockefeller Center; E•F to 53rd St

☆ TAKASHIMAYA ♂A8

A very elegant Japanese department store, where every object has been carefully chosen. Whether you're looking for the perfect tea service, chic home furnishings, or an opulent item of clothing, this is your store. The jungle-like garden shop on the ground floor is filled with fresh flowers by Christian Tortu, and the tea room in the basement is appropriately serene.

693 Fifth Avenue, Midtown ☎ 350-0100 Ⓜ F to 53rd St

À Détacher
$E12

Local artists have decorated the walls of this lofty space, filled with spare city clothes and housewares to match.

262 Mott Street, Noho ☎ 625-3380 Ⓜ J•M•Z•6 to Canal St

Alpana Bawa
$F11

Luxurious, brightly hued, modern clothes (for both sexes), with bold, graphic shapes. Men love her filmy, embroidered shirts in muted colours.

41 Grand Street, Soho ☎ 965-0559 Ⓜ A•C•E to Canal St

Anna
$A12

Showcases the work of designer Kathy Kemp whose beautifully cut, limited edition pieces are a hit with downtown girls who appreciate unusual detailing.

150 E 3rd Street, East Village ☎ 358-0195 Ⓜ F to 2nd Ave

☆ ANNA SUI
$D11

Always young, fresh, fun, and more than a little bit rock 'n' roll, this purple boutique is filled with clothes for the sartorially courageous, including a small men's collection popular with rock stars and male models. All of this NY designer's leather coats are perfection, her shoes are the funkiest, and the accessories legendary. Recently, Sui's own make-up line (including lots of sparkly nailpolish) has been added to the mix.

113 Greene Street, Soho ☎ 941-8406 Ⓜ N•R to Prince St

☆ ANTIQUE BOUTIQUE
$B11

This space-age store offers some of the best downtown fashion around. There are lots of up-and-coming local designers represented, plus many burgeoning European stars too. Things are grouped according to colour rather than designer, and err towards the avant-garde.

712 Broadway, Nolita ☎ 460-8830 Ⓜ N•R to 8th St NYU; 6 to Astor Pl

☆ APC
$D11

The high-style basics from this French design company keep all those fashion-insider types well-dressed. Classically-cut clothes are made in interesting, contemporary fabrics. The T-shirts and underwear are luxe.

131 Mercer Street, Soho ☎ 966-0069 Ⓜ N•R to Prince St

Atsuro Tayama
$D11

Check out the boldly asymmetric, deconstructed garments – but only if you're feeling confident.

120 Wooster Street, Soho ☎ 334-6002 Ⓜ N•R to Prince St

Behrle ♬F11
If you're only going to buy one pair of leather trousers in your life, make sure they're from this store.
89 Franklin Street, Tribeca ☎ 334-5522 Ⓜ 1•9 to Franklin St

☆ **BETSEY JOHNSON** ♬D11
Soho fashion pioneer, Betsey Johnson, has decorated her flagship store in her signature and ultra-girly flower print, and it looks a bit like an upscale bordello. The clothes are directed at femmes of all shapes, sizes and ages: when you wear one of Betsey's frocks, you know you'll have lots of fun.
138 Wooster Street, Soho ☎ 995-5048 Ⓜ N•R to Prince St

Big Drop ♬D11
Houses a colourful collection of clothing, including lots of little sweaters and items by New York Industry or Earl Jean.
174 Spring Street, Soho ☎ 966-4299 Ⓜ C•E to Spring St; 6 to Spring St

Blue ♬A12
For the total made-to-measure experience, presided over by the brilliant Christina Kara. Kara can rustle up a thoroughly modern outfit in weeks.
125 St Mark's Place, East Village ☎ 228-7744 Ⓜ 6 to Astor Pl

Blue Skirt ♬F10
...And this is Christina Kara's ready-to-wear outlet for gals who can't wait to have some Kara style.
137 Avenue A, East Village ☎ 253-6551 Ⓜ L to 1st Ave

Built By Wendy ♬C12
Showcases the talents of Wendy Mullen, whose urban cowgirl look continues to prove popular.
7 Centre Market Place, Noho ☎ 925-6538 Ⓜ J•M to Bowery

Burberry ♬B7
The luxury store embodies classic British chic with clothing and accessories for men and women.
9 E 57th Street, Midtown ☎ 371-5010 Ⓜ B•Q to 57th St

☆ **CALVIN KLEIN** ♬A8
In Klein's spartan house of minimalist chic, designed by Brit architect John Pawson, you'll find the full complement of the designer's unfussy, clean-lined clothing. Also here is the cheaper CK line, a wide range of accessories (including a new handbag collection), plus the latest bed and bath range from one of America's favourite designers.
654 Madison Avenue, UES ☎ 292-9000 Ⓜ 4•5•6 to 59th St

☆ CALYPSO ST BARTHS
♭D11

This store is filled with a vibrant collection of pretty and feminine clothes from various designers. Along with the I-enjoy-being-a-girl outfits, there are brilliant little bags and accessories that can make getting dressed up a pleasure. Owner Christiane Celle's mini-empire also includes the store selling the wonderful bags of Jamin Puech.

280 Mott Street, Nolita ☎ 965-0990 Ⓜ B•D•F•Q to Broadway-Lafayette St; 6 to Bleecker St

☆ CATHERINE
♭D11

Well-known Parisian stylist, Catherine Malandrino has created a shop that looks like a very groovy, mid-60s living room. It's filled with colour-coordinated clothes that range from pretty beaded skirts to leathers, and lots of perfect tops to complete the outfit. The owner is also known for her high-style cowgirl hat in an array of pastel colours.

468 Broome Street, Soho ☎ 925-6765 Ⓜ N•R to Prince St; C•E to Spring St

Chanel
♭B7

This sumptuous, luxury store carries the ready-to-wear line and accessories.

15 E 57th Street, Midtown ☎ 355-5050 Ⓜ B•Q to 57th St

Chloé
♭F6

Has recently opened its first American store on Madison to house the feminine womenswear by British star, Stella McCartney.

850 Madison Avenue, UES ☎ 717-8220 Ⓜ 6 to 68th St-Hunter College

Christian Dior
♭C8

Perfect tailoring from extravagant Brit, John Galliano, in a luxury store.

703 Fifth Avenue, Midtown ☎ 931-2950 Ⓜ E•F to 5th Ave

☆ COMME DES GARÇONS
♭D9

The far west Chelsea shop of these fashion pioneers is as happening as many of the area's trendy art galleries. The beautifully-made clothes are always experimental and while all this fabulousness doesn't come cheap, Rei Kawakubo's brilliance makes every piece highly collectible.

520 W 22nd Street, Chelsea ☎ 604-9200 Ⓜ C•E to 23rd St

☆ COSTUME NATIONAL
♭D11

In a store that looks like the inside of a very dark, monochrome space ship, Ennio Capasso's clothes are streamlined, sexy and artistic. While the fashion is pure genius, everybody really wants the shoes. Terminally trendy, the men's styles, especially, are unique and very flattering.

108 Wooster Street, Soho ☎ 431-1530 Ⓜ N•R to Prince St; C•E to Spring St

shops

Courtney Washington *off map*
The collection here is simply exquisite: flowing, clean-lined clothes in scrunchy natural fabrics, dubbed 'ethnic-European' and made on site.
674 Fulton Street, Fort Greene ☎ 1-718-852-1464 Ⓜ J•M•Z•2•3•4•5 to Fulton St

☆ **CYNTHIA ROWLEY** *D11*
Cute, sexy and all-girl is the theme at this wild and eclectic store. New York designer, Rowley does dresses the best: pretty fabrics, lots of beading and colour, plus cute accessories like charm bracelets and lipstick bags. Don't miss the fantastic collection of very femme shoes.
112 Wooster Street, Soho ☎ 334-1144 Ⓜ N•R to Prince St

☆ **DARYL K** *A12*
Transplanted from Ireland, Daryl K has become an international style luminary with a huge celebrity following (so much so her clothes are endlessly imitated by Seventh Avenue designers). In her futuristic cavern-of-a-store are sophisticated clothes under the Daryl K label, as well as funky and less expensive pants and tops from her K-189 collection.
21 Bond Street, East Village ☎ 777-0713 Ⓜ 6 to Astor Pl; N•R to Prince St

DDC.Lab *D12*
An all-white style palace, radiating sophistication and big price tags. Their limited-edition Reeboks at a mere $2500 are the ultimate in hedonism.
180 Orchard Street, LES ☎ 375-1647 Ⓜ F•J•M•Z Delancy St-Essex St

☆ **DKNY** *B8*
Donna Karan's flagship is where she keeps her younger, DKNY line – the shapes borrow from classic sportswear silhouettes and the T-shirts make a great NY souvenir.
655 Madison Avenue, UES ☎ 223-3569 Ⓜ 4•5•6 to 59th St

☆ **DL CERNEY** *F11*
Based mostly on vintage wear from the 40s, 50s, and 60s, this store's collection features casual, inexpensive, and well-cut clothing in good quality fabrics. Particularly strong on hand-tailored shirts, which are an essential basic, as well as blazers, fitted pants, and feminine shift dresses.
222 West Broadway, Tribeca ☎ 941-0530 Ⓜ 1•9 to Franklin St; A•C•E to Canal St

☆ DOLCE & GABBANA $F6

The Italian design duo's fabulously sexy clothing will bring out the Sophia Loren (or Marcello Mastroianni) in you. Choose between the glamorous, high-end label, or the 'cheaper' D&G line which repeats themes from the uptown collection like lavish embroidery and flashy metallics.

825 Madison Avenue, UES ☎ 249-4100 Ⓜ 6 to 68th St-Hunter College
D&G: 434 W Broadway, Soho ☎ 965-8000 Ⓜ B•D•F•Q to Broadway-Lafayette

Dosa $D11

This store has grown into a cult favourite with It girls. Using classic shapes, it's the special fabrics and interesting details that give these elegant pieces their appeal.

107 Thompson Street, Soho ☎ 431-1733 Ⓜ C•E to Spring St

Eileen Fisher $A12

Her loose-fitting lines in quiet colours are popular with women who want fashion without ostentation.

314 E 9th Street, East Village ☎ 529-5715 Ⓜ 6 to Astor Pl

Emilio Pucci $F6

For clothing, swimwear, undies, and home accessories featuring retro-style psychedelic swirls.

24 E 64th Street, UES ☎ 752-4777 Ⓜ B•Q to Lexington Ave

☆ EMPORIO ARMANI $E10

Armani is synonymous with high Italian style. Minimalist chic from the master means simple shapes, decorated with lots of glitter and shine, and classic men's suits in rich fabrics. Uptown at Giorgio Armani, Italian ingenuity is applied to more expensive designs.

110 Fifth Avenue, Gramercy Park ☎ 727-3240 Ⓜ L•N•R•4•5•6 to 14th St-Union Sq
Giorgio Armani: 760 Madison Avenue, UES ☎ 988-9191
Ⓜ 6 to 68th St-Hunter College

Etro $F6

For fabulous sweaters and leather goods from Italy

720 Madison Avenue, UES ☎ 317-9096 Ⓜ B•Q to Lexington Ave

☆ FENDI
♂C8

The fabulous Fendi sisters continue to create super-stylish, offbeat clothes, using lots of fake fur and funky leather. But what everyone craves, season after season, are the 'baguette' bags, designed by Karl Lagerfeld, decorated with big 'F' buckles and even bigger price tags.
720 Fifth Avenue, Midtown ☎ 767-0100 Ⓜ E•F to 5th Ave

4W Circle of Art
♂off map

More traditional African wear (by neighbourhood designers) as well as jewellery, candles and cards.
704 Fulton Street, Fort Greene ☎ 1-718-875-6500 Ⓜ J•M•Z•2•3•4•5 to Fulton St

Fragile
♂D12

A tiny shop showcasing a handful of designers such as Bill Tournade and Paris-based Lamine Kouyaté, whose pieces often feature his signature multi-textured, multi-coloured patchwork made from recycled materials.
189 Orchard Street, LES ☎ 334-9166 Ⓜ F•J•M•Z to Delancy St-Essex St

Frida's Closet
♂off map

A pristine space (inspired by Frida Kahlo) with racks of classic handmade women's clothes and jewellery.
296 Smith Street, Carroll Gardens ☎ 1-718-855-0311 Ⓜ F•G to Carroll St

Givenchy
♂D6

Alexander McQueen's genius couture is a marvel of tailoring and innovation.
954 Madison Avenue, UES ☎ 772-1040 Ⓜ 6 to 77th St

☆ GUCCI
♂B7

Tom Ford, who has radically changed the Gucci look, never fails to impress with his sensual, of-the-moment clothes for both sexes. The severely stylish also hanker after the beautiful handbags, amazing shoes, and unbelievably tasteful home furnishings.
10 W 57th Street, Midtown ☎ 826-2600 Ⓜ N•R to 57th St; B•Q to 57th St

The Harlem Collective
♂off map

Featuring clothes for men and women, accessories, jewellery, art, books and small pieces of furniture; many of the artisans and designers are locals, and much of the merch is ethnic.
2533 Eighth Avenue, Harlem ☎ 368-0520 Ⓜ A•B•C•D to 125th St

Hedra Prue   ♯C12
A mixture of groovy designs for girls from designers from around the world. The accessories are always irresistible.
281 Mott Street, Noho ☎ 343-9205 Ⓜ 6 to Spring St

☆ HELMUT LANG   ♯D11
Lang is beloved of fashionable New Yorkers, who never say no to lots of expensive black designs in 'interesting' shapes. The spartan store houses his stark, poetic clothing including stunning men's suits and seemingly simple, yet high-constructed, frocks for women.
80 Greene Street, Soho ☎ 925-7214 Ⓜ 6 to Spring St; N•R to Prince St

☆ HOTEL VENUS   ♯D11
The Soho outlet for downtown style maven Patricia Field, this is the place for outlandish, clubby wear with a dash of class. Hotel Venus carries labels like Courrèges and Stephen Sprouse, plenty of fetish-inspired outerwear, stilettos, adorable accessories from Japan, and rhinestones for every occasion.
382 W Broadway, Soho ☎ 966-4066
Ⓜ C•E to Spring St

☆ IF SOHO NEW YORK   ♯D11
With an intriguing mix of international fashion icons and brilliant newcomers, this store really gives any serious shopper a taste of the truly avant-garde. The entire Comme des Garçons collection is here, along with Martin Margiela and Dries Van Noten, plus designs from edgy local stars that change seasonally.
94 Grand Street, Soho ☎ 334-4964 Ⓜ N•R to Prince St; C•E to Spring St

L'Impasse   ♯B11
A wild collection of look-at-me garb for women.
29 W 8th Street, West Village ☎ 533-3255 Ⓜ 1•9 to Christopher St

Intermix   ♯C10
Innovative clothes from a group of rarely-found international designers.
125 Fifth Avenue, Gramercy Park ☎ 533-9720 Ⓜ N•R to 23rd St

Isabel Toledo Lab   ♯C10
Overlooks the city from its fifth-floor vantage point, and is the showcase for the Cuban-born designer. Check out her feminine yet architectural clothes for women; her capsule collection for men; pieces for the home, and pen-and-ink drawings by her artist husband, Ruben.
277 Fifth Avenue, Gramercy Park ☎ 685-0948 Ⓜ N•R to 23rd St

☆ ISSEY MIYAKE PLEATS PLEASE ♂D11
The store itself is as entertaining as the merch within – check out the windows which change from clear to opaque as you walk by. The clothes, which come in neutrals and bright patterns, are all totally pleated, and slide on the body like a second skin. It's a distinctive look, if you're feeling especially experimental.
128 Wooster Street, Soho ☎ 226-3600 Ⓜ N•R to Prince St; C•E to Spring St

☆ JANET RUSSO ♂B11
The homey shop of the former Madison Avenue fashion designer won't disappoint with its ultra-feminine floral print dresses, classic lines, and precious collectibles from around the world, like Vietnamese dolls and pyjamas. This may well be where you'll find that perfect, pretty little dress.
262 Mott Street, Nolita ☎ 625-3297 Ⓜ B•D•F•Q to Broadway-Lafayette St; 6 to Bleecker St; N•R to Prince St

☆ JEANNETTE LANG ♂D11
You don't have to be super skinny to fit into one of Lang's creations: there's no bias cut so anyone can enjoy her stretch silk looks, flowing lines, and sexy touches. The German designer infuses a general sensuality to her creations and, for women who really want to stand out in a crowd, she also makes custom dresses.
171 Sullivan Street, West Village ☎ 254-5676 Ⓜ 1•9 to Houston St; A•C•E•D•F•B•Q to West 4th St

Jill Anderson ♂A12
Lovely laid-back garb for women – fun dresses and separates in interesting fabrics.
331 E 9th Street, East Village ☎ 253-1747 Ⓜ 6 to Astor Pl

Joseph ♂F6
British favourite Joseph has two stores on Madison, one for his perfect-fit pants and the other for luscious knitwear.
804 Madison Avenue, UES ☎ 570-0077 Ⓜ 6 to 68th St-Hunter College

Juan Anon ♂D12
Providing yet another take on sleek, urban sportswear, where the colour palette is neutral to match the low-key vibe.
193 Orchard Street, LES ☎ 529-7795 Ⓜ F•J•M•Z Delancy St-Essex St

Katayone Adeli ♂A12
This art-gallery-style store is a great setting for the innovative yet very wearable designs for downtown girls. Her trousers fit to perfection.
35 Bond Street, Noho ☎ 260-3500 Ⓜ 6 to Bleecker St

☆ **KIRNA ZABÊTE** ⚡*D11*

Wonder where all the edgy fashion-forward women you see on the streets of Soho shop? Most likely it's at Kirna Zabête, the brainchild of two fashionista friends and always a safe bet for the coolest accessories and hottest looks of the season. Two levels of adornments and attitude include items from hard to find designers like Hussein Chalayan, Alain Tondowski, LuLu Guiness, and Martine Sitbon.

96 Greene Street, Soho ☎ 941-9656 Ⓜ B•D•F•Q to Broadway-Lafayette St; C to Spring St

Language ⚡*E12*

A rich and unusual line in higher-priced designer clothes and accessories (including pashmina shawls).

238 Mulberry Street, Noho ☎ 431-5566 Ⓜ J•M•Z•6 to Canal St

Louie ⚡*D11*

Showcases the talents of a small group of burgeoning style-stars, with a unique collection of accessories.

68 Thompson Street, Soho ☎ 274-1599 Ⓜ C•E to Spring St

☆ **MARC JACOBS** ⚡*D11*

Marc Jacobs has made a name for himself as the premier young American designer. Having been dubbed 'the new Calvin Klein', Jacobs lives up to the moniker with refined, minimalist designs that are continuously fun, fresh, and really expensive. His cashmere sweaters are so popular, there's rumoured to be a very long waiting list to get one.

163 Mercer Street, Soho ☎ 343-1490 Ⓜ N•R to Prince St

Margie Tsai ⚡*D11*

Another member of fashion's younger generation, consistently creating adorable, fun clothes with matching accessories.

4 Prince Street, Noho ☎ 334-2540 Ⓜ N•R to Prince St

Mark Montana ⚡*A12*

On an entirely feminine trip, his 'couture' suits and frocks are always colourful choice for a party.

434 E 9th Street, East Village ☎ 505-0325 Ⓜ 6 to Astor Pl

Mary Adams ⚡*D12*

Mary is mistress of distinctive, feminine party dresses.

159 Ludlow Street, LES ☎ 473-0237 Ⓜ F•J•M•Z Delancy St-Essex St

Max & Roebling
off map

Sells arty, interesting clothes from Brooklyn designers, as well as leather bags and beaded dresses from India.

189 Bedford Avenue, Williamsburg ☎ 1-718-387-0045 Ⓜ L to Bedford Ave

Mayle
C12

Brainchild of ex-model Jane Mayle features an eclectic selection of retro-inspired clothes for women.

252 Elizabeth Street, Noho ☎ 625-0406 Ⓜ F to 2nd Ave

Missoni
F6

Excels in unusual and sensuous knits in gem-like colours.

1009 Madison Avenue, UES ☎ 517-9339 Ⓜ 6 to 68th St-Hunter College

☆ MIU MIU
D11

This is the younger, sexier, slightly less expensive line from Prada. There are lots of little skirts, tops, dresses and coats that are modern yet flirtatious, with unique bags to match. Check out the super-trendy shoes too.

100 Prince Street, Soho ☎ 334-5156 Ⓜ N•R to Prince St

☆ MORGANE LE FAY
D11

The world of Morgane Le Fay is totally original: meant to be layered, one piece on top of the other, gypsy-meets-fairytale princess. This look is meant for the supremely-confident artsy type who likes to be noticed.

151 Spring Street, Soho ☎ 925-0144 Ⓜ N•R to Prince St; C•E to Spring St

Moschino
F6

Whimsical and pricey fashion (for men and women) is the order of the day, although there is a cheaper line for those who can't afford the four-figure price tags.

803 Madison Avenue, UES ☎ 639-9600 Ⓜ 6 to 68th St-Hunter College

Moshood
off map

The clothes are bold and simple, urban and African (and on weekends you'll see live mannequins modelling in the window).

698 Fulton Street, Fort Greene ☎ 1-718-243-9433 Ⓜ J•M•Z•2•3•4•5 to Fulton St

Nicole Farhi
B8

Elegant easy-to-wear clothing that also accommodates a stylish, in-store restaurant, Nicoles.

14 E 60th Street, UES ☎ 421-7720 Ⓜ N•R to Lexington Ave

shops

Nicole Miller

‡D11

Great for wearable evening dresses and chic separates.
134 Prince Street, Soho ☎ 343-1362 Ⓜ N•R to Prince St

☆ NOVA USA

‡D12

Surrounded by a haze of bright lights, this store carries occasionally severe, sporty clothes (like the perfect drawstring pants) meant for men, but worn by lots of women who appreciate the classic cut.
100 Stanton Street, LES ☎ 228-6844 Ⓜ F•J•M•Z Delancy St-Essex St

Nylon Squid

‡A12

This futuristic-looking store favours British designers. The interesting selection of streetwear couldn't be any more up-to-date if it tried.
222 Lafayette Street, Noho ☎ 334-6554 Ⓜ 6 to Bleeker St

☆ OLIVE & BETTE

‡A5

In this cute neighbourhood shop (there's a sister store on the UES), the focus is on happening young designers like Daryl K and Vivienne Tam, along with genius jeans from Earl, those must-have T-shirts from 3 Dot and the most recent thing from Fiorucci.
252 Columbus Avenue, UWS ☎ 579-2178 Ⓜ B•C to 72nd St

105 Stanton

‡D12

Designers include Min Lee, who specializes in classic clothes with a twist – chic numbers that can be worn all day and night when teamed with tiny evening bags.
105 Stanton Street, LES ☎ 375-0304 Ⓜ F•J•M•Z Delancy St-Essex St

Oriental Dress Company

‡C12

If you want your cheongsam custom-made for a fraction of what it would cost you at Dolce & Gabbana (and it will be nearly as amazing), drop by this place. You can choose from the shop's own luxurious silks (in a wide variety of colours), or provide your own fabric. Orders take about three weeks, long dresses cost around $280, short ones $250.
38 Mott Street, LES ☎ 349-0818 Ⓜ J•M to Bowery

Patch 155

‡D12

Designer Cal Patch's treasure trove of quirky clothes – urban and funky-pretty – includes exclusive labels such as It's an Exciting Time to Be Me!.
155 Rivington Street, LES ☎ 533-9995 Ⓜ F•J•M•Z Delancy St-Essex St

Patricia Field ♯A12
Catering to club-kids and drag queens who subscribe to her taste in clingy clothing, 6-inch stilettos and colourful accessories (there's also a wig salon).
10 E 8th Street, West Village ☎ 254-1699 Ⓜ 6 to Astor Pl

Philosophy di Alberta Ferretti ♯D11
Genius clothes that are almost upstaged by the architecture.
452 W Broadway, Soho ☎ 460-5500 Ⓜ C•E to Spring St

☆ **POLO RALPH LAUREN** ♯F6
This historic, Upper East Side mansion provides the perfect environment for Ralph Lauren's classic look for men and women. Just as the setting appropriates the trappings of an English country castle, the clothing encorporates Old World elegance and New World ease.
867 Madison Avenue, UES ☎ 606-2100 Ⓜ 6 to 68th St-Hunter College

Polo Sport ♯F6
Ralph Lauren's sportier creations for those who prefer the casual but preppy look.
79 W Broadway, UES ☎ 625-1660 Ⓜ 6 to 68th St-Hunter College

☆ **PRADA** ♯F6
No matter which lime green Prada store you happen into, plan on spending big bucks for some of the most modish clothes available anywhere. While her bags, shoes, and shapes are endlessly imitated in the chain stores, Miuccia Prada's original and clean-lined designs for men and women are worth every penny.
841 Madison Avenue, Midtown ☎ 327-4200 Ⓜ 6 to 68th St-Hunter College
724 Fifth Avenue, Midtown ☎ 664-0010 Ⓜ B•Q to 57th St

☆ **PRADA SPORT** ♯D11
How to look fabulous when you're actually doing something more than posing? For those who worship at the altar of Prada, this latest addition to Muiccia's empire is a must. Filled with highly designed sport clothes, utility wear and shoes.
116 Wooster Street, Soho ☎ 925-2221 Ⓜ N•R to Prince St; C•E to Spring St

Red Tape ♯A12
Showcases brilliant designer Rebecca Danenberg's bold, graphic pieces for women as well as those of other NYC designers.
E 9th Street, East Village ☎ 529-8483 Ⓜ 6 to Astor Pl

Roberto Cavalli $F6

This is the only boutique of the Latin-born designer in North America, providing a home for his outré, multimedia designs for women and men.
711 Madison Avenue, UES ☎ 840-5110 Ⓜ B•Q to Lexington Ave

Scheme $off map

A major fashion outpost carrying lots of labels like Iceberg and Moschino plus a wide array of edgy trainers and must-have boots. There's also a fashion-forward selection of leather jackets.
201–303 W 125th Street, Harlem ☎ 678-2146 Ⓜ 2•3 to 125th St

☆ SCOOP $D11

Owner Stephanie Grenfield's taste in clothing runs from girly frocks to bold separates: young designers from New York and Europe are the lure, with lots of cute accessories to finish the look. Don't miss colourful T-shirts by Juicy USA – the best bargains in the store.
532 Broadway, Soho ☎ 925-2886 Ⓜ C•E to Spring St

Searle $D6

An exclusive UES affair, which has no fewer than four stores on Madison. They specialize in clean-lined coats, sportswear and covetable knitwear.
1035 Madison Avenue, UES ☎ 717-4022 Ⓜ 6 to 77th St

Selia Yang $A12

Supremely pretty party frocks in diaphanous fabrics.
328 E 9th Street, East Village ☎ 777-9776 Ⓜ 6 to Astor Pl

Shack Inc $F11

As much an art gallery as a shop, features ethereal, romantic clothes (all hand-made and hand-dyed) plus home furnishings and handbags.
137 West Broadway, Tribeca ☎ 267-8004 Ⓜ 1•9 to Franklin St

☆ SHANGHAI TANG $A8

Ultra-luxe clothes from China are the main attraction in this impressive, brightly-coloured art-deco store, which includes lots of mandarin-style jackets and gorgeous cashmere sweaters, and an in-store tailor who makes up garments in rich, expensive silks (5th flr).
714 Madison Avenue, UES ☎ 888-0111 Ⓜ N•R to 5th Ave

Sorelle Firenze $B13

For a hip, feminine look, this store (run by two Italian sisters - natch), does a fine line in flirty skirts and tops, lacey dresses and accessories.
139½ Reade Street, Tribeca ☎ 571-2720 Ⓜ 1•2•3•9 to Chambers St; A•C to Chambers St

Stacia New York *♯off map*
The adorably feminine clothes are made by the owner, who used to work for Cynthia Rowley.
267 Smith Street, Carroll Gardens ☎ 1-718-237-0078 Ⓜ F•G to Bergen St

☆ **STEVEN ALAN** *♯D11*
The eponymous owner is famous for his ability to sniff out new, young design talent before anybody else. His main women's store regularly showcases young designers who combine casual chic with a downtown aesthetic. Just west of Sixth Avenue is his first men's boutique, filled with smart utilitarian styles and accessories.
women: 60 Wooster Street, Soho ☎ 334-6354 Ⓜ N•R to Prince St; C•E to Spring St
men: 558 Broome Street, Soho ☎ 625-2541 Ⓜ 1•9 to Canal St

☆ **TG-170** *♯C12*
Owner Terri Gillis was one of the original pioneers in the now happening LES fashion scene. This is one of the most distinctive and edgy collections in New York, and many a designer has been launched here. The prices are impressively low for all this daring style.
170 Ludlow Street, LES ☎ 995-8660 Ⓜ F to 2nd Ave

Tocca *♯D11*
A range of very girlie, but wearable designs as well as pretty bed linens.
161 Mercer Street, Soho ☎ 343-3912 Ⓜ N•R to Prince St

☆ **TRACEY FEITH** *♯D11*
The interior here is all elegant dark wood and white walls – the perfect place to display Feith's colourful and seductive dresses, many of them inspired by vintage silhouettes and fabrics. Darling shoes and bags, and Raj, the less-expensive, hippie-gypsy clothes, that all downtown girls love.
209 Mulberry Street, Nolita ☎ 334-3097 Ⓜ C•E to Spring St

TSE *♯F6*
Cashmere is the raison d'être at this store, where brilliant designer Hussein Chalayan spins the soft stuff into coats and sweaters. The funkier Tse Surface downtown is for a younger customer, with funkier colours and styles. Prices are a little less too, but nothing's cheap.
827 Madison Avenue, UES ☎ 472-7790 Ⓜ B•Q to Lexington Ave

☆ **UNTITLED** ♯A11

This two-storey abode carries a selection of clothes from hot, young designers from around the globe. Upstairs, the duds are mostly for dudes, and include desirable gear by Dirk Bikkemberg, Martin Margiela, Helmut Lang, Maharishi, Jean-Paul Gaultier, and more. Downstairs, the women's clothes are equally illustrious and the accessories are divine.

26 W 8th Street, West Village ☎ **505-9725** Ⓜ **A•B•C•D•E•F•Q to W 4th St-Washington Sq**

Valentino ♯F6

This elegant emporium is beloved of the neighbourhood's fur-coat-brigade.

747 Madison Avenue, UES ☎ **772-6969** Ⓜ **6 to 68th St-Hunter College**

☆ **VERSACE** ♯F6

Beloved by exhibitionist types (including lots of celebs), the entire Versace collection shines in a multi-level shop that is as lavish and vivid as the clothes it contains. Even if the colossal price tags are out of your league, stop in just for the wild Versace experience.

815 Madison Avenue, Midtown ☎ **744-6868** Ⓜ **6 to 68th St-Hunter College**

Vivienne Tam ♯D11

Sleek, exotic clothes – form-fitting, beaded dresses; saucy suits; handbags and loungewear with an oriental flair – have become a staple of fashionable gals, including Julia Roberts.

99 Greene Street, Soho ☎ **966-2398** Ⓜ **N•R to Prince St**

☆ **VIVIENNE WESTWOOD** ♯D11

British icon Vivienne Westwood's first stateside store. The space (once a Soho art gallery) is filled with the entire range of Westwood's quirky English tailoring, including the hard-to-find Anglomania and her MAN collections. There are also loads of distinctive bags.

71 Greene Street, Soho ☎ **334-5200** Ⓜ **N•R to Prince St**

☆ **YOHJI YAMAMOTO** ♯D11

Yamamoto's all-white shrine of a store pushes forward the boundaries of fashion – so no wonder the sales help behave as if every item were a work of art. Consistently inventive and surprisingly wearable, Yamamoto's designs are like nothing else you'll see.

103 Grand Street, Soho ☎ **966-9066** Ⓜ **J•M•N•R•Z•6 to Canal St**

Zao   *D12*

This lifestyle boutique has the best up-and-coming designers from around the world: fashion, furniture, electronics – plus sexy sounds and happening art shows to boot.

175 Orchard Street, LES ☎ 505-0500 Ⓜ F•J•M•Z Delancy St-Essex St

Zero   *C12*

Sophisticated urban clothes are the order of the day.

225 Mott Street, Noho ☎ 925-3849 Ⓜ 6 to Spring St

discount stores

☆ **CENTURY 21**   *D13*

Even uptown fashionistas aren't beneath shopping at this infamous clearing house, featuring 16 departments with most designer names at 25–75% off – but it's a real endurance test to pluck the diamonds from the trash.

22 Cortlandt Street, Lower Manhattan ☎ 227-9092 Ⓜ N•R•1•9 to Cortlandt St

☆ **DAFFY'S**   *B9*

The masters of the outfit for under $100. Fight your way through the overcrowded racks for eveningwear, lingerie, and men's and women's clothes and shoes.

131 Broadway, Gramercy Park ☎ 736-4477 Ⓜ B•D•F•N•Q•R to 34th St-Herald Sq

☆ **FIND OUTLET**   *C12*

New stock arrives every week in this store in chic Noho where last season's designer wares and accessories are sold at up to 80% off the regular price. Feminine designs by Paige Novick, Joseph, Helmut Lang, and Jimmy Choo fill the neat, organized space.

229 Mott Street, Nolita ☎ 226-5167 Ⓜ 6 to Spring St

☆ **LOEHMANN'S**   *F9*

Known for carrying tremendous high-end designer merchandise from DKNY, Versace, Dries van Noten and many more – all at eye-popping prices.

101 Seventh Avenue, Chelsea ☎ 352-0856 Ⓜ 1•9 to 18th St

☆ **NICE PRICE $$$**   *B9*

Each week several designers offer up delicious samples of their clothing, old and new, at below bargain prices. Marc Jacobs, Donna Karan, Urban Outfitters, and Kenar, amongst other designers, have all tested their wares here.

2nd floor, 261 W 36th Street, Midtown ☎ 947-8748 Ⓜ A•C•E to 34th St-Penn Station

drink

☆ ASTOR WINES & SPIRITS
♭A12

Manhattan's biggest liquor store, with row upon row of bottles from around the world, including a trustworthy wine selection from New York State. The staff know their stuff and you can't beat the prices (check out the house brand liquors). Free wine tastings 3–6pm every Sat, and often 5–8pm Thu–Fri.

12 Astor Place, East Village ☎ 674-7500 Ⓜ 6 to Astor Pl

☆ BEST CELLARS
♭A6

Instead of classifying wines by grape or origin, here sections are labelled 'luscious', 'juicy', 'smooth', 'big', etc, so you can match them with mood or food. Better yet, every bottle is under $10 and has an evocative description to go with it. Free tastings daily from 5–8pm.

1291 Lexington Avenue, UES ☎ 426-4200 Ⓜ 4•5•6 to 86th St

electronics

☆ B & H PHOTO-VIDEO
♭B9

Home from home for many photographers looking for the best deal on professional quality lenses and bodies.

420 Ninth Avenue, Midtown ☎ 239-7500 Ⓜ A•C•E to 34th St-Penn Station

Circuit City
♭E10

Filled with great deals on everything you've ever wanted that plugs in, has an on button or takes a picture.

52 E 14th Street, Gramercy Park ☎ 387-0730 Ⓜ L•N•R•4•5•6 to 14th St-Union Sq

☆ J & R MUSIC & COMPUTER WORLD
♭A14

All the top-name computer and stereo equipment you could ever hope to use.

23 Park Row, Lower Manhattan ☎ 238-9100 Ⓜ J•M•Z•2•3•4•5 to Fulton St-Broadway Nassau; N•R•4•5•6 to City Hall

☆ NOBODY BEATS THE WIZ
♭C8

A major chain specializing in TVs and audio equipment and accessories. The bargains make up for the sluggish service.

555 Fifth Avenue, Midtown ☎ 557-7770
Ⓜ B•D•F•Q to 47–50th Sts-Rockefeller Center; E•F to 5th Ave

☆ **RADIO SHACK** *⌂D10*
For years, consumers have thought of the Radio Shack chain as a cheap imitation of the electronic big boys. But recently, their products have taken a giant step forward in quality, and the slightly higher costs reflect it.
626 Broadway, LES ☎ 677-7069 Ⓜ B•D•F•Q to Broadway-Lafayette St

☆ **SHARPER IMAGE** *⌂C8*
The *only* destination for gadget freaks.
W 57th Street, Midtown ☎ 265-2550 Ⓜ B•D•F•Q to 47th–50th Sts-Rockefeller Center

erotic boutiques

Naughty & Nice *⌂C5*
The neighbourhood's friendly sex store – the sign outside says 'Romance Boutique'. Inside are sex toys, naughty lingerie and erotic videos. This being the Upper West Side, it is only slightly tacky.
212 W 80th Street, UWS ☎ 787-1212 Ⓜ 1•9 to 79th St

Pink Pussycat Boutique *⌂A11*
A neighbourhood institution that's so unintimidating, the staff might as well be selling candy bars.
167 W 4th Street, West Village ☎ 243-0077 Ⓜ A•B•C•E•F•Q to W 4th St-Washington Sq

Pleasure Chest *⌂A11*
An erotic boutique, sleek as can be – prices here are reassuringly expensive and the window displays are often wildly imaginative.
156 Seventh Avenue S, West Village ☎ 242-2158 Ⓜ 1•9 to Christopher St

Toys in Babeland *⌂D12*
A hip sex shop with naughty lingerie and toys for girls home alone.
94 Rivington Street, LES ☎ 375-1701 Ⓜ F•J•M•Z Delancy St-Essex St

eyewear

☆ **ROBERT MARC** *⌂F4*
A New York staple for excellent eyewear, this tiny chain has a good selection including hard-to-find makes like Prosh and Beausoleil.
1300 Madison Avenue, UES ☎ 722-1600 Ⓜ 6 to 96th St

☆ SELIMA OPTIQUE ⌖D11
Selima's sexy, sleek line of eyewear is known for its cult-like following of everyone from the Dior-clad lady to edgy hipsters. There are loads of other designer frames stocked too.
59 Wooster Street, Soho ☎ 343-9490 Ⓜ C•E to Spring St

fabrics

Kaarta Imports ⌖off map
The place for all kinds of African fabrics and almost all of it 100% cotton.
121 W 125th Street, Harlem ☎ 866-4062 Ⓜ 2•3 to 125th St

food stores

☆ BALDUCCI'S ⌖A11
Open since 1946, this virtual horn of plenty will astound you with its exquisite fruits and vegetables as well as lovely cheeses, pastries, chocolates, charcuterie and prepared foods. Most of it's costly, so sometimes it's just fun to look.
424 Sixth Avenue, West Village ☎ 673-2600 Ⓜ A•B•C•D•E• F•Q to W 4th St-Washington Sq

☆ CHELSEA MARKET ⌖F9
A mini mall open daily for gourmets, offers and offering a mouthwatering array of international delicacies: Amy's Bread, Thai and Italian import goods, an exclusive wine store, and incredible ice-cream from Ronnybrook Farm Dairy.
75 Ninth Avenue, Chelsea ☎ 243-5678 Ⓜ A•C•E to 14th St; L to 8th Ave

☆ DEAN & DELUCA ⌖D11
A huge white gallery with hundreds of mustards, vinegars, olive oils and herbs, as well as gourmet cheeses, gorgeous breads, exotic flowers, professional kitchenware and cookbooks. Up at the front of the store is a popular espresso bar.
560 Broadway, Soho ☎ 226-6800 Ⓜ N•R to Prince St

☆ ELI'S BREAD AT THE VINEGAR FACTORY ⌖A6
Eli's is famous citywide for its cavernous warehouse (a former vinegar factory!) of grocery items. The salad bar holds dozens of choices and 10 fresh soups, but the seafood counter, homemade potato chips and fresh squeezed juices also make it worth the trek. Upstairs is a café and exclusive housewares department.
431 E 91st Street, UES ☎ 987-0885 Ⓜ 4•5•6 to 86th St

Fairways   ⌖C5
A UWS deli that wows foodies, and is open 24 hours.
2127 Broadway, UWS ☎ 595-1888 Ⓜ 1•9 to 79th St

☆ **GARDEN OF EDEN**   ⌖D9
Both the Chelsea and East Village locations display exotic, fascinating
fruits you've never heard of: 'ugly fruit' from Jamaica, gold tamarilo from
New Zealand, kiwana-horned melons, sweet feijoa, etc. This is a global,
decently-priced farmers' market with dozens of types of marinated
olives, fantastic prepared foods and cured meats.
162 W 23rd Street, Chelsea ☎ 675-6300 Ⓜ 1•9 to 23rd St
314 Third Ave, East Village ☎ 255-4200 Ⓜ L•N•R•4•5•6 to 14th St-Union Sq

Godiva Chocolatier   ⌖B7
Exquisite chocolates from Belgium.
701 Fifth Avenue, Midtown ☎ 593-2845 Ⓜ B•Q to 57th St

☆ **GOURMET GARAGE**   ⌖D11
Groovy, food-conscious downtown types are always roaming the aisles
here, filling their baskets with organic produce, European cheeses, house
olive oil, salsa, tortilla chips and ice cream. Also a funky stop for bagels,
sandwiches and soups to go.
453 Broome Street, Soho ☎ 941-5850 Ⓜ N•R to Prince St

Jefferson Market   ⌖A11
The selection is enormous and prices affordable; the people who work
here are without the attitude found in more elitist food venues.
450 Sixth Avenue, West Village ☎ 533-3377 Ⓜ 1•9 to Christopher St

M&I   ⌖off map
The serious gourmet store, but be persistent to get anyone to wait on you.
249 Brighton Beach Avenue, Brighton Beach ☎ 1-718-615-1011
Ⓜ D•Q to Brighton Beach

Mrs Stahl's Knishery   ⌖off map
Cheap, rib-sticking snacks to go, in flavours like mushroom and potato
or blueberry.
1001 Brighton Beach Avenue, Brighton Beach ☎ 1-718-648-0210
Ⓜ D•Q to Brighton Beach

☆ MURRAY'S CHEESE SHOP ♪A11
Manhattan's oldest cheese purveyor (opened 60 years ago) is beloved by foodies and locals alike – an old-world cornucopia of well-chosen international dairy produce, sold by a knowledgeable staff who have the gift of the gab. A fun Village stop for antipasti and sandwiches as well.
257 Bleecker Street, West Village ☎ 243-3289 Ⓜ 1•9 to Christopher St

Odessa ♪off map
This elegant store offers fancy foods like duck legs with apples and coubiliac of salmon.
1113 Brighton Beach Avenue, Brighton Beach ☎ 1-718-332-3223 Ⓜ D•Q to Brighton Beach

Philip's Candy Store ♪off map
It's been selling made-on-the-premises candies for over 40 years.
1237 Surf Avenue, Coney Island ☎ 1-718-372-8783 Ⓜ B•D•F•N to Stiwell Ave Coney Island

Richart ♪C8
Empyreal French delicacies almost too exquisite to eat
7 E 55th Street, Midtown ☎ 371-9369 Ⓜ E•F to 5th Ave

☆ RUSS & DAUGHTERS ♪C12
This cherished, spic-and-span Jewish deli has survived since World War I due to personalized service, and top quality smoked salmon (eight varieties), chopped liver, whitefish salad, sophisticated cheeses and dried fruits. So proud of their stock, they urge tastings on you (Eat!).
179 E Houston Street, LES ☎ 475-4880 Ⓜ F to 2nd Ave

Teuscher ♪C8
From Switzerland , this store has a divine selection of chocolates.
620 Fifth Avenue, Midtown ☎ 246-4416 Ⓜ E•F to 5th Ave

☆ UNION SQUARE MARKET ♪E10
An open air farmers' market selling seasonal produce, maple syrup, jams, flowers, and plants, and open Monday, Wednesday, Friday and Saturday, all year round.
bet. 17th St & Broadway, Gramercy Park ☎ no phone Ⓜ L•N•R•4•5•6 to 14th St-Union Sq

☆ ZABAR'S   *C5*

Beloved by New Yorkers and tourists alike, this landmark, labyrinthine store has a dizzying array of cheeses, coffee beans, bargain caviar, imported candies, baked goods and smoked salmon. Upstairs are housewares at the cheapest prices in town. Nutty on the weekends.

2245 Broadway, UWS ☎ 787-2000 Ⓜ 1•9 to 79th St

gifts & stationery

Alphaville   *D11*

An amusing selection of market-style collectibles, including tin toys, pop novelties and vintage movie posters in an all-white setting

226 W Houston Street, West Village ☎ 675-6850 Ⓜ 1•9 to Houston St

Chelsea Garden Store   *F9*

Specializes in essential tools and interesting gifts for the green-fingered.

207 Ninth Avenue, Chelsea ☎ 741-6052 Ⓜ A•C•E to 14th St

Isay's Leather   *off map*

Crammed with interesting items from the former USSR: amber jewellery, dolls, hand-painted boxes, and leather goods.

292 Brighton Beach Avenue, Brighton Beach ☎ 1-718-769-8775 Ⓜ D•Q to Brighton Beach

Kate's Paperie   *A11*

Holds no fewer than 5000 different kinds of paper, many of them handmade. Beautiful journals, pens and greeting cards are also carried.

8 W 13th Street, West Village ☎ 633-0570 Ⓜ 1•9 to Christopher St

Main Street Ephemera/Paper Collectibles   *off map*

Everything to satisfy your schlock-horror movie-poster needs.

272 Smith Street, Carroll Gardens ☎ 1-718-858-6541 Ⓜ F•G to Carroll St

Maxilla & Mandible   *A5*

The question most often asked at this store is 'are they real?'. 'They' refers to the human bones for sale at this extraordinary place, and the answer is 'yes'. If dem bones aren't your thing, the store also has fascinating fossils, seashells, bugs, butterflies and other natural history-related phenomena.

451 Columbus Avenue, UWS ☎ 724-6173 Ⓜ 1•9 to 86th St

Oriental Gifts   *E12*

Has a nice variety of Chinoiserie, from vases to fans, lanterns and woks.

96 Bayard Street, LES ☎ 608-6670 Ⓜ J•M•Z•6 to Canal St

☆ PEARL RIVER MART ♫E12
This Chinese emporium is packed with goodies: the top floor stocks a vast assortment of kimonos, silk and embroidered pyjamas and underwear, slippers, cheongsam dresses, and padded jackets. On other floors are kitschy home furnishings, trinkets, Chinese music, videos, and food: you're bound to see some celebrity picking through the treasures.
277 Canal Street, LES ☎ **431-4770** Ⓜ **J•M•Z•6 to Canal St; N•R to Canal St**

Sears & Robot ♫A12
For trinkets and T-shirts make your way to this wacky store specializing in Japanese imports and other kitschery.
120 E 7th Street, East Village ☎ **253-8719** Ⓜ **6 to Astor Pl**

☆ SHI ♫B11
Spare, sleek and modern is the style of this store, and everything in it from tiny lights on strings to perfectly-shaped ash trays. Very Zen.
233 Elizabeth Street, Nolita ☎ **334-4330** Ⓜ **6 to Bleecker St**

☆ TROY ♫D11
Troy's superb collection of strong design pieces by various New York and European names is offset by a sleek, all-white space. Hunt for the best in 90s design: unique lamps, small furniture and cool accessories like clocks and candles. Everything has a strong graphic edge.
138 Greene Street, Soho ☎ **941-4777** Ⓜ **N•R to Prince St; C•E to Spring St; 6 to Bleecker St**

Village Chess Shop ♫D11
In business since 1972. Folks of all ages come here for the huge selection of boards and pieces, or to pick up a game at one of the store's small café tables.
230 Thompson Street, West Village ☎ **475-8130** Ⓜ **C•E to Spring St**

hats

☆ AMY DOWNS ♫C12
Her hats are outrageous, and take a degree of courage to wear; some make you think the Cat in the Hat went couture.
103 Stanton Street, LES ☎ **598-4189** Ⓜ **F to 2nd Ave**

☆ KELLY CHRISTIE ♫D11
Beautifully crafted, handmade hats, there's something for everyone.
235 Elizabeth Street, Nolita ☎ **965-0686** Ⓜ **N•R to Prince St**

shops

☆ ABC CARPET & HOME $E10
One of the most popular and unique stores in NYC, it's got six floors crammed with the most luxurious items for bed, bath, table and kitchen – plus fine fabrics and trim, antiques and, of course, carpets. On the ground floor there's a great café and an exotic food shop.
888 Broadway, Gramercy Park ☎ 473-3000 Ⓜ L•N•R•4•5•6 to 14th St-Union Sq

☆ AD-HOC SOFTWARE $D11
Ad-Hoc Software's creative items always manage to fit the bill. Along with covetable bed and bath accessories (including some of the finest sheets and towels anywhere), there are lots of luxuries like French scented candles, gorgeous table linens, edgy dishware and cutlery, and even the latest in watch design.
136 Wooster Street, Soho ☎ 925-2652 Ⓜ N•R to Prince St

African Paradise $off map
A showcase for all things African – garments, home furnishings, art, and tie-dye fabrics.
27 W 125th Street, Harlem ☎ 410-5294 Ⓜ A•B•C•D to 125th St

Amalgamated Home $A11
The place for furniture, lamps, and home accessories.
9 Christopher Street, West Village ☎ 255-4160 Ⓜ 1•9 to Christopher St

Amalgamated Hardware $A11
Interesting drawer pulls, door handles, hooks and other finishing touches.
19 Christopher Street, West Village ☎ 691-8695 Ⓜ 1•9 to Christopher St

Anandamali $F11
Over-the-top, quirky glamour comes in the shape of bureaux, tables and mirrors decorated (mosaic-style) with antique china.
35 North Moore Street, Tribeca ☎ 343-8964 Ⓜ 1•9 to Franklin St

Antik $F11
A covetable selection of 20th-century collectibles, including lots of Scandinavian ceramics and furniture.
104 Franklin Street, Tribeca ☎ 343-0471 Ⓜ 1•9 to Franklin St

Apartment 48 ♯F9
A store laid out to resemble the pad of some clever interior decorator. The overall feel is traditional-casual chic, with a mixture of flea market finds, designer knick-knacks and useful kitchen implements.
48 W 17th Street, Chelsea ☎ 807-1391 Ⓜ 1•9 to 18th st

Astroturf ♯off map
Homewares (cocktail shakers, clunky lamps and spindly dinette sets) can be found at this all-retro store.
290 Smith Street, Carroll Gardens ☎ 1-718-522-6182 Ⓜ F•G to Carroll St

☆ AUTO ♯F9
Modern, must-have designs for the home, office and body. Off the beaten path, this immaculate shop-cum-showroom features items by young, free-thinking American designers like Elizabeth Powell, Fred Flare, and Kathleen Lewis. Auto's owners also represent the designers who've been snapped up by outlets like Barney's New York, Colette in Paris and DKNY.
805 Washington Street, Chelsea ☎ 229-2292 Ⓜ A•C•E to 14th St

☆ BED BATH AND BEYOND ♯F9
This gigantic superstore is the first place to check out when you're furnishing a new apartment. It carries a vast range of things for the home – some of it high-end and expensive, some of it a real bargain. For people used to shopping in crowded spaces with limited options, this place is a real treat, and the quality of the merchandise is pretty good.
620 Sixth Avenue, Chelsea ☎ 255-3550 Ⓜ 1•9 to 18th St; F to 23rd St

Campagna Home Shop ♯C10
Full of imported painted porcelain, pots and pans too gorgeous to actually cook with, and other snazzy objects.
29 E 21st Street, Gramercy Park ☎ 420-1600 Ⓜ N•R to 23rd St

Cobblestones ♯A12
A tiny boutique filled to the brim with *tchotchkes* as well as selection of accessories.
314 E 9th Street, East Village ☎ 673-5372 Ⓜ 6 to Astor Pl

Crate & Barrel ♯A8
The famous Chicago home furnishings outpost, has a beautiful and spacious NY store. On offer are high quality yet functional and chic furniture, dishwares, and other home accessories – all at affordable prices.
650 Madison Avenue, Midtown ☎ 2308-0011 Ⓜ N•R to 5th Ave

Dom
♯D11

For the ultimate in cheap and cheerful, yet well-designed home furnishings. You can get colourful home accessories for a song, along with whimsical lighting and inflatable furniture that's easy to store.

382 W Broadway, Soho ☎ 334-5580 Ⓜ C•E to Spring St

Eclectic Home
♯D9

Offers a sleek, post-modern aesthetic; its lamps, clocks and other accessories have a colourful, kooky edge.

224 Eighth Avenue, Chelsea ☎ 255-2373 Ⓜ C•E to 23rd St

☆ FISHS EDDY
♯E10

Dishes are the name of the game at Fishs Eddy. The owners of this clever shop buy up sets of decorated dishes from country clubs, schools, hotels and other unlikely institutions, and sell them here. They also do their own retro designs – the one with the New York skyline is fab.

889 Broadway, Gramercy Park ☎ 420-9020 Ⓜ L•N•R•4•5•6 to 14th St-Union Sq; N•R to 23rd St

☆ GRACIOUS HOME
♯F6

Taking up almost both sides of one block, Gracious Home has all you need to line your nest. Everything here, from hardware to cleaning products, imported linens and towels, is sleek and highly-designed.

1217 & 1220 Third Avenue, UES ☎ 517-6300 Ⓜ 6 to 68th St-Hunter College

H
♯A12

Home to elegantly modern lamps and furniture as pared down as the store's name.

335 E 9th Street, East Village ☎ 477-2631 Ⓜ 6 to Astor Pl

Hold Everything
♯F9

This store does just that – stocking containers, dividers and racks for all your worldly possessions.

104 Seventh Avenue, Chelsea ☎ 633-1674 Ⓜ 1•2•3•9 to 14th St

It's a Mod, Mod World
♯F10

No vintage per se, but it does carry lamps and clocks recycled from such disposables as cereal boxes.

85 First Avenue, East Village ☎ 460-8004 Ⓜ L to 1st Ave

☆ JONATHAN ADLER
♭D11

Designer of the moment, Adler is known for his whimsical home accessories blessed with bold, graphic designs. He has assembled a charming and aesthetically-pleasing selection of vases and tableware, along with other desirable objects culled from trips to flea markets – clearly his obsession.

465 Broome Street, Soho ☎ 941-8950 Ⓜ N•R to Prince St

La Maison Moderne
♭F9

A tiny, cluttered shop, has plenty of precious accessories, such as vintage silver knives and beaded lampshades.

144 W 19th Street, Chelsea ☎ 691-9603 Ⓜ 1•9 to 18th St

☆ LAS VENUS
♭C12

A staple for fashionable downtowners, this is all about 20th-century pop culture. The store carries lots of graphic furniture and other colourful home furnishings (some of them quite kitsch) that any trendster would crave.

163 Ludlow Street, LES ☎ 982-0608 Ⓜ F to 2nd Ave

☆ MOSS
♭D11

A showcase of the best designs past and present: if you like things for your home that are both functional and slick, Moss is nirvana. There are silver pieces from Alessi, fanciful glassware, jewel-toned Swedish crystal, and vases made from resin. The shop sometimes serves as a gallery for up-and-coming designers.

146 Greene Street, Soho ☎ 226-2190 Ⓜ N•R to Prince St

Mxyplyzyk
♭F9

The store that nobody can pronounce, carries lots of highly designed items to make every aspect of your home utterly groovy.

125 Greenwich Avenue, Chelsea ☎ 989-4300 Ⓜ A•C•E to 14th St; L to 8th Ave

Orange Chicken
♭F12

A more traditional take on furnishing your home.

152 Franklin Street, Tribeca ☎ 431-0037 Ⓜ 1•9 to Franklin St

Oser
♭B13

If Hawaiian bamboo furniture is up your alley, then you will love Oser. Here you can sip coffee at the bar, watch an old surf movie, and admire the hot line of own brand swimsuits or the giant shark you've bought to hang on your wall.

148 Duane Street, Tribeca ☎ 571-6737 Ⓜ 1•2•3•9 to Chambers St; A•C to Chambers St

Portico Bed & Bath *♭C12*

The lifestyle pioneers in Soho. They offer the finest, most elegant linens and other accessories that will make your home positively scream 'good taste'.

139 Spring Street, Soho ☎ 941-7722 Ⓜ 6 to Spring St

☆ **POTTERY BARN** *♭D11*

As quintessentially American as Gap, this is a mass-market outlet for well-designed, countrified home furnishings at reasonable prices. It's hard to find anyone in New York who doesn't shop here.

600 Broadway, Nolita ☎ 219-2420 Ⓜ B•D•F•Q to Broadway-Lafayette St

Quilted Corner *♭F10*

Stacks of vintage fabric, bedding and linens.

120 Fourth Avenue, East Village ☎ 505-6568 Ⓜ L to 3rd Ave

☆ **SHABBY CHIC** *♭D11*

No false advertising here – the name says it all. The owners of this influential design store have made quite an impact with their laid-back take on contemporary elegance (think cozy, over-stuffed sofas and piles of downy pillows). The sheets made from T-shirt material have been much imitated.

93 Greene Street, Soho ☎ 274-9842 Ⓜ C•E•6 to Spring St; N•R to Prince St

Shi *♭C12*

Zen merchandise, from the tiny, distinctive tea lights to an engaging collection of ceramics.

233 Elizabeth Street, Noho ☎ 334-4330 Ⓜ F to 2nd Ave

☆ **TOTEM** *♭F11*

One of the most modern home furnishing stores in the city, everything here is beautifully designed; colourful, slick and functional. They carry loads of stylish plastic accessories, along with clean-lined furniture and distinctive rugs.

71 Franklin Street, Tribeca ☎ 925-5506 Ⓜ 1•9 to Franklin St

☆ **WILLIAMS-SONOMA** *♭F9*

A big chain store from California, everything here is top-of-the-line: there are dishes from Italy, Calphon pans, plenty of glassware, food and gadgets that you can't do without. The real bargains here are the linens and napkins that look expensive but aren't.

110 Seventh Avenue, Chelsea ☎ 633-2203 Ⓜ 1•9 to 18th St; 1•2•3•9 to 14th St

Wyeth
‰F11

A huge array of flawless 20th-century collectibles, mostly from the 40s and 50s.

151 Franklin Street, Tribeca ☎ 925-5278 Ⓜ 1•9 to Franklin St

☆ ZONA
‰D11

Zona brings a bit of country life to the urban jungle. Filled with furniture and other items from around the world; the stock here is eclectic, deluxe and colourful. There are lots of little doodads that will brighten your pad, and don't cost much. The cult item here is the store's own hand-rolled candles that come in a rainbow of colours.

97 Greene Street, Soho ☎ 925-6750 Ⓜ C•E to Spring St; 6 to Spring St

jewellery

Bamboozle Studio
‰off map

If you're really into making a total statement, you'll need an 'ear spear' by designer Lavalais. These heavy but elegant carved earrings are in both artistic and tribal styles.

171 E 118th Street, Harlem ☎ 360-6848 Ⓜ B•C to 116th St; 2•3 to 116th St

Cartier
‰C8

Purveyor of movie star jewellery offers extravagant retail therapy.

653 Fifth Avenue, Midtown ☎ 753-0111 Ⓜ E•F to 5th Ave

☆ FRAGMENTS
‰D11

Owner's Goldman and Moore keep this pretty Soho store filled with the inventive creations of 30 or so designers. Expect anything from Indian beadwork to rhinestone-studded bracelets, and even the occasional diamond.

107 Greene Street, Soho ☎ 334-9588 Ⓜ 6 to Spring St; N•R to Prince St

Gregg Wolf
‰A12

Excellent silver cufflinks, rings and chains – mainly for men.

346 E 9th Street, East Village ☎ 529-1784 Ⓜ 6 to Astor Pl

Home Boy of Harlem
‰off map

Looking for a trendy name necklace? Have yours made where the fashion pack get theirs at this den of glinting gold jewellery. Plenty of bargains and a custom service for initial rings and name pendants.

166 W 125th Street, Harlem ☎ 316-1320 Ⓜ A•B•C•D to 125th St

☆ ME & RO
♢B11

Bohemian jewellery styles that subtly beautify the body are what's on offer here. Soon after designers Robin Renzi and Michelle Quan opened shop, a celebrity following appeared: Liz Taylor and Kate Moss are amongst those who love the religious-inspired artifacts, Indian style bell-drop earrings, and charm bracelets.

239 Elizabeth Street, Nolita ☎ 917-237-9215 Ⓜ 6 to Bleecker St

Sarah Samoiloff
♢F10

A talented local – her silver pieces accented with feathers have a punky edge.

149 Avenue A, East Village ☎ 460-5392 Ⓜ L to 1st Ave

Tiffany's
♢B7

The famous blue boxes decadently scream 'I've just spent a pile of money and don't give a damn!'. Alternatively, you can window shop...

727 Fifth Avenue, Midtown ☎ 755-8000 Ⓜ B•Q to 57th St

lingerie

Le Corset
♢D11

Crammed with frilly items from around the world, including some vintage pieces.

80 Thompson Street, Soho ☎ 334-4936 Ⓜ C•E to Spring St

Nocturne
♢F6

Specializes in sleepwear. It's also one of the only places in town to stock up on cult favourite Lily Pulitzer's flowered frocks and separates.

698 Madison Avenue, UES ☎ 750-2951 Ⓜ 6 to 68th St-Hunter College

Only Hearts
♢C5

Showcases the store's own line of dreamy cotton-lycra lingerie. The rest of the store is replete with great PJs, dressing gowns and gift-items, most of which are heart-shaped.

386 Columbus Avenue, UWS ☎ 724-5608 Ⓜ 1•9 to 79th St

markets

☆ ANNEX FLEA MARKET
♢D9

Every Saturday and Sunday, from sunrise to sunset, this fleamarket – the city's biggest and best – sells anything and everything, from furniture and clothing to jewellery and silver. $1 admission fee.

Sixth Avenue and 26th Street, Chelsea ☎ 243-5343 Ⓜ F to 23rd St

☆ COLUMBUS CIRCLE MARKET
⊕B7

Peddling art and antiques; this daily market (11am–7pm) is a known hot spot for tourists, so prices tend to be higher.

58th Street & Eighth Avenue, Midtown ☎ 242-1217 Ⓜ A•B•C•D•1•9 to **59th St-Columbus Circle**

☆ COLUMBUS FLEA MARKET
⊕B5

Similar to, but on a much smaller scale than the Annex.

77th St & Columbus Avenue, UWS ☎ no phone Ⓜ B•C to 81st St-**Museum of Natural History**

☆ MALCOLM SHABAZZ HARLEM MARKET
⊕off map

A daily outdoor market with a vast range of colourful African imports.

118 Lenox Avenue, Harlem ☎ 987-8131 Ⓜ 2•3 to 116th St

Mart 125
⊕off map

All under one roof are many different outlets for African food, clothes, fabrics, music and more. Open daily, the market is very much the local shopping hub.

260 W 125th Street, Harlem ☎ 316-3340 Ⓜ A•B•C•D to 125th St

☆ ORCHARD STREET MARKET
⊕D12

The street is closed to traffic on Sundays so local vendors can sell underwear, leather goods, and toys to the masses.

Orchard Street, LES ☎ no phone Ⓜ F•J•M•Z to Delancey St-Essex St

☆ PS 44 MARKET
⊕C5

Upscale antiques, needlework, and various other arts and crafts are all available at this Sunday market.

Columbus Avenue, UWS ☎ no phone Ⓜ 1•9 to 79th St; B•C to 81st St

☆ PS 183 MARKET
⊕F6

Similar to PS44, with indoor and outdoor stalls. Held every Saturday.

419 E 67th Street, UES ☎ no phone Ⓜ 6 to 68th St-Hunter College

☆ SPRING STREET MARKET
⊕D11

This daily street market has a particularly good selection of affordable knock-offs.

Spring & Wooster Sts, Soho ☎ no phone Ⓜ C•E to Spring St.

☆ TOWER FLEA MARKET
⊕D11

At weekends, this small but crowded lot is filled with stalls selling knitted caps, T-shirts, and tapes.

Broadway, Nolita ☎ no phone Ⓜ B•D•F•Q to Broadway-Lafayette St

Beau Gosse *♭B11*
Tight T-shirts and sharp separates for men who like to show off.
27 W 8th Street, West Village ☎ 598-0314 Ⓜ N•R to 8th St-NYU

Hotel of the Rising Star *♭D11*
Caters for men looking for an eminently wearable, minimalist look.
13 Prince Street, Noho ☎ 625-9657 Ⓜ N•R to Prince St

Lee's Mardi Gras *♭F9*
For certain men only! Truly outrageous large-size dresses, beard-covering make-up, costume-jewellery and size-15 pumps beloved of drag queens and trannies.
400 W 14th Street, Chelsea ☎ 645-1888 Ⓜ A•C•E to 14th St

☆ PAUL SMITH *♭E10*
Paul Smith's clothes are at once classically English and slightly wacky. His shirts and sweaters are brilliantly designed and made from luxe (ie expensive) materials, the ties often whimsical, and the suits amazing for both style and quality. And there's a wonderful selection of toney accessories and stylish objects for the home too.
108 Fifth Avenue, Gramercy Park ☎ 627-9770 Ⓜ L•N•R•4•5•6 to 14th St-Union Sq

Raymond Dragon *♭F9*
Stretchy, second-skin numbers and swimwear for men that requires regular trips to the gym.
130 Seventh Avenue, Chelsea ☎ 727-0368 Ⓜ 1•9 to 18th St

Recon *♭C12*
All camouflage paint and razor wire, selling T-shirts and hi-tech toys – testosterone rules here.
237 Eldridge Street, LES ☎ 614-8502 Ⓜ F•J•M•Z to Delancy St-Essex St; F to 2nd Ave

Savoia *♭A12*
Send your male escort to this store for a classic 40s-style suit, either off the rack or made-to-measure.
125 E 7th Street, East Village ☎ 358-9182 Ⓜ 6 to Astor Pl

☆ SEAN ⚡D11

A recent addition to the menswear scene, Sean offers sporty clothes that are stylish without trying too hard. Ranging from corduroy shirts to tailored jackets, everything here is very wearable, with reasonable price tags.
132 Thompson Street, Soho ☎ 598-5980 Ⓜ N•R to Prince St

Steinberg & Sons ⚡C12

Decorative designer Martin Keehn fills his store with gorgeous, custom-made shirts worn by celebs as diverse as David Bowie and the late John Kennedy Jr – along with men's essentials inspired by workwear.
229 Elizabeth Street, Noho ☎ 625-1004 Ⓜ F to 2nd Ave

Tom of Finland ⚡F9

Favoured by Chelsea's gay male residents (affectionately known as 'Chelsea boys'), offering fashion-forward clothes for men who aren't afraid to stand out in the crowd.
261 W 19th Street, Chelsea ☎ 229-1375 Ⓜ 1•9 to 18th St

☆ YVES SAINT LAURENT RIVE GAUCHE ⚡D11

The elegant and spacious store is one of the few really stylish men-only outlets in Soho. With a new designer (Hedi Slimane) at the wheel, YSL Men is recycling the classics, but there's also a modern (and very dapper) aesthetic for guys who aren't afraid to make a fashion statement.
88 Wooster Street, Soho ☎ 274-0522 Ⓜ N•R to Prince St; C•E to Spring St

museum stores

☆ COOPER-HEWITT, NATIONAL MUSEUM OF DESIGN STORE ⚡A6

The former music room of the Carnegie Mansion offers unexpected and unusual items that often tie in with the exhibitions: unique building toys, kitchen gadgets, stationery and artsy books.
2 E 91st Street, UES ☎ 849-8355 Ⓜ 4•5•6 to 86th St

☆ GUGGENHEIM MUSEUM STORE ⚡A6

Pricey merchandise for the art lover (and materialist) in you: Chinese paint and ink sets, geometric-shaped Japanese mobiles, decorated chopsticks as well as museum store staples like posters, prints, scarves, T-shirts and shoulder bags.
1071 Fifth Avenue, UES ☎ 423-3615 Ⓜ 4•5•6 to 86th St

☆ **METROPOLITAN MUSEUM OF ART STORE**   *♪A6*
The mother of all museum shops, the Met's three spacious, colourful floors are an ode to art and commerce, and the book department can equal any art bookstore in the city.
Fifth Avenue, UES ☎ 650-2850 Ⓜ 4•5•6 to 86th St

☆ **MUSEUM OF MODERN ART STORE**   *♪C8*
Most of the goods in the MoMA shop relate directly to the museum's permanent exhibits: its calendars, posters, monographs and books all make great gifts. Don't miss the MoMA design store across the street, which features rugs and kitchen accessories as well as contemporary remakes of furniture by designers like Charles Rennie Mackintosh.
11 W 53rd Street, Midtown ☎ 708-9700/767-1050 Ⓜ E•F to 5th Ave

Studio Museum Gift Shop   *♪off map*
At the centre of Harlem is the Studio Museum, devoted to modern African-American culture. The shop stocks all manner of related goodies – books, posters and decorative objects.
144 W 125th Street, Harlem ☎ 864-0014 Ⓜ A•B•C•D to 125th St

shoes

☆ **CHRISTIAN LOUBOUTIN**   *♪D6*
Red-soled ultimate style statements will satiate even the most serious shoe shopper.
941 Madison Avenue, UES ☎ 396-1884 Ⓜ 6 to 77th St

☆ **JIMMY CHOO**   *♪C8*
Brit import Jimmy Choo has made a real splash with his snazzy boutique which houses a collection of pretty heels and mules in the unusual, ultra-luxury category.
645 Fifth Avenue, Midtown ☎ 593-0800 Ⓜ E•F to 5th Ave

☆ **JOAN & DAVID**   *♪F6*
For a more conservative look, this store has a reliable, stylish selection of footwear with price tags to match.
816 Madison Ave, UES ☎ 772-3970 Ⓜ 6 to 68th St-Hunter College

☆ **JUNO'S**   *♪C10*
Edgy footwear for ladies, as well as a competitive selection of men's shoes.
170 Fifth Avenue, Gramercy Park ☎ 995-0162 Ⓜ N•R to 23rd St

☆ KENNETH COLE ♯D11
A favourite with smart, young New Yorkers of both sexes who flex their plastic for his cool, wearable styles (his bags and sharp separates are here too).
567 Broadway, Soho ☎ 965-0283 Ⓜ B•D•F•Q to Broadway-Lafayette St

☆ MANOLO BLAHNIK ♯C8
If your credit is limitless and you aren't afraid of vertigo, Manolo Blahnik's heels are the kind no fashionista leaves the house without.
31 W 54th Street, Midtown ☎ 582-3007 Ⓜ E•F to 5th Ave

☆ MARK SCHWARTZ ♯C12
Huge but super feminine skyscraper heels can be found inside this tiny downtown boutique.
45 Spring Street, Nolita ☎ 343-9292 Ⓜ 6 to Spring St

☆ 9 & CO ♯E5
A fashion-friendly chain, in a cheaper price bracket than even Nine West.
148 Columbus Ave, UWS ☎ 787-9499 Ⓜ 1 9 to 66th St-Lincoln Center

☆ NINE WEST ♯D11
The ubiquitous chain store always has plenty of well-priced styles which 'pay hommage' to the likes of Prada and Gucci.
577 Broadway, Soho ☎ 941-1597 Ⓜ B•D•F•Q to Broadway-Lafayette St

☆ OTTO TOOTSI PLOHOUND ♯D11
A mini chain for the best selection of high-fashion shoes by various big names such as Free Lance.
413 W Broadway, Soho ☎ 925-8931 Ⓜ N•R to Prince St; 6 to Spring St

☆ PAYLESS ♯A11
For the ultimate bargain – this store has footwear for men and women for as little as $10. Just don't expect these shoes to outlive the month.
388 Avenue of the Americas, West Village ☎ 375-0976
Ⓜ A•B•C•E•F•Q to W 4th St-Washington Sq

☆ PETIT PETON ♯A11
A one-off, which stands out from the crowd thanks to a good range of European imports and the store's own line. Prices here, as with other stores on the block, are generally quite reasonable.
27 W 8th Street, West Village ☎ 677-3730
Ⓜ A•B•C•D•E•F•Q to W 4th St-Washington Sq

☆ ROCKPORT $D11

If your feet are worn out after looking for something to slip them into, you can get complimentary reflexology at this downtown 'concept' store where, thankfully, comfy footwear is the lure.

465 W Broadway, Soho ☎ 529-0209 Ⓜ N•R to Prince St

☆ SACCO $A5

An excellent outpost for women's shoes and boots – although prices are a little higher than some of the other chains, sophistication is the payoff.

2355 Broadway, UWS ☎ 874-8362 Ⓜ 1•9 to 86th St

☆ SIGERSON MORRISON $D11

Less pricey and infinitely inventive 60s-style, mod designs on offer at one of the best little shoe stores in town.

242 Mott Street, Nolita ☎ 219-389 Ⓜ B•D•F•Q to Broadway-Lafayette St

☆ STÉPHANE KÉLIAN $A8

Outlandish European creations in the high-end price bracket; a good choice to join the ranks of Madison's well-heeled.

717 Madison Avenue, UES ☎ 980-1919 Ⓜ N•R to 5th Ave

Steve Madden $D11

Ostentatious platforms and fun sneakers are on offer at this store, whose shoes are beloved of the dazed and confused set.

540 Broadway, Soho ☎ 343-1800 Ⓜ N•R to Prince St

☆ TOD'S $A8

The brand's beloved (and expensive) leather 'driving loafer' is the kind worn by slumming movie stars.

650 Madison Avenue, UES ☎ 644-5945 Ⓜ N•R to 5th Ave

sports gear

☆ FOOT LOCKER $B9

A good selection of sportswear and trainers at very competitive prices.

43–45 W 34th Street, Midtown ☎ 971-9449 Ⓜ B•D•F•N•Q•R to 34th St-Herald Sq

Malia Mills $C12

Stocks the latest and best swimwear which practically guarantee you'll look hot on the beach.

199 Mulberry Street, Noho ☎ 625-2311 Ⓜ 6 to Spring St

☆ **MODELL'S** ♯B9
Especially good for sporting equipment and clothing.
901 Sixth Avenue, Midtown ☎ 594-1830 Ⓜ B•D•F•N•Q•R to 34th St Herald Sq

☆ **PARAGON** ♯E10
A well-stocked, brand-orientated retail paradise for sports addicts of all kinds, Paragon has simply been providing the best in sportswear for nearly 100 years.
876 Broadway, Gramercy Park ☎ 255-8036 Ⓜ L•N•R•4•5•6 to 14th St-Union Sq

☆ **REEBOK CONCEPT STORE** ♯E5
New York's most prestigious gym carries requisite sweats and cycle shorts at this in-house store. For looking good when you work out.
160 Columbus Avenue,UWS ☎ 595-1480 Ⓜ 1•9 to 66th St-Lincoln Center

streetwear

Air Market ♯F10
A repository of all things Japanese including clubby asymmetric clothing and Hello Kitty backpacks.
97 Third Avenue, East Village ☎ 995-5888 Ⓜ L to 3rd Ave

Anthropologie ♯F11
Best described as a grown-up Urban Outfitters, this is the kind of place where labels are less important than the look. Think colourful cowgirl chic, Latin flounces and ruffles, and lots of lovely housewares and furnishings.
375 W Broadway, Soho ☎ 343-7070 Ⓜ N•R to Canal St

Barney's Co-Op ♯F9
Branch of the midtown store, focusing on more casual lines of clothes (Daryl K, Maharishi etc) reflecting the tastes of the local residents and young edgy crowd who love to shop here. It also has shoes, cosmetics and plenty of accessories.
236 W 18th Street, Chelsea ☎ 826-8900 Ⓜ 1•9 to 18th St

☆ **CANAL JEAN CO** ♯D11
Hit the lower level of this NY institution to find racks of vintage and new Levis, polyester shirts, jackets, and accessories at OK prices.
504 Broadway, Soho ☎ 226-1130 Ⓜ 6 to Spring St; N•R to Prince St

Dave's New York $D9

A tiny, 30-year old jeans outlet with a great selection of utilitarian work-wear (Levis, Hanes, Schott, Carhartt) at excellent prices. And, the staff really know their stuff.

779 Sixth Avenue, Chelsea ☎ 989-6444 Ⓜ F to 23rd St

☆ DIESEL $B8

The riotous Diesel flagship can sometimes seem as surreal as those ubiquitous adverts. Amidst the loud music and the 'art exhibits', you'll find urban, streetwise clothes that are casual with a cutting-edge twist. Even the underwear is trendy. Take a break from it all at the in-store café.

770 Lexington Avenue, UES ☎ 308-0055 Ⓜ N•R to Lexington Ave-59th St

Exodus Industrial Sport $off map

A small place that carries sombre, yet chic, clothes.

771 Fulton Street, Fort Green ☎ 1-718-246-0321 Ⓜ J•M•Z•2•3•4•5 to Fulton St

Stussy $D11

The epicentre for upscale skatewear, meant for men but worn by everybody.

104 Prince Street, Soho ☎ 274-8855 Ⓜ N•R to Prince St

Supreme $A12

If skating is more your thing, then this store has all the necessary hats, baggy pants, T-shirts and other neat stuff that boarders hoard.

**274 Lafayette Street, Noho ☎ 966-7799
Ⓜ 6 to Bleecker St**

☆ TRUFAUX $F11

PC animal prints and ultra-suede jackets, dresses and skirts at affordable prices. This is the place to shop for faux fur trim, giraffe print wrap dresses and washable and weatherproof leather-inspired looks that won't break your bank or your principles.

301 West Broadway, Soho ☎ 334–4545 Ⓜ 1•9•A•C•E to Canal St

Working Class $B13

This store has elevated workwear to a new level of elegance, seen in their vintage jeans with leather pockets, handmade clogs and workboots, and schoolboy satchels – all in bright shades.

**168 Duane Street, Tribeca ☎ 941-1199 Ⓜ 1•2•3•9 to Chambers St;
A•C to Chambers St**

X-Large *♪A12*
Easy and refined streetwear for skate kids who've grown up a bit.
267 Lafayette Street, Noho ☎ **334-4480** Ⓜ **6 to Bleecker St**

theme stores

☆ **DISNEY STORE** *♪C12*
Strictly for kids and their adult companions, Disney is Mickey and more in an OTT setting.
711 Fifth Avenue, Midtown ☎ **702-0702** Ⓜ **E•F to 5th Ave**

Firefighter's Friend *♪A12*
So you wanna be a fireman, or just look like one? Then stop in at this outlet for authorized (and very snappy) NY Fire Dept merchandise, including standard-issue firemen's coats.
263 Lafayette Street, Noho ☎ **226-3142** Ⓜ **6 to Bleecker St**

NBA Store *♪C8*
Holds a full-range of merchandise from every NBA basketball team – you can get kitted out just like Shaq.
666 Fifth Avenue, Midtown ☎ **515-6221** Ⓜ **E•F to 5th Ave**

☆ **NIKETOWN** *♪A8*
Few people leave New York without a visit to this ultimate megastore. Five floors of gear with the 'swoosh' in a suitably futuristic interior, and a huge screen showing polished Nike commercials. The experience of visiting is invigorating, even if the service is slow.
6 E 57th Street, Midtown ☎ **891-6453** Ⓜ **E•F•N•R to 5th Ave**

☆ **ORIGINAL LEVI'S STORE** *♪A8*
Four floors of this all-American brand, including non-denim clothing and accessories. Can't find a pair that fits? The store will custom-make some for you.
3 E 57th Street, Midtown ☎ **838-2188** Ⓜ **E•F•N•R to 5th Ave; B•Q to 57th St**

☆ **SONY STYLE** *♪C8*
Shop for gadgets or simply test drive the Playstations in this technophile's paradise.
550 Madison Avenue, Midtown ☎ **833-8800** Ⓜ **E•F to 5th Ave**

☆ WARNER BROS STUDIO STORE ♫B7

Products galore from the WB's cartoons, movies and TV shows plus interactive games on the top floor.

1 E 57th Street, Midtown ☎ 754-0305 Ⓜ E•F•N•R to 5th Ave; B•Q to 57th St; 4•5•6 to 59th St

thrift stores

Filth Mart ♫F10

You'll have to look hard to find something worth taking home at this no-frills thrift store, but when you do, it'll definitely be a bargain.

531 E 13th Street, East Village ☎ 387-0650 Ⓜ L to 1st Ave; L to 3rd Ave

☆ HOUSING WORKS THRIFT SHOP ♫F9

The clothing (especially men's suits), books, furniture and trinkets are exceptionally low in price. Benefits AIDS charities.

143 W 17th Street, Chelsea ☎ 366-0820 Ⓜ 1•9 to 18th St

☆ OUT OF THE CLOSET ♫A6

One of the biggest thrift stores in town, the merchandise is pristine and varied thanks to wealthy neighbourhood types who regularly donate unwanted treasures. Bargains are likely and sales benefit AIDS charities.

220 E 81st Street, UES ☎ 472-3573 Ⓜ 4•5•6 to 86th St

toys

Enchanted Forest ♫C12

Toys Я Art rather than Toys Я Us. Handmade stuffed animals, puppets, masks and instruments are discreetly displayed in the branches of this shop's mock forest. Highly recommended for beautiful, top-quality, one-of-a-kind toys.

85 Mercer Street, Soho ☎ 925-6677 Ⓜ 6 to Spring St

FAO Schwarz ♫A8

The larger-than-life stuffed animals, huge music box-cum-clock and extensive train set will have you and the kids marvelling at this, the granddaddy of all toy stores. Highly commercial, it has everything a child could want.

767 Fifth Avenue, Midtown ☎ 644 9400 Ⓜ E•F•N•R to 5th Ave

Penny Whistle Toys

An uptown treasure-trove of time-tested toys for newborns through to teens. Parents will love their high-quality, educational aspects, while the bubble-blowing bears outside and the satisfying toys inside keep the children happy.

448 Columbus Avenue, UWS ☎ 873-9090 Ⓜ B•C to 81st St; 1•9 to 79th St

vintage clothes

Allan & Suzi   ⚑A5

The racks here are filled with a riot of barely-worn and vintage couture. Versace and Gaultier are the designers of preference, and although you can find jeans, they'll probably be studded with rhinestones.

416 Amsterdam Avenue, UWS ☎ 724-7445 Ⓜ 1•9 to 86th St

☆ **CHERRY**   ⚑C12

A store devoted to collectible clothing and accessories (sometimes complete with original tags) from post-World War II forward.

185 Orchard Street, LES ☎ 358-7131 Ⓜ F to 2nd Ave

☆ **EACH AND THEM**   ⚑C12

Purveyors of groovy yet chic threads, shoes, sunglasses and bags from the 60s, 70s and 80s.

216 Lafayette Street, Noho ☎ 925-9699 Ⓜ 6 to Spring St

Domsey's Warehouse Outlet   ⚑off map

A megastore for the thrifty, with racks and racks of used clothing and housewares, for literally next-to-nothing.

431 Kent Avenue, Williamsburg ☎ 1-718-384-6000 Ⓜ L to Bedford Ave

FAB 208   ⚑A12

Home to a colourful mix of kooky vintage and brand new duds for both sexes.

77 E 7th Street, East Village ☎ 673-7581 Ⓜ 6 to Astor Pl

The Fan Club   ⚑F9

OTT glamorous garb (some of it donated by celebrities) from the 20s to the 90s. All proceeds go to charity.

22 W 19th Street, Gramercy Park ☎ 929-3349 Ⓜ 1•9 to 18th St

☆ **FOLEY & CORINNA**   ⚑D12

In addition to glorious vintage clothing, this store sells new bags made from antique fabrics as well as previously-loved models by Gucci and Fendi.

108 Stanton Street, LES ☎ 529-2338 Ⓜ F•J•M•Z to Delancey St-Essex St

☆ INA
♂D11

For the finest selection of pre-owned designer duds, go to Ina, which has separate stores for men and women.

women: 101 Thompson Street, Soho ☎ 941-4757 Ⓜ A•C•E to Spring St; N•R to Prince St

men: 21 Prince Street, Nolita ☎ 334-9048 Ⓜ A•C•E to Spring St; N•R to Prince St

Metropolis
♂F10

A favourite with the NYU set, sells new and used clothing with a funky feel, including never-before-worn utilitarian gear.

43 Third Avenue, East Village ☎ 358-0795 Ⓜ L to 3rd Ave

Rags a Go Go
♂A12

Great for cheap vintage togs especially jeans and good-quality basics.

73 E 7th Street, East Village ☎ 254-4771 Ⓜ 6 to Astor Pl

119 St Mark's Place, East Village ☎ 254 4772 Ⓜ 6 to Astor Pl

☆ RESURRECTION
♂A12

Crammed with museum-quality antique and vintage pieces, which acts as a magnet for models and stylists.

123 E 7th Street, Nolita ☎ 228-0063 Ⓜ F to 2nd Ave; L to 1st Ave; 6 to Astor Pl

☆ SCREAMING MIMI'S
♂A12

A NY institution where there is never a shortage of genius clothes (for men and women), mostly from the 60s, 70s and beyond.

382 Lafayette Street, Noho ☎ 677-6464 Ⓜ N•R to 8th St; 6 to Astor Pl

☆ STELLA DALLAS
♂A11

This store has a girly collection of dresses, slips and nighties from the 30s and 40s at reasonable prices.

218 Thompson Street, West Village ☎ 674-0447 Ⓜ A•B•C•D•E•F•Q to W 4th St-Washington Sq

☆ TIMTOUM
♂C12

Acts as a magnet for those who attend the owner's club night: lovely used garb, clothing by local designers, utilitarian bags and an eclectic selection of vinyl are the lure.

179 Orchard Street, LES ☎ 780-0456 Ⓜ F to 2nd Ave

Junk
$off map

In this store you're sure to find that Depression-era glass candy dish, or electric beer sign that you've always been looking for.

324 Wythe Avenue, Williamsburg ☎ **1-718-388-8580** Ⓜ **L to Bedford Ave**

Lively Set
$D11

For funkier flea market-style finds, this store has an immaculate collection of furniture, pottery and lamps from the 40s to the 70s.

33 Bedford Street, West Village ☎ **807-8417** Ⓜ **1•9 to Houston St**

R
$off map

A good, if pricey, source of covetable post-World War II furniture.

326 Wythe Avenue, Williamsburg ☎ **807-8417** Ⓜ **L to Bedford Ave**

restaurants & cafés

New York has always been a major chowtown but never so much as today – even the most dedicated foodie has trouble keeping up. You'd need a King Kong appetite and a Rockefeller-sized fortune to try it all, so sample what you can of the amazing variety of eateries – high-priced and low – in neighbourhoods all over the city.

african & caribbean

Africa   *♭F1*
Very authentic, mellow Senegalese restaurant adorned with African fabrics and chairs carved with animal figures. Look out for grilled fish, couscous and lamb stew with peanut butter.
247 W 116th Street, Harlem ☎ 666-9400 Ⓜ B•C to 116th St $

Brisas del Caribe   *♭C12*
A ramshackle Cuban luncheonette, which attracts a mixed bag of raga-muffins and cool Soho-ites. This is a good choice for a quick fix as the menu features basic breakfasts, rice and beans, and sandwiches.
489 Broadway, Soho ☎ no phone Ⓜ 6 to Spring St $

Chez Es Saada   *♭C12*
A fashionable upscale casbah, has a cramped dining-room, but there are roomier, candlelit lounges downstairs. Dazzling cocktails and savoury Moroccan-inspired food like chicken *bisteeyah* with saffron lemon sauce come at a price.
42 E 1st Street, East Village ☎ 77-5617 Ⓜ F to 2nd Ave $$

Keur 'n' Dye   *♭off map*
Satisfying Senegalese cooking in a pleasant, calming environment.
737 Fulton Street, Fort Greene ☎ 1-718-875-4937 Ⓜ G to Fulton St $–$$

Mekka   *♭B12*
A comfy, sociable place, serving a selection of soulful southern Caribbean dishes (you can't beat the fried chicken). The happening bar scene is popular with music-industry types, and great tunes are guaranteed to be always spinning.
14 Avenue A, East Village ☎ 475-8500 Ⓜ F to 2nd Ave $–$$

Negril
♭D9

Feast to a reggae beat on Jamaican chicken and roti bread. Swaying plants, beachside murals and an aquarium behind the bar give you that island feel.

362 W 23rd Street, Chelsea ☎ 807-6411 Ⓜ C•E to 23rd St $–$$

Obaa Koryoe
♭off map

A friendly, relaxed nook attached to a shop stocked with unique *tchotchkes*. Specializing in exotic West African cuisine, it is particularly busy on Sundays when people flood in for the great value all-you-can-eat buffet brunch.

3143 Broadway, Harlem ☎ 316-2950 Ⓜ 1•9 to 125th St $

american

Alley's End
♭F9

The speakeasy entrance promises an illicit evening. There is a romantic atmosphere – the candlelit dining room facing a picture-perfect garden is sure to seduce, and the American bistro menu and boutique wine list crackle with creativity.

311 W 17th Street, Chelsea ☎ 627-8899 Ⓜ A•C•E to 8th Ave; L to 14th St $$–$$$

Astor Restaurant & Lounge
♭A12

An art deco brasserie that bears a passing resemblance to Balthazar, attracts a young clientele. The menu is superb (crawfish corn chowder, braised lamb with pistachio couscous), providing ballast for when you retire to the Moroccan-style downstairs lounge to finish the evening with just another cocktail.

316 Bowery, Noho ☎ 253-8644 Ⓜ 6 to Bleecker St $$

Bayou
♭D1

Dishes out Creole food at its best; the New Orleans chef makes a sinful *pain perdu* (New-Orleans-style french toast).

308 Lenox Avenue, Harlem ☎ 426-3800 Ⓜ 2•3 to 125th St $$

☆ B-BAR & GRILL
♭A12

Here, in the sexy, aviary-themed dining room, in the huge bar and out on the enclosed patio, interesting faces and fashions are sure to be seen. Even though it's been around a few years, B-Bar (formerly the Bowery Bar) still hosts tons of private music biz parties, and there's always a line of stretch limos purring outside. American favourites, like crab cakes and roast chicken with mash, are dead certs.

40 E 4th Street, Noho ☎ 475-2220 Ⓜ 6 to Astor Pl $–$$$

☆ BOULEY BAKERY ♯B13

Some describe the space at Bouley as 'intimate' – others go for 'cramped'. But regardless, everyone agrees on the food: it's succulent and flavourful, an unadulterated party for your tastebuds. Chef David Bouley has long been revered for his creations, and despite the name 'Bakery' this is a fully-fledged NY culinary hotspot. Think filo-crusted shrimp with Maine crab meat and baby squid, Maple Leaf Farm duck with glazed turnips. While the service is often quite surly, tables are booked way ahead, and even though the prices get steep, no one seems to mind or complain.

120 W Broadway, Tribeca ☎ 964-2525 Ⓜ 1•2•3•9 to Chambers St $$$

☆ BLUE RIBBON ♯D11

The waiting-in-line situation is absurd (even at 3am), but the people-watching (super-chic and supermodels) is almost an essential part of the experience. While it tends to get sceney, it's never obnoxious – because everyone is there for one thing... fabulous, eclectic, innovative food, like the flavour-bursting fondue, roasted duck club sandwich and whole steamed flounder. Calorie counters, beware: it's impossible to stick to your diet here... and with a menu this diverse and tempting, you wouldn't want to.

67 Sullivan Street, Soho ☎ 274-0404 Ⓜ C•E to Spring St $–$$$

Bryant Park Grill & Café ♯E8

Offers a retreat from the hustle of Midtown. The Café wins hands down in the summer with an ample supply of alfresco seating (singles flock here on Thursday evenings), while the classy Grill serves top-notch New American food and has huge windows affording a great view.

25 W 40th Street, Midtown ☎ 840-6500 Ⓜ 7 to 5th Ave;
B•D•F•Q to 42nd St $$–$$$

☆ CAFETERIA ♯F9

Don't be fooled by the name – this is the furthest thing from a typical cafeteria. In fact, it's one of the city's sleeker hot spots, so try not to gawp when Kate Moss, Calvin Klein or Evan Dando sit at the cushy booth right next to you and order from a menu packed with cholesterol-rich comfort food like old-fashioned macaroni cheese, fries, milk shakes, and jaw-breakingly huge sandwiches. Downstairs, there's a funky lounge where late-night crawling lizards may languish.

119 Seventh Avenue, Chelsea ☎ 414-1717 Ⓜ 1•2•3•9 to 14th St $$

Candela
⌖E10

As dark and gothic as a medieval castle. Along with a hyper bar and singles scene is surprisingly thoughtful food, such as an abundant seafood platter, and asparagus, goat's cheese and basil purée.

116 E 16th Street, Gramercy Park ☎ 254-1600 Ⓜ L•N•R•4•5•6 to 14th St-Union Sq $$

Canteen
⌖D11

Featuring colourful decor, this 60s-style eatery attracts a very cool crowd. The food ain't bad either – from the rather nostalgic macaroni cheese to the thoroughly modern pumpkin-crusted red snapper – though it is a little overpriced.

142 Mercer Street, Soho ☎ 2431-7676 Ⓜ N•R to Prince St $$–$$$

Commune
⌖C10

This buzzy, super-chic restaurant is proving a favourite with movie premiere parties. Presided over by Matthew Kenney (of Canteen fame), the restaurant serves up satisfactory American-inspired dishes, although you're more likely to be here to be seen, rather than to eat.

12 E 22nd Street, Gramercy Park ☎ 777-2600 Ⓜ 6 to 23rd St $$–$$$

☆ COPELAND'S
⌖off map

For a fun night out in Harlem, head here, especially on Saturdays when live jazz plays all night. There's a veneer of formality and decor that recalls a 70s-style country club. The wine list is economical and the homey Southern cooking accomplished: fried chicken, collard greens, spicy Louisiana gumbo, and delectable candied yams. Sunday brunch features gospel.

547 W 145th Street, Harlem ☎ 234-2357 Ⓜ 1•9 to 145th St $–$$$

Cowgirl Hall of Fame
⌖F11

Round up those kiddies and bring them to this Western wonderland of cowhide, lassos and steer horns. The full kids' menu has a Tex-Mex, Southern feel, and there's a great room in the back for romping around with other kids, which is stocked with toys and games. Crayons and colouring materials are also available.

519 Hudson Street, West Village ☎ 633-1133 Ⓜ A•C•E to 14th St; 1•9 to Christopher St

Danal
⌖A12

One of the neighbourhood's sweetest, most romantic restaurants, which has a daily-changing but tantalizing American-Mediterranean menu.

90 E 10th Street, East Village ☎ 982-6930 Ⓜ 6 to Astor Pl $$

☆ ELEVEN MADISON PARK ♪C10

Danny Meyer, restaurateur supreme scores another success with this swanky eatery located in a former bank. It's his most corporate place, from the lobby-like soaring marble-floored room to the Yankee-French food and the suits at the tables. Menus read like a butcher's display: foie gras several ways (with pomegranate essence, toasted walnuts and sage), braised pork shoulder, dry-aged sirloin strip, loin of lamb, saddle of venison, roast chicken (with potato speck tart); accompaniments are invariably hearty. Not for vegetarians, anorexics or dates.

11 Madison Park, Gramercy Park ☎ 889-0905 Ⓜ N•R to 23rd St $$–$$$

Fanelli ♪D11

A dark-wood corner tavern that opened in 1847. The crowd is interesting, dressed-down and boisterous, and it's a safe bet for burgers, chilli, and chicken pot pie.

94 Prince Street, Soho ☎ 431-5744 Ⓜ N•R to Prince St $

☆ FIRST ♪A12

First has an undeniable groove, even though you'd never notice it passing by. The commodious booths are ideal for groups, and dim lighting enhances everybody's appearance. The new American cuisine is generously portioned, so beware the addictive warm bread with infused olive oil. Martinis are served in their own cute pitchers on ice, keeping them cold for refills. Pizza with condiments on the side (like fresh pesto) is wonderful, as is the vegetable extravaganza and grilled lamb steak.

**87 First Avenue, East Village ☎ 674-3823 Ⓜ 6 to Astor Pl;
F to 2nd Ave $–$$$**

Five Points. ♪A12

The accomplished American-Mediterranean cooking here is complemented by a beautifully decorated room bisected by a flowing 'creek'; weekend brunches feature eye-opening egg dishes, and irresistible donuts and hot chocolate.

31 Great Jones Street, Noho ☎ 253-5700 Ⓜ 6 to Bleeker St $$–$$$

☆ FRESSEN ♪F11

Organically-focused American cuisine. The seasonal menu changes daily, but you'll always find pristine fish, crispy Amish chicken and tender grilled meats, along with fresh-off-the-farm vegetables. The concrete industrial space is warmed by oxblood lacquered walls, and the dimly-lit dining room is split up by handsome mahogany screens. Overzealous, slickly groomed boulevardiers sully it at weekends; stick to weeknights.

**421 W 13th Street, Meatpacking District ☎ 645-7775 Ⓜ A•C•E to 14th St;
L to 8th Ave $$–$$$**

restaurants & cafés

☆ GOTHAM BAR AND GRILL ♩E10
Alfred Portale's edible sculptures have been amazing New Yorkers since 85. His kitchen has been a training ground for several of the city's top chefs, educated in his visionary architecture of flavours and beauty. The soaring room is lit by billowy parachutes, a great environment to carefully savour sweetwater shrimp salad with papaya, and seared yellowfin tuna with pappardelle and caponata. The polished, friendly service sets the standard, and the crowd is sophisticated too.
12 E 12th Street, West Village ☎ 620-4020 Ⓜ L•N•R•4•5•6 to 14th St-Union Sq $$$

Grace ♩F11
Innovative American food and an interesting buzz. The kichen's open 'til 4am, and there's a great bar scene too.
114 Franklin Street, Tribeca ☎ 343-4200 Ⓜ 1•9 to Franklin St $$–$$$

☆ GRAMERCY TAVERN ♩C10
If your pocket's not up to it, you can sidestep the gastronomic *prix fixe* dinner at this extremely popular and lively temple to New American cuisine by sauntering into the tavern area (no reservations needed) where lower-priced à la carte items are featured. The wine selection is excellent, and they'll open just about anything for you to try by the glass. Everything is well prepared, such as fondue of sea urchin and crabmeat with curry essence, and roasted monkfish with pancetta and truffle vinaigrette. Lunch is happening, too, with a more reasonable set menu.
42 E 20th Street, Gramercy ☎ 477-0777 Ⓜ N•R to 23rd St $$–$$$

☆ GRANGE HALL ♩A11
So homey, you'll feel like you're dining in your friend's ultra-cool art deco apartment. And the fact that it's nestled on one of NYC's most beautiful streets makes this restaurant even more of a draw. The service is sweet and the portions are waist-strainingly huge, so go hungry and prepare to scarf down some old-fashioned comfort food like creamy garlic mashed potatoes, herb-breaded organic chicken, and a big slab of aged shell-steak with pickles. This popular eatery always brings in a crowd, especially for brunch.
50 Commerce Street, West Village ☎ 924-5246
Ⓜ 1•9 to Christopher St $$–$$$

The Grocery ♩off map
Features a minimalist decor and food inspired by the seasons; the desserts are particularly delicious.
288 Smith Street, Carroll Gardens ☎ 1-718-596-3335 Ⓜ F•G to Carroll St $$–$$$

Home
♭A11

The owners are from the Midwest and proud of it, presenting comfort food, along with alcohol-spiked lemonade. Though tiny, Home, whose motto is 'fine wines, fine ketchup', has a garden.

20 Cornelia Street, West Village ☎ 243-9579 Ⓜ A•B•C•D•E•F•Q to W 4th St-Washington Sq $$

The Independent
♭F11

A local hangout in warm, rustic surroundings. The menu is inspired and moderately priced

179 W Broadway, Tribeca ☎ 219-2010 Ⓜ 1•9 to Franklin St $$$

Joanie's
♭A10

With bordello-red walls and whimsical décor, this is prime for romance. The food is expensive but worth it for originality and flavour, such as blue crab chowder, and apple-curry pasta with seafood.

126 E 28th Street, Gramercy Park ☎ 689-5656 Ⓜ 6 to 28th St $$$

The Lenox Room
♭D6

A genteel option, with a great raw bar and exceptional new American food. The polished dining room attracts affluent, mature types until 9pm, when a younger crowd arrives for drinks and elevated snacks.

1278 Third Avenue, UES ☎ 772-0404 Ⓜ 6 to 77th St $$$

Lucian Blue
♭off map

An American menu, with African accents, in a spacious bar-restaurant that wouldn't look out of place in Soho.

63 Lafayette Avenue, Fort Greene ☎ 1-718-422-0093 Ⓜ G to Fulton St $$

☆ MERCER KITCHEN
♭D11

You can't go wrong with anything you order in this ultra-cool, roomy subterranean restaurant in the fashionable Mercer Hotel. The food (prepared by one of New York's most acclaimed chefs, Jean Georges Vongerichten) is superb, though the crowd, decked out in the latest creations by Gucci, Prada and Helmut do their best to outshine the menu. Whether you're a fashionista or Madonna, so long as you look the part, the staff will treat you like a star. Book way ahead.

147 Mercer Street, Soho ☎ 966-5454 Ⓜ N•R to Prince St $–$$$

☆ MESA GRILL ⧸E10

Everything is oversized in the design of this airy, two-level space, from the huge pillars to the blown-up pop art, to fans as big as propellers on a B-52. The Southwestern flavours are tremendous, too. There's nothing cowardly about sweet potato and Scotch bonnet pepper ravioli, Yucatan-spiced venison or red snapper with poblano sauce. Cut down on the cost by visiting the long bar and sampling margaritas and spicy appetizers. Brunch is a standout, with Bloody Marys to knock your socks off.

102 Fifth Avenue, Gramercy Park ☎ 807-7400 Ⓜ L•N•R•4•5•6 to 14th St-Union Sq $$–$$$

Miss Ann's ⧸off map

A true hole-in-the-wall, serving sublime Southern dishes – but only to 12 people at a time.

86 Portland Avenue, Fort Greene ☎ 1-718-858-6997 Ⓜ G to Fulton St $

New City Bar & Grill ⧸off map

Offers French-American bistro food in a cool, airy setting.

25 Lafayette Avenue, Fort Greene ☎ 1-718-875-7197 Ⓜ D•Q•2•3•4•5 to Atlantic Ave $–$$

Nathan's Famous Restaurant ⧸off map

Serving the best hot dog in the universe (together with sublime fries and sauerkraut) in basic surroundings.

1310 Surf Avenue, Coney Island, Brooklyn ☎ 1-718-946-2202 Ⓜ B•D•F•N to Stillwell Ave-Coney Island $

☆ THE ODEON ⧸B13

If Downtown had to eliminate all but one restaurant, the vote would definitely be to keep Odeon. This is the ideal place for all occasions (date, birthday, hunger), all hours (still busy at midnight on Mondays), all moods (it can cure misery), and all types (though predominantly arty and cool). During the short boom of the early 1980s, it was the place to be seen ,frequented by Warhol et al. After this period the restaurant died a little, but now it is clear it is here to stay. Food is American bistro (burgers, seared tuna, beet and fennel salad, steak frites); service is brisk. Even if you can't get a table, it's fun to observe the action from the bar. Big tables for brunching parties: forever cool.

145 W Broadway, Tribeca ☎ 233-0507 Ⓜ A•1•2•3•9 to Chambers St $$–$$$

☆ OLD DEVIL MOON ⚹C12

This is where your 'white trash diner' meets the edgy East Village. The decor and atmosphere resemble a funky-looking flea market with mismatched chairs, booths, kitsch and fairy lights. Gigantic portions of meatloaf with mash, stews, salads and – the best dish – country ham are served by the unbelievably sweet waitpersons. The pies (peanut butter cream and the like) are so loved, that you can place orders for whole pies, to go.

511 E 12th Street, East Village ☎ 475-4357 Ⓜ F to 2nd Ave $–$$

☆ PARK VIEW AT THE BOATHOUSE ⚹F6

A shuttle bus leaves from Fifth Avenue and 72nd Street every ten minutes to ferry customers to this rustic chalet in the middle of Central Park. Open all year round, the cozy interior glows from the slate fireplace in winter and there's a bar where you can warm up on hot toddies. In good weather the outdoor tables are romantically lakeside. The American menu with global touches is strong on seafood, such as Indian-spiced salmon tartare with mango, and spinach and potato crusted monkfish with Barolo sauce.

Central Park (bet. East Park Drive & 74th St), UES ☎ 517-2233
Ⓜ 6 to 68th St-Hunter College $$–$$$

☆ PRUNE ⚹C12

So sweet and charming, this tiny spot is dear to many, though cramped seating might gall anti-social types. The creative, very personal menu is often revised by chef owner Gabrielle Hamilton: grilled artichokes with fried fava beans; pasta kerchiefs with asparagus, ham and poached egg; and roasted slab bacon with okra and pickled radish are all boldly flavoured. Desserts are equally singular, such as strawberry-rhubarb cobbler with brown sugar ice cream, and chocolate cashew tart with sour cherry compote. Sunday night 'firehouse suppers' are family affairs, with everyone getting the same thing.

54 E 1st Street, East Village ☎ 677-6221 Ⓜ F to 2nd Ave $$

☆ QUILTY'S ⚹D11

Chef Katy Sparks knows how to wow and woo diners with her spectacularly innovative cuisine. It is American food taken to a higher form of evolution, with Asian and French influences that accent each other in an eloquent way. For instance, you've never tasted anything quite like her tuna medallions with sesame-wilted Savoy cabbage, papaya coulis and macadamia couscous.

The far-reaching wine list is nearly as amazing. Moneyed corporate types impress clients here with the cool Soho vibe, so go later for more quiet romance.

177 Prince Street, Soho ☎ 254-1260 Ⓜ N•R to Prince St $$$

Red Cat ♫F11

Try the Amero-Mediterranean food at this restaurant (open evenings only) and you'll leave grinning like a Cheshire puss. Not only is the menu sorely tempting – a sweet pea risotto cake with oysters and a champagne cream, perfect chicken and mash, and grown up desserts like caramelized banana tart – but the prices aren't bad either.

227 Tenth Avenue, Chelsea ☎242-1122 Ⓜ A•C•E to 14th St $$

Restaurant 147 ♫F11

Red firehouse doors conceal this formerly super-hot restaurant. The fire may have burnt itself out, but it's still a groovy setting for caviar, crab cakes – and a spot of live jazz.

147 W 15th Street, Chelsea ☎929-5000 Ⓜ A•C•E to 14th St $$–$$$

Savoy ♫D11

A romantic haven, but their menu – salt-crust baked duck with braised kale, blood oranges and black olives – is sometimes overly ambitious.

70 Prince Street, Noho ☎ 219-8570 Ⓜ N•R to Prince St $$$

☆ SCREENING ROOM ♫F11

All under one roof, at The Screening Room you can enjoy cinematic cocktails at the bar (the 'Clockwork Orange', the 'Lolita'), tuck into rapturous dishes like pan-fried artichokes and cedar-planked salmon, and then move into the 40s-style theatre showing independent and foreign films. The attractive dining room is downtown casual, and the best deal is the $30 prix fixe, which includes three courses plus the screening. Brunch is also fun when they regularly show old cult favourites like Breakfast at Tiffany's and Valley of the Dolls.

54 Varick Street, Tribeca ☎ 334-2100 Ⓜ A•C•E•1•9 to Canal St $$–$$$

Serendipity 3 ♫B8

Kids are wild about their dreamy 'frozen hot chocolate', fountain sodas and ice-cream sundaes. The whimsically nostalgic setting also houses a general toy store out front. They serve standard American lunches and dinners, but leave plenty of room for their famously outrageous desserts.

225 E 60th Street, UES ☎ 838-3531 Ⓜ 4•5•6 to 59th St

☆ 71 CLINTON FRESH FOOD *D12*

A tatty Lower East Side block is luring uptown, moneyed patrons who brave the unsavoury journey to partake of Wylie Dufresne's far tastier, inspired American cooking. Yet this is no place for stiffs; it's small and boisterous and attracts hip locals, too. The precocious young chef was tutored for years by the fabled Jean-Georges Vongerichten, and it shows in his diverse, market-driven menu. Think yummy but not fussy.

71 Clinton Street, LES ☎ 614-6960 Ⓜ F•J•M•Z to Delancey St-Essex St $$–$$$

Sugar Shack *A1*

Poets and rappers take to the stage at this homey soul-food restaurant with open-mic nights.

2611 Eighth Avenue, Harlem ☎ 491-4422 Ⓜ B•C to 135th St

Sylvia's *D1*

The 'queen of soul food' attracts bus loads of tourists so the food is not as carefully prepared. Still, skip church and get your gospel here, along with church lady fashions.

328 Lenox Avenue, Harlem ☎ 996-0660 Ⓜ 2•3 to 125th St $–$$

☆ TABLA *C10*

Chef Floyd Cardoz may be a Bombay native but he's more influenced by his training in haute cuisine at Lespinasse. Tabla's food is actually contemporary American with a profusion of Indian spices, the flavours intense and controversial, provoking feelings of love and hatred. See which way you turn with dishes like tandoori rabbit, or lobster with pink lentils and five-spice sauce. The fricassee of shellfish comes with turmeric mash and curry leaves. The beautiful, two-level space has dynamic views of Madison Square Park; downstairs is the more casual Bread Bar (lentil soup and lamb tandoori are delicious); upstairs there's a set menu.

11 Madison Avenue, Gramercy Park ☎ 889-0667 Ⓜ N•R•6 to 23rd St $$$

The Tonic *F9*

A fashionable (read: pricey) enterprise, featuring sumptuous new American cuisine. If you want to say you've been there but don't want to pay top dollar, their handsome bar next door (the Tavern) serves a full menu including Yankee pot roast and fish and chips.

108–110 W 18th Street, Chelsea ☎ 929-9755 Ⓜ 1•9 to 18th St $$–$$$

Tribeca Grill *F11*

A warehouse-sized restaurant with cross-cultural American food and an award-winning wine list.

375 Greenwich Street, Tribeca ☎ 941-3900 Ⓜ 1•9 to Franklin St $$$

☆ '21' CLUB

♫C8

What?! You might harrumph at paying such prices for a hamburger (potatoes and green beans included!), or chicken hash (Joe DiMaggio's favourite). But this Prohibition-era speakeasy is such a charming landmark it's hard to be curmudgeonly. Newish chef Erik Blauberg, a culinary historian, has taken standards to a new level of excellence. Flaming baked Alaska and caramelized banana flan lit with Malibu rum produce exciting pyrotechnics. Hang out at the bar and feel the tippling spirits of old regulars Ernest Hemingway and Humphrey Bogart.

21 W 52nd Street, Midtown ☎ 941-3900 Ⓜ E•F to 5th Ave; B•D•F•Q to 47th-50th St-Rockefeller Center **$$$**

☆ UNION SQUARE CAFÉ

♫E10

You can see clear to America's heartland through chef Michael Romano's vibrant cooking, matched by a brilliant wine list. The ambience is streamlined and comfortable. With such innovative delights as risotto with foie gras, savoy cabbage and sage, and lobster 'shepherd's pie', it is not surprising that this is many New Yorkers' favourite restaurant. If you can't get a table, swing by and request a seat at the bar, order some wine, a hamburger and hot garlic chips, and you'll feel like the smartest cookie in town.

21 E 16th Street, Gramercy Park ☎ 243-4020 Ⓜ L•N•R•4•5•6 to 14th St-Union Sq **$$$**

☆ VERBENA

♫E10

If Edith Wharton were alive today, she would probably dine at Verbena; she lived nearby and the place manages to be civilized and daring at the same time. The townhouse setting is lovely and spare and the courtyard garden is bordererd by herbs and vegetables, which chef-owner Diane Forley employs in American dishes like butternut squash ravioli with roasted oranges and sage, and red snapper with braised cabbage and salsify.

53 Irving Place, Gramercy Park ☎ 260-5757 Ⓜ L•N•R•4•5•6 to 14th St-Union Sq **$$$**

☆ VERITAS

♫C10

This muted, shimmering room gets rave reviews for one of the most astonishing wine lists in the city. What's more, bottles are not overpriced – certainly not for the quality and rare vintages. Owners Gino Diaferia and Scott Bryan are sharp guys, already having the extremely good Indigo and Siena restaurants under their belts. Veritas is their real showplace, with subtle yet exhilarating contemporary American inventions like warm truffled oysters with Riesling, roasted squab with foie gras emulsion, and pepper-crusted venison with sour cherry-Armagnac sauce.

43 E 20th Street, Flatiron District ☎ 353-3700 Ⓜ N•R to 23rd St **$$$**

australian

Eight Mile Creek *♯C12*
Brings interesting Aussie treats (including native ingredients like yabbie and kangaroo) to Downtown.
240 Mulberry Street, Noho ☎ 431-4635 Ⓜ 6 to Spring St $$–$$$

bagels (see also delicatessens)

Bagels by the Park *♯off map*
Respectable bagels (12 kinds), plus knishes and burritos, are available at this low-key eatery.
323 Smith Street, Carroll Gardens ☎ 1-718-246-1321 Ⓜ F•G to Carroll St $

☆ ESS-A-BAGEL *♯D8*
Don't let the varnished panelling and tacky chandeliers dissuade you from stopping in for arguably the best and biggest bagels in town. There are also smoked fish platters and a range of calorie-laden desserts.
831 Third Avenue, Midtown ☎ 980-1010 Ⓜ E•F to Lexington Ave $

belgian

Markt *♯F11*
A bona fide reproduction of a stylish Belgian brasserie, its kettles of mussels and beer-braised seafood are superb especially when washed down with world-class Belgian brews.
401 W 14th Street, Chelsea ☎ 727-3314 Ⓜ L to 8th Ave;
A•C•E to 14th St $$–$$$

Petite Abeille *♯F9*
This Belgian café is cheerful, and adorned with Tintin posters. Omelettes, sandwiches, and beefy carbonade offer sturdy daytime refuelling.
107 W 18th Street, Chelsea ☎ 604-9350 Ⓜ 1•9 to 18th St $

Pommes Frites *♯A12*
Totally unhealthy and absolutely addictive this little nook is dedicated to paper cones of golden Belgian-style fries. Dozens of inventive sauces are at hand for dipping, and although there are a couple of benches to sit on, most customers just eat on the hoof.
123 Second Avenue, East Village ☎ 674-1234 Ⓜ 6 to Astor Pl $

☆ WATERLOO ⚓A11

If you aren't in a good mood when you arrive here, you will be when you leave – the party-on atmosphere is up there with the best. The industrial, flatteringly-lit dining room is filled with arty types, and the tight seating promotes merrymaking. Sharing a black kettle of mussels and frites over a delicious Belgian beer is a bonding experience, and you'll also want to dig into each other's full-flavoured Belgian-accented chocolatey-rich desserts. One of the best of Manhattan's crop of Belgian eateries.
145 Charles Street, West Village ☎ 352-1119 Ⓜ 1•9 to Christopher St $$$

bistros

☆ BALTHAZAR ⚓C12
When this spot-on facsimile of the perfect Parisian bistro opened in 1997, it was a too-hot-to-handle celebrity-model nightmare, but now it's assumed its rightful place as the young sibling of New York's most lovable restaurant, Odeon. Order very good renditions of French faves, all accompanied by fine sourdough bread baked at the next-door boulangerie. This is a guaranteed fun meal out.
80 Spring Street, Nolita ☎ 965-1414 Ⓜ N•R to Prince St; 6 to Spring St $$–$$$

The Brasserie ⚓C8
Recently reopened after a massive makeover. Its new super-cool interior and upscale bistro food are a big draw at all hours (open 'til 1 am).
100 E 53rd Street, Midtown ☎ 751-4840 Ⓜ E•F to 5th Ave $$–$$$

Casimir ⚓F10
A stylish bar-bistro with a French-accented menu and crowd to match.
105 Avenue B, East Village ☎ 358-9683 Ⓜ L to 1st Ave $–$$

Guastavino ⚓B8
The food is simple, pricey, yet kind of tasty. Experience Terence Conran's first New York venture simply for the spectacular setting. Conran has revamped the cavernous Bridgemarket, a former farmer's market under the 59th Street Bridge. Next door there's a food hall and the Conran Shop.
409 E 59th Street, Midtown ☎ 980-2455 Ⓜ 4•5•6 to 59th St; N•R to Lexington Ave $$–$$$

Indigo ⚓A11
The food at this unassuming neighbourhood bistro is pure poetry. Service is professional, prices modest and the eclectic American cuisine exceptional – especially the wild mushroom strudel.
142 W 10th Street, West Village ☎ 691-7757 Ⓜ 1•9 to Christopher St $$

Jules
A12

A traditional French bistro with nightly live jazz in a cozy, very Parisian setting. Salade niçoise, cheesy onion soup and steak frites are ace.
65 St Mark's Place, East Village ☎ 477-5560 Ⓜ 6 to Astor Pl $$

☆ LA BONNE SOUPE
C8

Utterly retro, this adorable bistro anachronism makes a fantastic Midtown bolt-hole. Ignore the terrifying menu prose ('this omelette masterpiece, almost austere in its simplicity', 'transformed by the art of France into a sophisticated delight'), because the food is just fine. Onion soup; Emmenthal fondue; great brandade and quiche; and little tables in two straight lines are the essence of cozy.
48 W 55th Street, Midtown ☎ 586-7650 Ⓜ E•F to 5th Ave $–$$

☆ LE JARDIN BISTROT
C12

One hesitates to recommend this perfect bistro for fear of its being overwhelmed by success, but Breton chef-patron, Gérard Maurice, can surely handle it. The bucolic garden is full of grape vines, herb and tomato plants and Gérard's extensive collection of frog tchotchkes. Satisfy your yearnings for bouillabaisse, cassoulet, steak (or tuna) tartare, steak, moules-frites and coq au vin; there is not a bad dish on the menu, though desserts (tarte tatin, chocolate marquise, creme caramel) tend not to be as successful.
25 Cleveland Place, Nolita ☎ 343-9599 Ⓜ 6 to Spring St $$–$$$

Le Tableau
C12

Offers lovely, innovative bistro renditions of wild mushroom casserole, calamari tagine with houmous, and bacon-wrapped monkfish. Live combos make it festive, and sometimes overly loud.
511 E 5th Street, East Village ☎ 260-1333 Ⓜ F to 2nd Ave $$

Lucky Strike
F11

A rollicking bistro that also serves competent (if unexciting) food into the wee hours. It's the ideal place to nibble and drink your way closer to solving the world's problems – or at least your vacation agenda; it's also one of Manhattan's smokers' havens.
59 Grand Street, Soho ☎ 941-0479 Ⓜ A•C•E to Canal St $–$$

Montrachet
F11

A minimalist bistro serving ravishing nouvelle French cuisine.
239 W Broadway, Tribeca ☎ 219-2777 Ⓜ 1•9 to Franklin St $$$

restaurants & cafés

☆ PASTIS
⌖F11

Über-restaurateur Keith (Balthazar) McNally set out to make his latest enterprise, Pastis, an everyday sort of bistro. Intents aside, he created a monster. The casual, faux-aged setting is an impeccable re-creation of a Provençal village café, so appealing that some nights it feels like all of Manhattan is trying to squeeze inside. Go early or very late (at midnight), as a two-hour wait during prime hours is standard, due to a no reservations policy. Dishes such as hearty pastas, roasted chicken with garlic confit, and supple braised beef are reliable and modestly priced.
9 Ninth Avenue, Meatpacking District ☎ **929-4844** Ⓜ **A•C•E to 14th St; L to 8th Ave $$**

Patois
⌖off map

A French-American bistro that is jammed in the evenings; fortunately, its waiting area (out back, under casbah-like drapes) is beguiling.
255 Smith Street, Carroll Gardens ☎ **1-718-855-1535** Ⓜ **F•G to Carroll St $$**

☆ PAYARD PATISSERIE & BISTRO
[→teas & patisseries]

Soho Steak
⌖D11

Owned by respected restaurateur Jean-Claude Iacovelli, who prides himself on serving quality bistro fare at affordable prices.
90 Thompson Street, Soho ☎ **226-0602** Ⓜ **C•E To Spring St $$**

Village
⌖A11

A cool clientele who enjoy this restaurant's take on French bistro food, with some home-grown dishes thrown in for good measure (evenings only).
62 W 9th Street, West Village ☎ **505-3355** Ⓜ **1•9 to Christopher St $$–$$$**

breakfast & brunch

Le Gamin
⌖D9
[→cafés & coffeshops]

Jerry's
⌖D11
[→diners]

Mesa Grill
⌖E10
[→american]

The Odeon
⌖B13
[→american]

7A ♯*A12*
[→cafés]

Sylvia's ♯*D1*
[→american]

Three of Cups ♯*C12*
[→italian]

burgers

Big Nick's Burger ♯*C5*
24-hour Upper West Side dump that inspires affection; loosen your belt.
2175 Broadway, UWS ☎ 362-9238 Ⓜ 1•9 to 79th St $

Corner Bistro ♯*F11*
Join the night owls at this dark, old mahogany-stained pub with a television broadcasting sports. During and after drinking bouts, there's nothing like their cheap, messy burgers.
331 W 4th Street, West Village ☎ 242-9502 Ⓜ A•C•E to 14th St; L to 8th Ave $

Island Burgers & Shakes ♯*D7*
Move over McDonald's. You can have it any way you like it here. But no fries.
766 Ninth Avenue, Midtown ☎ 307-7934 Ⓜ C•E to 50th St $

Jackson Hole ♯*B6*
Get lots of napkins for these messy burgers, especially good for kids.
1270 Madison Avenue, UES ☎ 427-2820 Ⓜ 4•5•6 to 86th St $

Rialto ♯*C12*
Groovy bistro with lots of inventive choices but nothing beats their thick, quality hamburgers (or veggie burgers) and crispy fries. Has a fantastic back garden, plus a sexy lounge and a good vibe at the bar.
265 Elizabeth Street, Noho ☎ 334-7900 Ⓜ F to 2nd Ave $$

Walkers ♯*F11*
A friendly watering hole, serving burgers with beer on tap. Settle in and enjoy the live jazz.
16 North Moore Street, Tribeca ☎ 941-0412 Ⓜ 1•9 to Franklin St $$–$$$

ABC Parlour Café
♪*C10*

If you've maxed out on shopping, take a tranquil break at the back of this magical furniture store.

38 E 19th Street, Gramercy Park ☎ 677-2233 Ⓜ N•R to 23rd St $–$$

Brooklyn Moon Café
♪*off map*

There's a lively scene at this intimate café, where the chatty crowd gets big at the Friday open-mic sessions.

745 Fulton Street, Fort Greene ☎ 1-718-243-0424 Ⓜ G to Fulton St

Café Gitane
♪*C12*

Immensely popular, with a super-cool crowd often spilling onto the pavement. They come here to smoke, drink coffee, chat, read and occasionally eat low-priced, decent salads and sandwiches.

242 Mott Street, Noho ☎ 334-9552 Ⓜ 6 to Spring St $

Café Lalo
♪*A5*

This pretty, European-style café is an ideal date place which has a full coffee and liquor menu as well as light salads and sandwiches – make sure you save room for their luscious desserts.

201 W 83rd Street, UWS ☎ 496-6031 Ⓜ 1•9 to 86th St $

Café Restaurant Volna

A basic café which is a favourite with the locals.

3145 B 4th Street, Brighton Beach ☎ 1-718-332-0341 Ⓜ D•Q to Brighton Beach

Chez Brigitte
♪*F11*

Open for 40 years, Brigitte herself is long gone, but her spirit lives on in hearty, low-priced stews, light omelettes and heavy desserts. Seats only 11 people at a time.

77 Greenwich Avenue, West Village ☎ 929-6736 Ⓜ A•C•E to 14th Street $

City Bakery
♪*E10*

Huge cookies and other mouth-watering sweets, plus a line-up of fresh soups, sandwiches and prepared foods – to go or eat-in at several small tables (closes 6pm).

22 E 17th Street, Gramercy Park ☎ 366-1414
Ⓜ L•N•R•4•5•6 to 14th St-Union Sq $

Drip
A5
A place to meet your match. This cafe-cum-bar has a noticeboard, where, for a small fee, you can display your lonely heart details.
489 Amsterdam Avenue, UWS ☎ 875-1032 Ⓜ 1•9 to 86th St

Dojo's
A12
Its proximity to NYU makes it a student fixture, and in all kinds of weather they'll take sidewalk tables so they can smoke between courses of wholesome soy burgers and brown rice stir-fries.
24 St Mark's Place, East Village ☎ 674-9821 Ⓜ 6 to Astor Pl $

DT-UT (DownTown-UpTown)
B6
You'll feel like you're in an episode of Friends in this mellow coffeehouse (they have beer and wine too) with comfy chairs for reading.
1626 Second Avenue, UES ☎ 327-1327 Ⓜ 4•5•6 to 86th St $

Eisenberg Sandwich Shop
C10
This rather dowdy café (closes at 5pm) has been open since 1929, and one hopes it'll last forever. Thank the counterman for your chocolate shake and cheap, thick tuna sandwich and he'll respond, 'My pleasure, darling.' How often do you hear that in New York?
174 Fifth Avenue, Gramercy Park ☎ 675-5096 Ⓜ N•R to 23rd St $

Fall Café
off map
A place to find Brooklyn's true bohemians – a haven of big sofas, little tables, cool music, art on the walls, and artistic types dawdling over chilli, sandwiches and coffee.
307 Smith Street, Carroll Gardens ☎ 1-718-403-0230 Ⓜ F•G to Carroll St $

Flavors
E9
An illustrious catering company, with a market/café outpost selling assorted breakfast and lunch items, as well as a fantastic salad bar and beautiful desserts (closes 6.30pm).
8 W 18th Street, Gramercy Park ☎ 647-1234 Ⓜ F to 14th St; L to 6th Ave $

Habib's Place
F10
Habib serves up yummy street food, fresh, cheap and abundant falafels to the sound of Louis Armstrong.
438 E 9th Street, East Village ☎ 979-2243 Ⓜ L to 1st Ave $

Halcyon
off map
In this absolutely unique, record store-cum-coffee shop is where you can also shop for flea market finds. Weekly events feature DJs and local artists.
227 Smith Street, Carroll Gardens ☎ 1-718-260-9299 Ⓜ F•G to Carroll St

Herban Kitchen
C11

A dimly lit, engaging café, serving uncommonly tasty organic specialties.
290 Hudson Street, Soho ☎ 627-2257 Ⓜ 1•9 to Houston St $-$$

Krispy Kreme's
C1

Try the light glazed donuts from its outpost near the Apollo Theatre –
one taste and you'll be hooked.
280 W 125th Street, Harlem ☎ 531-0111 Ⓜ A•B•C•D to 125th St $

L Café
off map

Good sandwiches and salads, mismatched tables and chairs.
189 Bedford Avenue, Williamsburg ☎ 1-718-388-6762
Ⓜ L to Bedford Ave $–$$

Le Gamin
D9

In a charming brick townhouse, this café attracts an artsy crowd, serving
French crepes, interesting salads and big bowls of coffee. Service is
leisurely, and the atmosphere especially magnetic at weekend brunch.
183 Ninth Avenue, Chelsea ☎ 243-8864 Ⓜ C•E to 23rd St $-$$

Lotus Club
D12

This boho hang-out has healthy sandwiches and arty magazines to
peruse or purchase.
35 Clinton Street, LES ☎ 253-1144 Ⓜ F•J•M•Z to Delancey St-Essex St $

Mezze
E8

A sunny, casual Mediterranean café near Grand Central Station. Breakfast
coffee can be savoured with rich pastries, and at lunch there are quality,
pre-cooked meat, seafood and vegetable selections (closes at 5pm).
10 E 44th Street, Midtown ☎ 697-6644 Ⓜ B•D•F•Q to 42nd St $–$$

Nougatine
B8

The café adjacent to Jean-Georges and slightly more affordable.
Trump International Hotel, 1 Central Park W, UWS ☎ 299-3900
Ⓜ A•B•C•D•1•9 to 59th St-Columbus Circle $$

Once upon a Tart
D11

Offering terrific baked goods, crusty sandwiches, and salads in a relaxed
café atmosphere. Take a table, spread your newspaper and ease those
tired feet.
135 Sullivan Street, Soho ☎ 387-8869 Ⓜ C•E to Spring St $

restaurants & cafés

Papaya King *♭B6*
For the best hot dog/shake combo around: the hot dogs are delicious and the shakes freshly made (unsurprisingly papaya is the specialty here).
179 E 86th Street, UES ☎ 369-0648 Ⓜ 4•5•6 to 86th St $

7A *♭A12*
Cheap, hangover heaven. Bring sunglasses for sidewalk tables and reading material for the wait.
109 Avenue A, East Village ☎ 673-6583 Ⓜ 6 to Astor Pl $

Tatiana Café *♭off map*
Whatever the weather, or time of day, you'll find hardy fur-clad locals sitting outside among the seagulls at this elegant café.
3145 B 4th Street, Brighton Beach ☎ 1-718-646-7630
Ⓜ D•Q to Brigton Beach $–$$

☆ TEA & SYMPATHY *♭F9*
Anglos and Anglophiles alike can't get enough of Tea & Sympathy which is why it's often packed tight. Authentic English breakfasts, typical pub items (shepherd's pie, bangers and mash) and tea from mismatched pots are low-priced and satisfying. It looks like your favourite auntie's living room, the one who still cries over Diana (Royals' memorabilia is everywhere).
108 Greenwich Avenue, West Village ☎ 807-8329
Ⓜ A•C•E•1•2•3•9 to 14th St $–$$

The Tea Box *♭B7*
A calming, minimalist café inTakashimaya, the fancy Japanese department store, which serves bite-sized sandwiches, elegant bento boxes and lovely afternoon tea (11am– 6pm).
693 Fifth Avenue, Midtown ☎ 350-0180 Ⓜ B•Q to 57th St $–$$

Tillie's of Brooklyn *♭off map*
An arty coffee bar with jazz on the weekends (and occasional sightings of Rosie Perez who lives locally).
248 DeKalb Avenue, Fort Greene ☎ 1-718-783-6140 Ⓜ G to Fulton St $

Tossed *♭C10*
For the ultimate salad fix. Choose from eight types of lettuce, and vegetable toss-ins with dressings such as champagne-raspberry (closes 10pm).
295 Park Avenue S, Gramercy Park ☎ 674-6700 Ⓜ 6 to 23rd St $

Tuscan Square ♯D7
Within the Rockefeller Center is this busy Italian marketplace. The down-stairs self-service café dishes up tasty prepared foods, delicious soups and has a great salad bar (closes at 8pm).
16 W 51st Street, Midtown ☎ 977-7777 Ⓜ C•E to 50th St $–$$

cambodian

SEA Cambodian ♯off map
NY's only Cambodian restaurant. The fragrant, spicy food is great value.
87 S Elliott Place, Fort Greene ☎ 1-718-858-3262 Ⓜ G to Fulton St $–$$

chinese

First Wok ♯B6
Good quality fare and fast service. The Chinese dishes are ample, but the real incentive is their free, unlimited house wine.
1570 Third Avenue, UES ☎ 410-7747 Ⓜ 4•5•6 to 86th St $

Grand Sichuan ♯E12
A bare-bones, spicy Szechuan restaurant. As well as Chinese standards, they serve ethnic specialties you won't find elsewhere.
125 Canal Street, LES ☎ 625-9212 Ⓜ B•D•Q to Grand St $-$$

Great Shanghai ♯E12
A sleek, dimly-lit ambience; the sweet-and-sour fish and sauteed baby shrimp are excellent.
27 Division Street, LES ☎ 966-7663 Ⓜ J•M•Z•6 to Canal St $-$$

Hong Kong Egg Cake Co ♯C12
Aka the Egg Cake Lady. Look for her fading red shack tucked down a side street (11am–5pm Wed–Thu & Sat–Sun), and slip her $1 for a sack of a dozen hot cakes with custard filling.
Mott & Mosco Sts, LES ☎ no phone Ⓜ 6 to Spring St $

Jing Fong ♯E12
During the day, the Chinese parade to this cavernous eatery for dim sum carts loaded with sumptuous tidbits. It's noisy and service might be brusque, but it's also the real McCoy.
**20 Elizabeth Street, LES ☎ 964-5256 ☎ 966-7663
Ⓜ J•M•Z•6 to Canal St $-$$**

☆ JOE'S SHANGHAI ♭E12

The best joint in Chinatown. Sure, the insane queues, borderline rude service and communal tables may be frustrating, but there is nothing like their soup dumplings (scoop 'em up in a spoon, bite the top off, drink the soup inside, and then eat the crab meat and pork filling) and fried ricecakes. Get the real Shanghai experience, over-order, over-eat and share with friends...

9 Pell Street, LES ☎ 233-8888 Ⓜ N•R•6 to Canal St; B•D•Q to Grand St $–$$$

New Wonton Garden ♭E12

With lights bright enough to cause sunburn, this is good for cheap, quick, quality eats.

56 Mott Street, LES ☎ 966-4886 Ⓜ J•M•Z•6 to Canal St $

New York Noodle Town ♭E12

This restarant is a bright and lively magnet for both Chinese and Westerners. Pan-fried noodles are tossed with poultry, seafood, and vegetables.

28 Bowery, LES ☎ 349-0923 Ⓜ J•M•Z•6 to Canal St $–$$

delicatessens

☆ ARTIE'S NEW YORK DELICATESSEN ♭A5

Grab some cholesterol from this Jewish-style deli, which is new for its breed, but attracts all sorts of New Yorkers with its great old-time favourites like its fine pastrami and garlicky frankfurters.

2290 Broadway, UWS ☎ 579-5959 Ⓜ 1•9 to 86th St $$

Balducci's ♭A11

Open since 1946, this virtual horn of plenty will astound you with its exquisite fruits and vegetables as well as lovely cheeses, pastries, chocolates, charcuterie and prepared foods. Most of it's costly, so sometimes it's just fun to look.

424 Sixth Avenue, West Village ☎ 673-2600 Ⓜ A•B•C•D•E•F•Q to W 4th St-Washington Sq

☆ BARNEY GREENGRASS ♭A5

A beloved deli that's been around forever, Barney Greengrass serves top-notch Jewish specialities. If few tables are completely packed for weekend brunches, stop in during the week for bagels, pickled herring, velvety lox and knishes big as baseballs. (closes 6pm, and all day Monday).

541 Amsterdam Avenue, UWS ☎ 724-4707 Ⓜ 1•9 to 86th St $–$$

Buffa's Delicatessen
♯D11

A no-frills hangout, staffed by smart alecks slapping down cheap break-fasts and honest lunch items for its regular actor and director customers (Mon–Fri, closes at 4pm).

54 Prince Street, Noho ☎ 226-0211 Ⓜ N•R to Prince St $

☆ KATZ'S DELI
♯C12

One of the only Jewish eateries remaining in Lower East Side, Katz's is a funky cafeteria with incredible pastrami and chopped liver, around forever for good reason. Although a bit frayed at the edges, it's still popular with locals and American presidents alike (look for proudly displayed letters from Reagan and Clinton).

205 E Houston Street, LES ☎ 254-2246 Ⓜ F to 2nd Ave $–$$

☆ SECOND AVENUE DELI
♯A12

People of all ages love this old Jewish kosher favourite. Their matzoh ball soup, homemade pickles, corned beef and pastrami are legendary – as are the wise-cracking staff. Portions are huge and sharing costs extra, so give up and pig out. Always a line but worth it.

156 Second Avenue, East Village ☎ 677-0606 Ⓜ 6 to Astor Pl $–$$

diners

Bubby's
♯F11

A neighbourhood favourite for unpretentious food like roast chicken, and pancakes: its weekend brunches are terrific.

120 Hudson Street, Tribeca ☎ 219-0666 Ⓜ 1•9 to Franklin St $–$$

☆ COMFORT DINER
♯B6

New York is filled with greasy spoon diners with acceptable grub, but at the Comfort Diner (two locations), it's butter, not bacon grease, that will shoot up your cholesterol level. Owned by a nostalgic soul named Ira Freehof, the place is polished to a sheen. The idea is kitschy, but also authentic, with crunchy grilled cheese sandwiches, macaroni and cheese, and thick chocolate malteds. Soups and lighter sandwiches cater to healthier tastes. No alcohol served.

142 E 86th Street, UES ☎ 369-8628 Ⓜ 4•5•6 to 86th St $–$$

Diner
♯off map

Serves vaguely French cuisine in an actual chrome-and-tile diner.

85 Broadway, Williamsburg ☎ 1-718-486-3077 Ⓜ Z•M•J to Marcy Ave $–$$

Ellen's Stardust Diner *♪D7*
Owned by Ellen Hart, Miss Subway 1959, this vintage subway car-shaped diner with a dinnertime show was made for kids. The food is standard American with cleverly named kids' dishes, inspired by hugely popular kids' TV channel Nickelodeon.
1650 Broadway, Midtown ☎ 956-5151 Ⓜ 1•9 to 50th St

Empire Diner *♪D9*
Comfort food sassily served 24 hours a day, often accompanied by live piano music.
210 Tenth Avenue, Chelsea ☎ 243-2736 Ⓜ C•E to 23rd St $-$$

Great Jones Café *♪A12*
A cramped roadhouse serving Cajun specialities. Rambunctious customers throng the bar, downing cold beers, spicy jalapeño martinis and Bloody Marys, while honky tonk and country plays on the jukebox.
54 Great Jones Street, Noho ☎ 674-9304 Ⓜ 6 to Bleecker St $

☆ JERRY'S *♪D11*
Nearly the only soulful restaurant in the Soho 'mall', Jerry's red booths, mosaic-tiled floor, zinc bar and zebra-striped walls have held up well over time, as has much of the American comfort food with slight pretensions – well, mostly. Portions – of roast chicken; seasonal vegetable plate; cajun shrimp salad; devilishly good chocolate brick cake – aren't exactly diner-sized, but the French toast, made with baguette, is the best in town. Watch out for the brunch crush and occasionally deranged service.
101 Prince Street, Soho ☎ 966-9464 Ⓜ N•R to Prince St $$

Joe Jr's *♪F9*
Cinematic diner dollhouse with lots of heart but no vitamin content.
482 Sixth Avenue, Chelsea ☎ 924-5220 Ⓜ F to 14th St; L to 6th Ave $

Jones Diner *♪A12*
The genuine free-standing variety – another favourite for budget breakfasts and cheeseburgers.
371 Lafayette Street, Noho ☎ 673-3577 Ⓜ 6 to Bleecker St $

Junior's *♪off map*
The blintzes and world-famous cheesecakes are showstoppers. Go on, live a little.
386 Flatbush Avenue, Flatbush ☎ 1-718-852-5257 Ⓜ D•M•N•Q•R to De Kalb Ave $$

Kitchenette
♯B13
A sweet American roadside stop with hearty country cooking (open 'til 10pm).
80 W Broadway, Tribeca ☎ 267-6740 Ⓜ 1•2•3•9 to Chambers St $

Mayrose
♯C10
Popular for turkey burgers, milkshakes and big breakfasts (served at any time). The food isn't amazing but it's abundant and popular with pre- and post-cinema goers.
920 Broadway, Gramercy Park ☎ 533-3663 Ⓜ N•R to 23rd St $

Moondance Diner
♯F11
A friendly shack heavy on bygone charm. Satisfy your appetite with hearty soups, big sandwiches and piles of fries.
80 Sixth Avenue, Soho ☎ 226-1191 Ⓜ A•C•E to Canal St $

Tom's Restaurant
♯A3
Immortalized by Seinfeld, with satisfying greasy-spoon specialties for student budgets.
2880 Broadway, Harlem ☎ 864-6137 Ⓜ 1•9 to 110th St-Cathedral Pkway $

Vynl Diner
♯C7
This diner in Hell's Kitchen is super-friendly, with mosaic tabletops and camp decor. In addition to American staples like grilled cheese and meat-loaf, there are also dishes such as Thai-accented curries and stir-fries on offer.
824 Ninth Avenue, Midtown ☎ 974-2003 Ⓜ C•E to 50th St $

east european

Kasia's
♯off map
Tasty Polish and diner grub in a log-cabinesque setting.
146 Bedford Avenue, Williamsburg ☎ 1-718-387-8780 Ⓜ L to Bedford Ave $

Leshko's
♯F10
A former no-frills Ukrainian coffee shop is now as sleek and stylish as they come. Indulge in too many of its *pierogis* though and you'll be waving your silhouette goodbye.
111 Avenue A, East Village ☎ 777-2111 Ⓜ L to 1st Ave

Russian Tea Room
♯B7
The OTT decor includes Tiffany stained-glass ceiling and mirrored walls. The food is hardly the lure, so head for the upstairs lounge where you can sup on caviar and cocktails.
150 W 57th Street, Midtown ☎ 974-2111 Ⓜ N•R to 57th St $$–$$$

Teresa's,   *$F10*
An authentic Polish diner, may have a new look but still serves the same old-fashioned *kielbasa*, stuffed cabbage and *blintzes*.
103 First Avenue, East Village ☎ 228-0604 Ⓜ L to 1st Ave $

Winter Garden   *$off map*
A winning combination of location (on the Boardwalk), excellent food (cherry dumplings, breast of duck), and a 'groovy' floorshow (perfumed smoke, glamour, and 70s sounds). Call to book, wear all your jewellery, go in a rowdy group (if you can), and call a car to get home.
3152 B 6th Street, Brighton Beach ☎ 1-718-934-6666
Ⓜ D•Q to Brighton Beach

french

Alison on Dominick Street   *$D11*
Pure romance – a small, out-of-the-way place with straightforward French and new American food. You go there to kiss and share bites, not to be blown away by innovative cuisine.
38 Dominick Street, Soho ☎ 727-1188 Ⓜ C•E to Spring St $$$

Avenue   *$B5*
A French country charmer with brick walls and dark wooden tables. Quality food at moderate prices, including delicious baked goods.
520 Columbus Avenue, UWS ☎ 579-3194 Ⓜ B•C to 86th St $$

☆ BAYARD'S   *$C14*
Maritime history and gentlemen's club elegance evoke an aura of privilege. Everyone who walks through the hallowed India House doors is treated like royalty by one of the best-trained, most personable staffs in the city. Sensational contemporary French cuisine is by chef Luc Dendievel; sautéed Hudson Valley foie gras, poached Maine lobster, and loin of venison in red wine are all divine, as is the wine list.
India House, 1 Hanover Square, Lower Manhattan ☎ 514-9454 Ⓜ 2•3 to Wall St $$$

☆ CAFÉ BOULUD
♪D6

Since chef/owner Daniel Boulud is busy over at his four-star restaurant Daniel, he has appointed rising star Andrew Carmellini to man the stove at the smaller, more relaxed Café Boulud. His take on traditional French (chicken fricassee), seasonal specialties (smoked salmon latkes with caviar), vegetarian creations (cassoulet of root vegetables with garlic crust), and featured world cuisines (anything from Basque to Louisiana cooking) is subtle and deeply resonant. The warm, cosmopolitan room is plushly upholstered and usually filled with powerbrokers (but ties aren't required).

20 E 76th Street, UES ☎ 772-2600 Ⓜ 6 to 77th St $$$

☆ CAFÉ DES ARTISTES
♪E5

Intimate and extravagantly filled with flowers and sensual murals, Café des Artistes is not for the claustrophobic. Patrons are well-heeled and it's perfect for cozy dates and smart family dinners. The French fare is consistent and classic. Hungarian owner George Lang has also sneaked in some of his native dishes (like chicken paprika, and goulash soup). Service is cutely formal, and it's tough getting a reservation. The polished bar is romantic for drinks.

1 W 67th Street, UWS ☎ 877-3500 Ⓜ 1•9 to 66th St-Lincoln Center $$$

☆ CAPSOUTO FRÈRES
♪F11

The out-of-the-way address may exasperate your cab driver, but it really does exist, and it's well worth seeking out. Three brothers with lots of savvy opened this gracious Tribeca loft-space nearly 20 years ago, and new chef Eric Heinrich has recently reinvigorated the French cuisine. The temple to magnificent soufflés, saucisson chaud and fork-tender duckling now boasts creative specials like tian of venison with parsnip purée. Brunch is fab, the crowd distinguished but dressed down.

451 Washington Street, Tribeca ☎ 966-4900 Ⓜ 1•9 to Canal St $$–$$$

Chanterelle
♪F11

One of NY's top-rated restaurants – creative French cooking in a friendly environment.

2 Harrison Street, Tribeca ☎ 966-6960 Ⓜ 1•9 to Franklin St $$$

Country Café
♪D11

Coloured lights welcome you into its tiny interior, which is filled to the brim with charming knick-knacks. The French and Moroccan food is richly prepared and served by an affable staff.

69 Thompson Street, Soho ☎ 966-5417 Ⓜ C•E to Spring St $$

☆ DANIEL ♭F6

Daniel Boulud is a god-like chef, and this pink parlour vindicates his reputation. He does serious, sit-up-straight French cuisine: incredible dishes include a chestnut-celery root soup with a braised apple slice and a tranche of foie gras immersed within; a boeuf aux carottes – perfect, peasanty braised beef and carrots; or roasted Arctic char with béarnaise and baby vegetables. Desserts are equally sublime – an espresso cup of foamy chocolate with a thick chocolatey bottom; a fruit soup with apple beignets... To die for.

60 E 65th Street, UES ☎ 288-0033 Ⓜ 6 to 68th St-Hunter College $$$

☆ FLORENT ♭F11

Fêted institutions should often be avoided, but this drag queens' French diner on a cobblestone street is so much fun. You'll go away hoarse and deaf (especially late on weekends) and will eat amply, if not memorably. Best bets are roast chicken with mustard sauce and mash, boudin noir and fries, mussels, smoked trout, French toast, or steak frites. It's an ideal pitstop on your way home after an exhausting evening. Best to be decisive about what you want because some of the waiters are verging on cruel.

69 Gansevoort Street, Meatpacking District ☎ 989-5779 Ⓜ A•C•E to 14th St $–$$

French Roast ♭E10

Stays open 24 hours, 365 days a year, and is good for strong coffee, red wine and a repertoire of well-prepared French classics. The casual milieu is pure Parisian flea market.

78 W 11th Street, West Village ☎ 533-2233 Ⓜ L to 6th Ave $–$$

Jean Claude ♭D11

Seating is tight at this restaurant serving classic French cuisine. The benefit of this is that it renders conversation with your neighbour effortless.

137 Sullivan Street, Soho ☎ 475-9232 Ⓜ C•E to Spring St $$

restaurants & cafés

☆ JEAN GEORGES   ♢B7

Jean-Georges Vongerichten's signature showplace astonishes palates with new French flavour combinations. The eclectic menu includes black sea bass with Sicilian pistachio crust, and loin of lamb dusted with black trumpet mushrooms and leek purée. The dining room's floor-to-ceiling windows and neutral canvas of colours is a soothing backdrop for the smart, refined clientele, who discuss their dishes in low, thrilled tones. The kitchen also turns out grilled meats, salads and cold soups for the Mistral Terrace (summer only) which overlooks Central Park. Tables are booked 30 days in advance.

Trump International Hotel, 1 Central Park W, UWS ☎ 299-3900
Ⓜ A•B•C•D•1•9 to 59th St-Columbus Circle $$$

JoJo   ♢F6

A jewel box of a townhouse restaurant. The crowd is refined, the staff unfailingly pleasant, with inventive French cooking the speciality – the prix-fixe lunch is a bargain.

160 E 64th Street, UES ☎ 223-5656 Ⓜ B•Q to Lexington Ave $$$

La Lunchonette   ♢F11

Feels like a French version of a frontier saloon, a lively, red-hued affair with richly-flavoured Gallic classics.

130 Tenth Avenue, Chelsea ☎ 675-0342 Ⓜ L to 8th Ave; A•C•E to 14th St $$

☆ LESPINASSE   ♢A8

The grandest of Gotham City's French restaurants is named after Mademoiselle Lespinasse who, during Louis XV's reign, entertained philosophers, nobles and diplomats in her Paris salon. The restaurant's exquisite atmosphere may evoke a past era, but you'll hear big money deals discussed more than ideas. Chef Christian Delouvrier is highly trained in classic French techniques, using only the best ingredients in dishes like hare stew in red wine, and confit of baby pig in rich cassoulet. Before or after dinner, take time to luxuriate in the glowing King Cole Bar.

St Regis Hotel, 2 E 55th Street, Midtown ☎ 339-6719 Ⓜ E•F to 5th St $$$

Lucien   ♢C12

To get into this tiny popular French bistro, go early or very late to avoid the crush. Classic dishes are richly seasoned and excellent value, with a smart wine list to match.

14 First Avenue, East Village ☎ 260-6481 Ⓜ F to 2nd Ave $$

The Terrace $E1
Situated Morningside Heights at the top of an elegant residential building, this is a pricey French restaurant with breathtaking views of the city, even if its interior resembles that of a cruise ship.
400 W 119th Street, Harlem ☎ 666-9490 Ⓜ A•B•C•D to 125th St $$$

Titou $A11
A beautiful, leafy venue, with French specialties, and a good deal on wine.
259 W 4th Street, West Village ☎ 691-9359 Ⓜ 1•9 to Christopher St $$

global & fusion

☆ AMERICAN PARK $F13
Smack dab on the harbour and near the Staten Island ferry, American Park's towering windows afford an incomparable view of passing boats and the Statue of Liberty. But this is no tourist trap. The seafood tastes of the sea it just came from, and is swimming with global influences. How about grilled *mahi mahi* with Vietnamese rice noodles, Japanese eggplant and shiitake mushrooms in spicy lemongrass coconut broth? It works. A table on the outdoor patio at sunset is a lovely experience and service is friendly and proficient.
Battery Park (opposite 175 State Street), Lower Manhattan ☎ 809-5508 Ⓜ 1•9 to South Ferry; 4•5 to Bowling Green $$–$$$

Asia de Cuba $E8
The trendy, attitude-heavy scene can be over the top, so it's not for everybody. If, however, you want to lounge in a creamy boudoir, share punch-bowl-sized tropical drinks and sample exotic, expensive Asian-Latin fusion dishes, step right up.
Morgans Hotel, 237 Madison Avenue, Midtown ☎ 726-7755 Ⓜ 4•5•6•7 to Grand Central-42nd St $$$

Bar Six $F9
French-Moroccan fare is satisfactory for late-night noshing ('til 2am), although the noise can be ear-splitting.
502 Sixth Avenue, West Village ☎ 691-1363 Ⓜ L to 6th Ave; M to 14th St $$

Bright Food Shop $D9
Southwestern cooking meets the Far East at this cute spot open all day. The staff are welcoming and the prices pocket-friendly.
216 Eighth Avenue, Chelsea ☎ 243-4433 Ⓜ C•E to 23rd St $–$$

Kitchen Club
C12

For something French, with just a hint of Asian, try this well run, and very civilized restaurant. They do magical things with mushrooms. Check out, too, their adjoining saké bar.

30 Prince Street, Noho ☎ 274-0025 Ⓜ 6 to Spring St $$

Lola
C10

Possesses a more assured sexiness, serving an inventive mix of American, Mediterranean and Asian cuisines; the live gospel music at Sunday brunch is especially rousing.

30 W 22nd Street, Gramercy Park ☎ 675-6700 Ⓜ N•R to 23rd St $$$

The Place
F9

Eating in this intimate, Mediterranean-inspired 'cottage' is more rewarding than its name implies. Treats such as leek and butternut squash risotto, and curry-crusted leg of lamb are nicely prepared, and 10% of sales go to charity.

310 W 4th Street, West Village ☎ 924-2711 Ⓜ L to 8th Ave; A•C•E 14th St $$

Radio Perfecto
F10

A hopping place, filled with illuminated Bakelite radios, and there's a charming garden at the rear. The wide-ranging menu mixes anything from Argentine *empanadas* to rotisserie chicken with delicious pesto dipping sauce.

190 Avenue B, East Village ☎ 477-3366 Ⓜ L to 1st Ave $

Rice
C12

This intimate restaurant is true to its name, stirring up a medley of different grains with Asian and Mediterranean toppings.

227 Mott Street, Noho ☎ 226-5775 Ⓜ 6 to Spring St $

Torch
D12

A swanky lounge and 40s-style supper club. Cabaret acts can be enjoyed along with cocktails and French/South American-inspired cuisine.

137 Ludlow Street, LES ☎ 228-5151 Ⓜ F•J•M•Z to Delancey St-Essex St $$

27 Standard
A10

If you're into jazz, head here (performances downstairs). The cavernous dining room offers superb eclectic dishes like pecan-crusted pork, and tuna sashimi wrapped in nori.

116 E 27th Street, Gramercy Park ☎ 447-7733 Ⓜ 6 to 28th St $$$

UN Delegates' Dining Room ♯E8
Book a table for something truly international. Expect an extravagant buffet and a room full of dignitaries with stunning river vistas (11.30am–2.30pm Mon–Fri). Allow 15 minutes to pass security (photo ID and jackets required).
45th Street, Midtown ☎ 963-7626 Ⓜ 4•5•6•7 to Grand Central-42nd St $$

☆ UNION PACIFIC ♯C10
At this smart restaurant, expect some of the most succulent and creatively prepared seafood your tongue could hope to tangle with. Sashimi-quality Taylor Bay scallops with sea urchin; wild sturgeon with morels; and for the non-fish-eaters, there's always steak and chicken and daring global creations, such as sauteed foie gras with green papaya and tamarind. The richly-decorated space is just as smart as the menu – a plush lounge filled with chic velvet sofas and over-stuffed chairs in the basement level – it's the perfect place to impress.
111 E 22nd Street, Gramercy Park ☎ 995-8500 Ⓜ 6 to 23rd St $$$

Yaffa Café ♯C12
A 24-hour dive, whose big plus is its vast back garden. Inside, the screw-ball decor is diverting, and the fusion food (much of it vegetarian) reasonably healthy.
97 St Mark's Place, East Village ☎ 674-9302 Ⓜ F to 2nd Ave $

greek

Periyali ♯C10
Features the most stupendous Greek seafood in town, served in a peaceful, civilized atmosphere.
35 W 20th Street, Gramercy Park ☎ 463-7890 Ⓜ N•R•6 to 23rd St $$$

ice cream

Chinatown Ice Cream Factory ♯E12
Try exotic flavours like lychee and red bean to perfectly cap off any meal.
65 Bayard Street, LES ☎ 608-4170 Ⓜ J•M•Z•6 to Canal St $

Lexington Candy Shop ♯D6
For a real old-fashioned soda fountain, this is the business; grab one of their amazing flavoured seltzers.
1226 Lexington Avenue, UES ☎ 288-0057 Ⓜ 6 to 77th St

Monteleone's
♭off map

Top off any lunch with Italian pastries or ices, (the delicate lemon ice is a winner).

355 Court Street, Carroll Gardens ☎ 1-718-624-9253 Ⓜ F•G to Carroll St $

indian

Café Spice
♭B11

Part of the contemporary Indian trend: a colourful bistro with vividly flavoured regional specialties.

72 University Place, West Village ☎ 253-6999 Ⓜ N•R to 8th St-NYU $$

Curry in a Hurry
♭A10

In the part of Lexington Avenue known as Little India this resembles an Indian McDonald's. Masala dosa – vegetarian pancakes stuffed with potatoes and peas – are the best item, and it's BYOB which makes it super-cheap.

119 Lexington Avenue, Gramercy Park ☎ 683-0900 Ⓜ 6 to 28th St $

Haveli
♭A12

The king of 6th Street's Indian restaurants. It's a spacious duplex with courtly service and superior dishes; they even have topnotch, though distinctly un-Indian, Belgian beers to cut the spice.

100 Second Avenue, East Village ☎ 982-0533 Ⓜ 6 to Astor Pl $–$$

☆ SURYA
♭A11

A former beauty queen from India is the hostess, setting the tone for a stylish room full of beautiful people. Exotic spices from Southern India blaze in dishes like dosai crêpes filled with sea bass, and grilled halibut with ginger and coconut cream. Unique vegetarian choices abound, making use of lentils in cakes, pancakes and soups; and spice-lifted aubergines, okra and potatoes in dishes served with mint rice or paratha. It's as modern as Indian restaurants get, also featuring spectacular, photogenic cocktails. The main dining room can be deafening, so when weather cooperates, opt for the serene courtyard.

302 Bleecker Street, West Village ☎ 807-7770 Ⓜ 1•9 to Christopher St $–$$$

irish

St Dymphna's
♭F10

Irish expats hang out at this affable pub, serving beef and Guinness casserole. Its low-key informality has attracted the likes of anti-scenesters Daniel Day Lewis and Ralph Fiennes.

118 St Mark's Place, East Village ☎ 254-6636 Ⓜ L to 1st Ave $–$$

S J South & Sons *♭F11*

A casual, pub-like atmosphere, serving classic British/Irish fare like beef stew and pints of Guinness.

273 Church Street, Tribeca ☎ 219-0640 Ⓜ 1•9 to Franklin St $$

italian

☆ **BABBO** *♭A11*

Everything good you have heard about Mario Batali's gorgeous place in the old Coach House is true. Two spacious lemon-yellow rooms and meticulous service are merely the backdrop to the most original Italian food around. Read and salivate: goat's cheese tortellini with dried orange and wild fennel pollen; chestnut gnocchi with wild boar – and that's just the primi. Entrées are equally imaginative and the desserts, such as poached kumquats with gorgonzola, are delectable.

110 Waverly Place, West Village ☎ 777-0303
Ⓜ A•B•C•D•E•F•Q to W 4th St-Washington Sq $$–$$$

☆ **BAR PITTI** *♭A11*

A simple Tuscan restaurant that's best in summer, when tables line up on the wide sidewalk, and the marble floors and white walls inside are super cool. The fettuna (bread salad) is the best dish on the menu, but the blackboard specials are all usually good, from spinach with garlic and lemon to marinated quail or homemade pasta. Bar Pitti feels genuinely European, as opposed to Eurotrashy (that's what Da Silvano, the expensive schmoozy joint next door, is for).

268 Sixth Avenue, West Village ☎ 982-3300
Ⓜ A•B•C•D•E•F•Q to W 4th St-Washington Sq $–$$

Bottino *♭D9*

A spare, attractive Tuscan restaurant with a wonderful back garden, luring a cool art and publishing crowd. Pasta dishes and fish are straightforward, and the adjacent take-out shop sells panini and other prepared foods during the day.

246 Tenth Avenue, Chelsea ☎ 206-6766 Ⓜ C•E to 23rd St $$

Carino *♭B6*

For old-fashioned Sicilian food (veal parmigiana, chicken marsala) in a charming, bygone atmosphere.

1710 Second Avenue, UES ☎ 860-0566 Ⓜ 4•5•6 to 86th St $$

Danube
F11

David Bouley's luxurious downtown tribute to Vienna, offering refined middle European fare in a sumptuous setting at seriously uptown prices (some say it is rather overpriced).

30 Hudson Street, Tribeca ☎ 791-3771 Ⓜ 1•9 to Franklin St **$$$**

Don Giovanni
F7

Pretensions are wonderfully absent at this Theater District favourite adorned with vintage actors' photos and straw-covered Chianti bottles. The terrific brick-oven pizzas are better than the pastas.

358 W 44th Street, Midtown ☎ 581-4939
Ⓜ A•C•E to 42nd St-Port Authority Bus Terminal **$–$$**

Esca
F7

Mario Batali's new Southern Italian seafood-themed restaurant is another Midtown hit. Convenient to Broadway's theatres, it's a classy, but not a stuffy affair.

402 W 43rd Street, Midtown ☎ 564-7272 Ⓜ A•C•E to 42nd St-Port Authority Bus Terminal **$$–$$$**

☆ GRIMALDI'S
off map

Beneath the Brooklyn Bridge lies a paean to pizza lovers and Frank Sinatra (walls are littered with autographed photos of him as well as other bygone celebrities). Even the 'small' pizza is obscenely huge, the crust slightly charred, the fresh mozzarella bubbling from the brick oven. Conventional toppings are generous, the only gourmet touches being fresh basil leaves and a twist of fresh ground pepper. It may look tacky, and crass pop plays more than Ol' Blue Eyes, but it's hard to find a better pie.

19 Old Fulton Street, Brooklyn Heights ☎ 1-718-858-4300
Ⓜ A•C to High St; 2•3 to Clark St **$$**

Helen's Place
off map

An old-fashioned Italian joint, with white tablecloths, a linoleum floor, and atmosphere courtesy of the radio and memory.

396 Court Street, Carroll Gardens ☎ 1-718-855-9128 Ⓜ F•G to Carroll St **$–$$**

☆ IL BAGATTO ♪A12

If you never had the stereotypical Italian mamma (you know... killer cook, killer instinct) but always felt the need, head to this charming restaurant, where there are two rules: no cheese on seafood pasta, and be on time. While the service is often offhand and the seating cramped, the homemade gnocchi and lasagne will leave you begging for more. Everything is stuffed full of the best, hand-picked ingredients and made with love, so it's no wonder that the jewel box of a space is always packed with a hip crowd of downtown gurus, models and celebs. Warning: smoking's allowed here, and everyone does – with gusto.

192 E 2nd Street, East Village ☎ 228-0977 Ⓜ F to 2nd Ave $

☆ `INO ♪A11

Tucked down a little West Village side street, this is exactly the kind of cheery nook you'd love to find on a roadside in Italy. The staff are warm and don't rush you, allowing time to sit and read, think, or chatter all afternoon and night. What's more, the light snacking food is delicious: marinated olives, bruschetta with a number of toppings and flavourful panini with quality ingredients. Smooth music and interesting wines served by the glass, half carafe and bottle help wash cares away.

21 Bedford Street, West Village ☎ 989-5769 Ⓜ A•B•C•D•E•F•Q to W 4th St-Washington Sq $

I Trulli ♪A10

A gracious, exquisite spot with an enchanting enoteca (wine bar) attached.

122 E 27th Street, Gramercy Park ☎ 481-7372 Ⓜ 6 to 28th St $$$

☆ LOMBARDI'S ♪C12

This place is satisfyingly cinematic, with its brick walls and chequered cloths, but the point is the 1905 coal oven and the pizza that emerges from it, which is the best in Manhattan. The crust is the crispest, the mozzarella the freshest, the toppings (pancetta, sweet Italian sausage, anchovies, roasted peppers, fresh basil, etc) the finest. They also do a fresh clam pie without tomato or cheese, and a white pizza (no tomato), with mozzarella, romano, ricotta and garlic, with a salad on the side.

32 Spring Street, Nolita ☎ 941-7994 Ⓜ 6 to Spring St $$

☆ LUPA ♯D11

Secluded on a West Village street, this Roman-style trattoria is delightfully lacking in pretension, with terracotta floors, and wooden tables set with candles. Mario Batali and Joseph Bastianich, of Po, Babbo and Esca fame, are the formidable team behind it, ensuring value at a fair price. The menu is replete with straightforward pastas (silky fettuce alfredo) and expertly prepared seafood (crusty salt cod with fennel and mint), along with paper-thin antipasti meats shaved to order. Courses can be matched with rustic Italian wines served by the quartino.

170 Thompson Street, West Village ☎ 982-5089 Ⓜ 1•9 to Houston St; N•R to Prince St $$

Max ♯F10

This southern Italian spot with a menu that features flavourful options like 'Mom's meat loaf' and 'Father's style' rigatoni, is guaranteed to make you feel right at home.

51 Avenue B, East Village ☎ 539-0111 Ⓜ L to 1st Ave $–$$

Peasant ♯A12

The decor is low-lit and low-key, but the food is as rustic as you'd like. Italian-inspired dishes such as grilled fish and rotisserie-roasted game are cooked over a fire in the open kitchen.

194 Elizabeth Street, Noho ☎ 965-9511 Ⓜ 6 to Bleeker St $$-$$$

☆ PEPE ROSSO ♯D11

Stop by Pepe Rosso's tiny Sullivan Street shop in Soho for a delicious hunk of focaccia to snack on while strolling around. With just a few cramped tables, it's not very comfortable to linger, so it's prime for take-out.. However, their larger outpost in the East Village is a destination on its own. Dirt cheap pastas, salads and grilled vegetables are robustly flavoured. The dark, funky setting is utterly without pretension and wine is poured in fat, stemless glasses. Service is haphazard but when the food's this cheap and good, who cares?

149 Sullivan Street, Soho ☎ 677-4555 Ⓜ C•E to Spring St $
110 St Mark's Place, West Village ☎ 677-6563 Ⓜ N•R to 8th St; 6 to Astor Pl $

Pepolino ♯B13

Homey, and even the most basic of pastas won't fail to please.

281 W Broadway, Tribeca ☎ 966-9983 Ⓜ A•C to Chambers St $$-$$$

☆ PÓ ⬧A11

Chef 'Molto' Mario Batali is famous for his colourful TV cookery programme, popular cookbooks and a clutch of fine Italian restaurants. Pó is the original, and is still packed after a number of years. The small, unfussy space resembles a well-oiled machine, with every detail seen to in a professional, unpretentious manner. Garlicky white bean bruschetta comes gratis, and pastas are big in size and flavour. The six-course tasting menu is a real deal: and goes on and on, and on...

31 Cornelia Street, West Village ☎ 645-2189 Ⓜ 1•9 to Christopher St $$

☆ ROSEMARIE'S ⬧F11

Considering this excellent northern Italian in Tribeca doesn't put a foot wrong, it's remarkably underpopulated. The room is calm and grown up, the service is caring, and the small menu is good-to-spectacular. Go for wild mushrooms with polenta, pancetta and sage, or white bean crostini; a half order of pasta (orecchiette with Manila clams or rigatoni with lamb bolognese); then seared skate with brown butter over red cabbage, or a veal chop with porcini sauce – and your stomach will be happy. Buzz factor is low.

145 Duane Street, Tribeca ☎ 285-2610 Ⓜ 1•9 to Franklin St $$–$$$

Slice of Harlem ⬧A1

A boisterous scene, with a huge mural of black history and pop culture – just the ticket for cheesy pizza by the slice, garlic knots and sausage rolls.

2527 Eighth Avenue, Harlem ☎ 862-4089 Ⓜ B•C to 135th St $

Three of Cups ⬧C12

Quentin Tarantino once got into a tussle in this Italian, which is great for big salads, hearty pastas and wood-fired pizza. Brunch is under $10 and includes a couple of Bloody Marys.

83 First Avenue, East Village ☎ 388-0059 Ⓜ F to 2nd Ave $

☆ TRATTORIA DELL'ARTE ⬧B7

The price of the cracker-thin, fresh clam pizza makes you wonder if the little molluscs were flown in first class from the ocean, but you know what? It's worth it. So is the creative antipasti, and there is a special fish dish every day. An illustrious set regularly gathers at this attractive, bustling Italian establishment, with Tina Brown, Steve Martin and actor William Baldwin being spotted in a single lunch sitting. If no stars are around, feast your eyes on the strange art bedecking the walls.

900 Seventh Avenue, Midtown ☎ 245-9800 Ⓜ N•R to 57th St $$–$$$

restaurants & cafés

Two Boots   *F10*
A boisterous, child-friendly Italian-Cajun-Creole hangout with big red booths. Pizza is tops – especially the spicy tomato sauce and cornmeal crust.
37 Avenue A, East Village ☎ 505-2276 Ⓜ L to 1st Ave $-$$

Va Tutto!   *C12*
The atmosphere is welcoming, the accent is on Tuscan cuisine and there's a pretty garden for the summertime.
23 Cleveland Place, Noho ☎ 941-0286 Ⓜ 6 to Spring St $$

Vinny's of Carroll Gardens   *off map*
Have lunch here if you want to soak up the sound of some authentic 'Brooklynese'. Whether you choose the clam spaghetti or the tortellini en brodo, portions are huge.
295 Smith Street, Carroll Gardens ☎ 1-718-875-5600 Ⓜ F•G to Carroll St $–$$

japanese

Avenue A Sushi   *F10*
For a trip back into the 80s, step into the clubby, ink-black restaurant. Have faith: even though you can't see what you're eating, the Japanese fare is great, and the DJ spins a fun mix nightly.
103 Avenue A, East Village ☎ 982-8109 Ⓜ L to 1st Ave $–$$

☆ BOND ST   *A12*
This is the three-storey Japanese restaurant that out-Nobus Nobu. The lower ground floor is a loud bar where you pick your sake by personality, eg 'cool, subtle and refined' or 'warm, rich and complex'; above, there are two floors of packed, dimly-lit, minimalist dining rooms. Drop your entire budget on osetra caviar sushi, select spotted sardine, needle fish and basil-smoked salmon nigiri, or get fab, fun rolls like sesame-crusted shrimp with orange curry dressing. Absolutely not your everyday sushi joint.
6 Bond Street, Noho ☎ 777-2500 Ⓜ B•D•F•Q to Broadway-Lafayette St; 6 to Bleecker St $$–$$$

☆ JAPONICA ♫E10

There has been a long-time debate in NY sushi-eating circles over which place serves the best. Now it's official – well at least among the sushi-eating set. Whether you're a die-hard Yama-ite, a Tomoe-addict or a dedicated Iso fan, Japonica has the best. The beautifully-presented sashimi and sushi is swimmingly fresh (albeit pricey), their cooked delights are delicious, and there's always a colourful selection of specials. It's short on atmosphere and long on queues (so book ahead), but it's about a taste of Japan, not the trend factor.

100 University Place, West Village ☎ 243-7752 Ⓜ L•N•R•4•5•6 to 14th St-Union Sq $$–$$$

Next Door Nobu ♫F11

Like Nobu, this is also part-owned by De Niro, but distinguishes itself by offering a range of noodle dishes and a no-reservations policy.

105 Hudson Street, Tribeca ☎ 334-4445 Ⓜ 1•9 to Franklin St $$$

☆ NOBU ♫F11

Nobu's nouvelle-Japanese morsels are remarkable in flavour, freshness and sheer artistry. Dinner for two in this dramatic blond-wood setting easily costs $200 with items like abalone and sea urchins on the menu, but eating here for half that amount is possible if you stick to regular sushi items with salmon, squid, mackerel and white fish. (The more intriguing-sounding sakes and seafood specialties can really add up.) Film and music big-shots, and a galaxy of pretty faces fill the soaring, dramatic stage where the sushi bar stools look like oversized chopsticks, wall sconces resemble crossed samurai swords, and lights are embedded within towering birch tree sculptures.

105 Hudson Street, Tribeca ☎ 219-0500 Ⓜ 1•9 to Franklin St $$$

Soba-ya ♫A12

A clean, stylish environment, with exceptional udon and soba noodles dishes. Service is polished, prices are low and the saké list is noteworthy.

229 E 9th Street, East Village ☎ 533-6966 Ⓜ 6 to Astor Pl $

Taka ♫A11

The sushi is superb, and what makes this unpretentious townhouse truly unusual is the fact that a woman is the chef/owner (sushi chefs being overwhelmingly male).

61 Grove Street, West Village ☎ 242-3699 Ⓜ 1•9 Christopher St $$

☆ TAKAHACHI   *♯C12*

Unless you come before 7pm, you'll have to join the long line of East Village locals who know that the sushi here is worth the wait. Takahachi scores on its perfect, delicate shumai (steamed dumplings), its insistence on fresh crab instead of the stringy reconstituted stuff, and, in fact, the consistent super-freshness of everything. As an extra plus, it's also not too expensive and the portions are generous. The space is ugly standard-issue – pine tables and bright white light, but it's the food that people come back for.

85 Avenue A, East Village ☎ **505-6524** 📵 **F to 2nd Ave $$–$$$**

Yama   *♯E10*

Hidden in the basement of a picturesque townhouse, dishing up plentiful sushi at decent prices served in the ambience of a Japanese living room.

122 E 17th Street, Gramercy Park ☎ **475-0969**
📵 **L•N•R•4•5•6 to 14th St-Union Sq $$**

jewish (see also delicatessens)

Yonah Schimmel's Knishery   *♯C12*

Founded in 1910, is a rather decrepit hole-in-the-wall, still beloved for dumpling-like potato knishes and homemade bagels.

137 E Houston Street, LES ☎ **477-2858**
📵 **F to 2nd Ave $**

Russ & Daughters   *♯D11*

For more of a DIY snack, check out this eatery, known locally as the Herring Kings. Among the tasty treats on offer are lox, scallion cream cheese, superb chopped liver, and chewy bagels to go.

179 E Houston Street, LES ☎ **475-4880** 📵 **B•D•F•Q Broadway-Lafayette St $**

Korean

☆ CHO DANG GOL   *♯B9*

This may be the only Korean restaurant that makes its own tofu, which sounds a missable experience, until, that is, you try the Doo-Boo-Doo-Roo-Chi-Gi (kimchi fermented cabbage with tofu and pork) or the Mo-Doo-Boo Nak-Ji-Bok-Um (octopus with tofu, vegetables and noodles), after your Pa-Jun – a delicious, thin, chewy pancake – and the Panjan of assorted fiery vegetable and fish side dishes. No place in Koreatown is friendlier. The lovely people seem to like helping neophytes with the mysteries of the menu.

55 W 35th Street, Midtown ☎ **695-8222** 📵 **B•D•F•N•Q•R to 34th St-Herald Sq $–$$**

Clay
♪C12

A stylish Korean spot, with steel-wrapped pillars and dramatic lighting. The seafood pancakes are sublime, as are the vegetable dumplings.
202 Mott Street, Noho ☎ 625-1105 Ⓜ 6 to Spring St; J•M to Bowery $$

Do Hwa
♪C11

Delicious Korean 'dinner guest fare' features on the menu at Jenny Kwak's restaurant. Pricier than her hip East Village eatery, Dok Suni, it's still a crowd-pleaser: there's also a late-night film series that's been instituted – Quentin Tarantino's an investor!
55 Carmine Street, West Village ☎ 414-2815 Ⓜ 1•9 to Houston St $$–$$$

Dok Suni
♪F10

A dimly-lit Korean joint, usually packed with a noisy, young crowd. Marinated beef, ribs and chicken dishes are high on the spiceometer.
119 First Avenue, East Village ☎ 477-9506 Ⓜ L to 1st Avenue $–$$

latin american

Café con Leche
♪C5

A casual hang, cramped and colourful, with great coffee, Cuban-style rice and beans, crispy chicken and roast pork. Their early-bird special (4–7pm Mon–Thu) offers a full dinner for around $8.
424 Amsterdam Avenue, UWS ☎ 595-7000 Ⓜ 1•9 to 79th St $

Café Habana
♪D11

A spiffy paean to a Latin luncheonette – the grilled corn-on-the-cob coated in chilli powder and cheese is irresistible.
17 Prince Street, Noho ☎ 625-2001 Ⓜ N•R to Prince St $

☆ CALLE OCHO
♪C5

Past a warren of secret loungey nooks is a cavernous, dazzling dining room lit by huge burlap lampshades that resemble hoop skirts. One wall is dominated by a dramatic, faux-aged Cuban mural, and more Cuban imagery is evoked when wonderful rolls and muffins arrive in a lined cigar box. Alex Garcia's stimulating Pan-Latino cooking radiates fragrance and spice (octopus and calamari with palm hearts, chick peas and olives, or side dishes like *malanga* mash and green plantains), while fun rum drinks like *mojitos* and *caipirinha*s prime the palate.
446 Columbus Avenue, UWS ☎ 873-5025 Ⓜ 1•9 to 79th St $$–$$$

Casa
♯A11

An animated and appealing Brazilian spot, could also be used as a movie location. The empanadas and *feijoada* are homey, and the crowd arresting enough for celluloid.

72 Bedford Street, West Village ☎ 366-9410 Ⓜ 1•9 to Christopher St $$

☆ CHICAMA
♯E10

The exclusive emporium ABC Carpet & Home now houses a festive Nuevo Latino restaurant that is festooned with Peruvian rugs and constructed from a Brazilian country inn that was imported beam by beam. The sprawling, evocative space notwithstanding, the real draw here is ex-Patria chef Douglas Rodriguez, who stimulates palates with crispy fried oysters, citrusy ceviches, and spicy Peruvian hen stew with blue potatoes. The wine list is heavy on earthy South American choices, but it's the frothy Latino-inspired cocktails that really get the party going.

35 E 18th Street, Gramercy Park ☎ 505-2233 Ⓜ L•N•R•4•5•6 to 14th St-Union Sq $$–$$$

Coffee Shop
♯E10

A stylish canteen, with an amazing S-shaped bar, that pulses until 6am. What it lacks in service it makes up for in robust Brazilian dishes including a feijoada brunch.

29 Union Square W, Gramercy Park ☎ 243-7969 Ⓜ L•N•R•4•5•6 to 14th St-Union Sq $–$$

Isla
♯C11

The restaurant's retro decor smacks of pre-revolutionary Cuba and produces Nuevo Latino dishes that most modern day *compañeros* could only dream of.

39 Downing Street, West Village ☎ 352-2822 Ⓜ 1•9 to Houston St $$–$$$

Flor's Kitchen
♯F10

A homey BYOB hole-in-the wall serving cheap, interesting Venezuelan snacking food.

149 First Avenue, East Village ☎ 387-8949 Ⓜ L to 1st Ave $–$$

Ideya
♯F11

Features a culinary tour of the Caribbean, Central and South America, and a range of potent tropical drinks. Homemade plantain chips and fresh salsa adorn every table at this warm and casual Latin American bistro.

349 W Broadway, Soho ☎ 625-1441 Ⓜ B•D•Q to Grand St $$–$$$

☆ PAMPA *♭E3*

If you're looking for a festive place to meet friends, you can't beat Pampa, even though they don't take reservations. It's a cool, lively spot and cheap enough for everyone. Argentine steaks, fries coated in garlic and parsley, juicy roasted chicken, flaky empanadas, and South American wines that start at $15 – all justify the trip Uptown. An added bonus is that the waiters are so cute and sweet you'll want to take them home.
768 Amsterdam Avenue, UWS ☎ 865-2929 Ⓜ 1•2•3•9 to 96th St $–$$

☆ PATRIA *♭C10*

Patria is the patriarch of the Nuevo Latino trend, and electrifying for lunch or dinner. Even though many other restaurants have copied its use of South American and Latin American ingredients, nobody can match chef Douglas Rodriguez's exceptional brilliance. The spacious, creatively-designed dining room sports mosaic touches reminiscent of Gaudi. The three-course set menu features dishes like incredible crispy oysters, 'fire and ice' tuna ceviche, and plantain-coated mahi mahi.
250 Park Avenue South, Gramercy Park ☎ 777-6211 Ⓜ 6 to 23rd St $$$

Sur *♭off map*

Try this rowdy, friendly eatery for organic steaks and Argentinian specialties.
232 Smith Street, Carroll Gardens ☎ 1-718-875-1716 Ⓜ F•G to Carroll St $–$$

malaysian

Nyonya *♭E12*

Malaysian cooking offering a wonderful hodgepodge of fried noodles, exotic casseroles and aromatic seafood preparations – it's cheap too!
194 Grand Street, Noho ☎ 334-3669 Ⓜ B•D•Q to Grand St $

Penang *♭D11*

A Malaysian outpost that combines an industrial design with hut-like booths and a waterfall. The exotic dishes are flavourful.
109 Spring Street, Soho ☎ 274-8883 Ⓜ N•R to Prince St $$

mediterranean

☆ ACQUARIO *♭A12*

Apparently, everybody in this small, cozy brick-lined restaurant, sister to the popular Il Buco, is from Europe, smokes and abuses cellphones, but don't let that discourage you. A Sicilian/Portuguese/Spanish menu offers no division between appetizers and mains, encouraging mix-and-match and sharing (Portuguese fish stew is a highlight).
5 Bleecker Street, Noho ☎ 260-4666 Ⓜ F to 2nd Ave; 6 to Bleecker St $-$$

Flor de Sol
♪F11

Reminiscent of a Spanish parador, this restaurant is an appealing option: its bar serves tapas too.

361 Greenwich Street, Tribeca ☎ 334-6411 Ⓜ 1•9 to Franklin St $$

☆ IL BUCO
♪A12

On any night of the week, well-coiffed young debs and their Newport-type dates mob this dark, romantic restaurant filled with vintage toys and bookshelves of wine bottles. Long-haired, carefully dishevelled downtown artists also gather around the big wooden tables. A rustic Spanish/Italian theme is carried through from the country decor to such luscious tapas plates as polenta with goose ragu and duck prosciutto. Pasta specials are heavenly, like penne with artichoke, pancetta and cream. The wine list is wide-ranging and discriminating.

47 Bond Street, Noho ☎ 533-1932 Ⓜ 6 to Bleecker St $–$$$

☆ SPARTINA
♪F11

Tribeca residents probably wish they could keep Spartina to themselves, but that's too bad. The warmth of the stylish room enfolds you, and the Mediterranean dishes further seduce. The place specializes in fish and seafood, such as roasted trout stuffed with brandade and wrapped in smoked bacon, but chef-co-owner Stephen Kalt also excels at slow-cooked short ribs and mash. Then there are the divine, crispy grilled pizzas, and over 80 types of wine. What more could you need?

355 Greenwich Street, Tribeca ☎ 274-9310 Ⓜ 1•9 to Franklin St $$–$$$

mexican

Casa Mexicana
♪D12

The kitchen puts a more sophisticated spin on Mexican food by marrying non-traditional combinations of ingredients with French culinary techniques.

133 Ludlow Street, LES ☎ 473-4100 Ⓜ F•J•M•C toDelancey St-Essex St; F to East Broadway $$

El Rey del Sol
♪F11

A dark, belowstairs hideaway, entices with an excess of tacky Mexican souvenirs and a back garden dappled with multi-coloured lights. Sangria and margaritas by the pitcher are the prelude to respectable enchiladas, fajitas and the like.

232 W 14th Street, Chelsea ☎ 229-0733 Ⓜ L to 8th Ave; A•C•E to 14th St $–$$

El Sombrero ♭C12

Frequented mostly by actors and musicians after performances. The (Mexican) food is cheap and pretty basic: the potent margaritas are the real appeal.

108 Stanton Street, LES ☎ 254-4188 Ⓜ F to 2nd Ave $

Gabriela's ♭E3

Guadalajara-style home cooking, highly popular for low-priced, massively portioned enchiladas, tamales and roast chicken. The atmosphere is old luncheonette crossed with a Mexican fiesta.

685 Amsterdam Ave, UWS ☎ 961-0574 Ⓜ 1•2•3•9 to 96th St $–$$

Los Dos Rancheros Mexicanos ♭F7

Some of the most authentic Mexican *moles*, *tamales* and *chiles rellenos* in New York. It's a funky cafeteria with few gringos so you know it must be the real thing.

507 Ninth Avenue, Midtown ☎ 868-7780 Ⓜ A•C•E to 42nd St-Port Authority Bus Terminal $

Mexican Radio ♭C12

Tasty and inventive south-of-the-border dishes as well as potent margaritas. Its new premises are roomier and lit by a myriad of candles and littered with Day of the Dead *tchotchkes*.

19 Cleveland Place, Noho ☎ 343-0140 Ⓜ 6 to Spring St $$

Rocking Horse Café Mexicano ♭D9

Perpetually jammed with a varied crowd, who sup ambrosial libations and eat very fresh Mexican *comidas* in colourful, contemporary surroundings.

182 Eighth Avenue, Chelsea ☎ 463-9511 Ⓜ C•E to 23rd St $$

Taqueria de Mexico ♭F9

Recommended for roasted tomato and tortilla soup with chipotle chilli, delicious fiery sandwiches, and uncomplicated soft tacos and burritos. It's convenient for take-out but the cheerful dining room is perfectly agreeable.

93 Greenwich Avenue, West Village ☎ 255-5212 Ⓜ 1•2•3•9 to 14th St $–$$

Vera Cruz ♭off map

Mexican food, Margaritas and, on Monday nights, mambo dancing.

195 Bedford Avenue, Williamsburg ☎ 1-718-599-7914 Ⓜ L to Bedford Ave $–$$

restaurants & cafés

Casa La Femme
♭D11

A candlelit Middle Eastern casbah, with tented booths and an incredible belly dancer. The food is good but not the point – especially for all the skinny models who slink in.

150 Wooster Street, Soho ☎ 505-0005 Ⓜ B•D•F•Q to Broadway-Lafayette St $$-$$$

Layla
♭F11

An opulent Middle Eastern palace (with bellydancers), featuring mezze, tajines, kebabs and couscous fit for a sultan.

211 W Broadway, Tribeca ☎ 431-0700 Ⓜ 1•9 to Franklin St $$$

Moustache
♭A11

A tiny treasure, serving tasty Middle Eastern pitzas.

90 Bedford Street, West Village ☎ 229-2220 Ⓜ 1•9 to Christopher St $

Oznot's Dish
♭off map

Where quirky decor meets Middle Eastern cuisine (and there's a garden).

79 Berry Street, Williamsburg ☎ 1-718-599-6596 Ⓜ L to Bedford Ave $$

oriental (see also cambodian, chinese, korean, japanese, thai & vietnamese)

The Elephant
♭C12

A neighbourhood magnet, with zesty Asian fusion creations, quirky decor and a constant hubbub at the door from those clamouring to get in.

58 E 1st Street, East Village ☎ 505-7739 Ⓜ F to 2nd Ave $$

Honmura An
♭D11

Has been esteemed for years as one of the city's top Asian restaurants. It's hard to imagine more artful noodle concoctions, and equally hard to imagine paying higher prices.

170 Mercer Street, Soho ☎ 334-5253 Ⓜ B•D•F•Q to Broadway-Lafayette St $$$

Kelley & Ping
♭D11

An Asian grocery and noodle shop, and a trendy, modestly priced spot best for the buzz at lunchtimes. The bustling open kitchen, healthy stir-fries and vast tea selection are the appeal.

127 Greene Street, Soho ☎ 228-1212 Ⓜ N•R to Prince St $–$$

Lucky Cheng's
♪C12

A colourful pan-Asian mecca for a mix of gay boys and suits. The average food is theatrically served by cross-dressing waiters, and raunchy drag shows provide entertainment.

24 First Avenue, East Village ☎ 473-0516 Ⓜ F to 2nd Ave $$

Rain
♪B5

A fun place for spicy and aromatic Thai-Vietnamese dishes. Golden hues, exposed brick and tropical plants evoke a colonial feel.

100 W 82nd Street, UWS ☎ 501-0776 Ⓜ B•C to 86th St $$

Republic
♪E10

The consummate Pan-Asian cafeteria: minimalist, capacious and cool. Brothy noodle soups and curried duck noodles are tasty and modestly priced.

37 Union Square W, Gramercy Park ☎ 627-7172 Ⓜ L•N•R•4•5•6 to 14th St-Union Sq $

portuguese

☆ O PADEIRO
♪D9

If you're in need of some hardcore carbohydrate action, then this adorable Portuguese bakery/tapas bar will be right up your alley. Their baked goods, and eclectic wine selections are outrageously good and their small-sized entrées (like salt cod layered with potato, chopped eggs and olives) demand indulgence. Every so often, a Portuguese singer adds a little more authentic flavour to the tile-embellished ambience.

641 Sixth Avenue, Chelsea ☎ 414-9661 Ⓜ 1•9 to 23rd St $$

scandinavian

☆ AQUAVIT
♪C8

Named after an icy eau de vie, Aquavit aptly offers a broad selection of fluid flavours infused with lemon, dill or anise. They go best with herring (four types of saltwater fillets are available), and other unusual Swedish specialties, like crispy smoked salmon with fingerling dumplings and dill-sevruga broth. Chef Marcus Samuelsson experiments with global influences, both in the intimate (and less expensive) upstairs café and in the formal downstairs atrium, which dramatically shoots up six storeys towards the skylights. A sculpted waterfall whispers in the background.

13 W 54th Street, Midtown ☎ 307-7311 Ⓜ E•F to 5th Ave $$$

F&B
⌀D9

Serving Belgian-style fries (fried twice to ensure maximum soft-on-the-inside crispness), this is the answer to every fast-food connoisseur's dream; wash down your Danish frankfurters and Swedish meatballs with mini bottles of Pommery champagne.

269 W 23rd Street, Chelsea ☎ 486-4441 ▣ 1•9 to 23rd St $

seafood

Aquagrill
⌀D11

Meeting friends for dinner, or looking for new ones? Singles gather here in the brightly decorated front lounge, or at the bar while waiting for a table at this perpetually jammed seafood restaurant.

210 Spring Street, Soho ☎ 274-0505 ▣ C•E to Spring St $$-$$$

Blue Water Grill
⌀E10

A sophisticated seafood restaurant with a great raw bar, fresh lobster, and grilled wild striped bass, plus a fab outdoor terrace.

31 Union Square W, Gramercy Park ☎ 675-9500 ▣ L•N•R4•5•6 to 14th St-Union Sq $$-$$$

Cello
⌀D6

Deluxe French seafood is the order of the day at this restaurant, which is one of the toughest (and most expensive) tickets in the UES.

53 E 77th Street, UES ☎ 517-1200 ▣ 6 to 77th Street $$$

☆ LE BERNARDIN
⌀D7

Chef Éric Ripert is so skilled he might spoil you for seafood prepared by anyone else. Based in corporate, moneyed Midtown, Le Bernardin has started to attract a cool, younger clientele flush with newfound-but-not-obnoxious wealth. The quiet, wood-lined dining room is Frank Lloyd Wright-inspired, embellished with gorgeous floral arrangements. It's flying first class all the way. Sit in the kitchen (six available seats) to observe the French master more closely, but only the very brave would try to duplicate dishes like roasted lobster tail with finely diced foie gras or skate in goosefat with caramelized confit of artichokes and fennel.

155 W 51st Street, Midtown ☎ 489-1515 ▣ N•R to 49th St; 1•9 to 50th St $$$

☆ OYSTER BAR ⚡E8

Somehow, visiting the Oyster Bar is a little like going to Coney Island: corny yet peculiarly charming. Essentially, it's expensive, ultra-fresh fish and seafood in an old-fashioned setting with gruff yet winsome servers who've been at it for decades. The vaulted space is vast and sitting at the counter for chowder, fresh oysters (tons of different types) and a glass of beer is an after-work treat. House specials include bouillabaisse, Maryland crab cakes and Arctic char. The big, dark bar at the back feels like a wood-lined steamship cabin.

Lower Level, Grand Central Station, Midtown ☎ 490-6650
Ⓜ 4•5•6•7 to Grand Central-42nd St $–$$$

Pearl Oyster Bar ⚡A11

This New England-style eatery is twice as nice in the daytime when there's more space. Crisp Caesar salad and clam chowder with smoked bacon are an ideal combination.

18 Cornelia Street, West Village ☎ 691-8211 Ⓜ A•B•C•D•E•F•Q to W 4th St-Washington Sq $–$$

☆ PISCES ⚡A12

What's so great about Pisces is that you can get really fresh seafood prepared in eclectic ways and still walk out with money in your pocket. At weekends it's a challenge to snag a table even though they open the second deck upstairs for the overflow. In summer, the wraparound windows are flung open, making it feel like you're out at sea on Avenue A. Brunch is also a big attraction, with several egg dishes for under $8, which includes a Mimosa (champagne and OJ) and coffee.

95 Avenue A, East Village ☎ 260-6660 Ⓜ F to 2nd Ave; 6 to Astor Pl $–$$

soups

Soup Kiosk ⚡D11

Every day the Soup Kiosk ladles out six steamy seasonal soups to slurp on the move.

Corner of Prince & Mercer Sts, Soho ☎ no phone Ⓜ N•R to Prince St $

Soup Kitchen International ⚡B7

Service might be strict and prices rather high, but the soups here (from which the famous 'Soup Nazi' Seinfeld episode was derived) are celestial (12–6pm Mon–Fri).

259a W 55th Street, Midtown ☎ 757-7730 Ⓜ B•D•E to 7th Ave $–$$

spanish

El Cid ♭F11
A frumpy yet cherished tapas joint attracting vivacious groups.
322 W 15th Street, Chelsea ☎ 929-9332
Ⓜ L to 8thAve; A•C•E to 14th St $–$$

Meigas ♭F11
Boasts a handsome, sophisticated, lofty space where chef Luis Angel Bollo seems destined for the same celebrity status enjoyed by Daniel Boulud and David Bouley for their creative take on traditional cuisine – in Bollo's case, that of Spain. Expect refined grilled fish and meat dishes plus options like roast suckling pig with honey and sherry vinegar sauce.
350 Hudson Street, Soho ☎ 627-5800 Ⓜ 1•9 to Canal St $$–$$$

sri lankan

Lakruwana ♭F7
An opulent Sri Lankan restaurant embellished with brass, crushed velvet curtains and wooden sculptures. Dishes are spicy, there's a good vegetarian selection, and it's BYOB.
358 W 44th Street, Midtown ☎ 957-4480 Ⓜ A•C•E to 42nd St-Port Authority Bus Terminal $$

steaks & grills

Keens Steakhouse ♭B9
Around since 1885, the bygone tavern decor is glorious and the dry-aged steaks and mutton chops legendary. Prices are steep but the brief bar menu is more affordable (closed Sun).
72 W 36th Street, Midtown ☎ 947-3636
Ⓜ B•D•F•N•Q•R to 34th St-Herald Sq $$$

Michael Jordan's The Steakhouse ♭E8
Eat enough of his steak and lamb chops and you too might grow tall and strong – just like Mike.
Grand Central, 23 Vanderbilt Ave, Midtown ☎ 655-2300
Ⓜ 4•5•6•7 to Grand Central-42nd St $$–$$$

Pearson's Texas Barbecue
off map
Serves up the best bbq in town. Get those fingers dirty and chow down.
71–04 35th Avenue, Long Island City ☎ 1-718-779-7715 Ⓜ N to Broadway **$$**

Peter Luger Steakhouse
off map
Don't ask for a menu: this century-old institution is strictly for carnivores who love the legendary dry-aged steaks. Go so hungry you could eat a cow – the portions are large.
178 Broadway, Brooklyn Heights ☎ 1-718-387-7400
Ⓜ Z•M•J to Marcy Ave **$$–$$$**

Virgil's Real BBQ
F7
Goodwill towards all – even children – reigns. It's big, fun and rambunctious.
152 W 44th Street, Midtown ☎ 921-9494 Ⓜ N•R•1•2•3•7•9 to Times Sq-42nd St **$$**

teas & patisseries

Hungarian Pastry Shop
off map
Across the street from the Cathedral of St John the Divine is this old, softly-lit café with pastries and great coffee. You can sit here long enough to write a book without anyone bothering you.
1030 Amsterdam Avenue, Harlem ☎ 866-4230 Ⓜ 1•9 to Cathedral Pkwy **$**

☆ PAYARD PATISSERIE & BISTRO
Children (and the child in you) will be filled with wonder at the tiers of tea cakes, tarts, éclairs, fancy pastries and handmade chocolates in the Parisian-style patisserie. A few small tables provide room for immediate gratification. Ladies who 'tea' will be entranced by the $14.50 afternoon delights of brioche, scones and madeleines. Those desirous of classic, but equally calorific, French fare can tuck into bouillabaisse and cassoulet in the bi-level bistro.
1032 Lexington Avenue, UES ☎ 717-5252 Ⓜ 6 to 77th St **$$–$$$**

Sweet Melissa
off map
Exquisite soufflé cakes, madeleines, and fruit tarts.
276 Court Street, Carroll Gardens ☎ 1-718-855-3410 Ⓜ F•G to Carroll St **$**

Veniero's
A12
Fabled for towering cakes, rich cheesecake and Italian cookies, this is a sweet place to retire to at the end of a date.
342 E 11th Street, East Village ☎ 674-7070 Ⓜ 6 to Astor Pl **$**

thai

Holy Basil
♯F10

Dark Thai restaurant where it's easy to hold a conversation. Their squid rings are the best, the seafood in general is superb, and the varied wine list is remarkable for a Thai place.
149 Second Avenue, East Village ☎ 460-5557 Ⓜ L to 3rd Ave $–$$

Plan-eat Thailand
♯off map

Excellent Thai food.
141 Ⓜ 7th Street, Williamsburg ☎ 1-718-599-5758 Ⓜ L to Bedford Ave $

Thailand Restaurant
♯E12

A favoured lunch spot – though the somewhat tacky, wood-panelled room looks better at night. The aroma from their classic dishes is incredible.
106 Bayard Street, LES ☎ 349-3132 Ⓜ J•M•Z•6 to Canal St $

turkish

Bereket
♯C12

A cheap bet, a bright beacon dispensing fresh Turkish fast food 24 hours a day.
187 E Houston Street, LES ☎ 475-7700 Ⓜ F to 2nd Ave $

vegetarian

☆ ANGELICA KITCHEN
♯E10

During the day Angelica Kitchen is a place to unwind over well-prepared dragon bowls of rice, beans, tofu and sea vegetables. Instead of salt and pepper on the tables, it's soy sauce and a shaker of sesame seeds. They also have good marinated tofu sandwiches and rich walnut-lentil paté. It's a homey, bright place with bronze Aztec-designed walls, an open kitchen and plain wood tabletops. At night it's more hectic so you won't absorb the same Zen-ness. Note: no alcohol served.
300 E 12th Street, East Village ☎ 228-2909 Ⓜ L•N•R•4•5•6 to 14th St-Union Sq $–$$

Hangawi
♯A10

An enchanting, serene temple devoted exclusively to vegetarianism. Wear good socks as shoes are left at the door.
12 E 32nd Street, Midtown ☎ 213-0077 Ⓜ 6 to 33rd St $$–$$$

Josie's
C5

An attractive, 'earth-friendly' hangout, is the place to be after dusk. Do your body a favour and feast on the myriad fresh juices, free-range meats and innovative vegan choices.

300 Amsterdam Ave, UWS ☎ 769-1212 Ⓜ 1•9 to 79th St $$

Vegetarian Paradise 3,
E12

A friendly, pastel-hued cafeteria with lots of tasty numbers.

33 Mott Street, LES ☎ 406-6988 Ⓜ J•M•Z•6 to Canal St $

☆ ZEN PALATE
E10

Luckily there is a Zen Palate Downtown, Midtown and Uptown so you never have to go too far to enjoy its meditative, unusual Asian compositions in a poetic atmosphere. The Union Square location is perhaps the most popular, with a busy downstairs area (and cheaper prices), and a tranquil, airy upstairs room (with fancier veggie offerings) affording views of the park. Patrons are chic but not horribly so. Real thought and creativity goes into dishes you feel you could eat into infinity. Note: no alcohol served.

34 Union Square E, Gramercy Park ☎ 614-9291 Ⓜ L•N•R•4•5•6 to 14th St-Union Sq $–$$

vietnamese

Indochine
A12

This restaurant attracts a faithful cadre of raffish musicians and their model girlfriends, who pick at the delicate Vietnamese dishes.

430 Lafayette Street, Noho ☎ 505-5111 Ⓜ N•R to 8th St; 6 to Astor Pl $$

Mekong
C12

Its sultry dining room is always filled with the delicious aroma of flavourful Vietnamese soups, pork and seafood dishes; its bar is part of the cool neighbourhood scene.

44 Prince Street, Noho ☎ 343-8169 Ⓜ 6 to Spring St $–$$

Miss Saigon
D6

A homey neighbourhood place, serving tasty, delicately prepared Vietnamese dishes at pocket-friendly prices. The whimsical architecture evokes a village hut, its walls adorned with Asian artefacts.

1425 Third Avenue, UES ☎ 988-8828 Ⓜ 6 to 77th St $–$$

restaurants & cafés

Nha Trang, *₱E12*
A rather charmless abode that pulls in crowds for its gorgeous, glossy platters of sauteed beef, seafood, and delicate vegetables.
87 Baxter Street, LES ☎ 233-5948 Ⓜ J•M•Z•6 to Canal St $

Uncle Pho *₱off map*
A delectable French-Vietnamese eaterie where the imaginative decor is matched by the menu. Try the coconut bouillabaise.
263 Smith Street, Carroll Gardens ☎ 1-718-855-8737
Ⓜ F•G to Carroll St $$–$$$

bars

New York's bars are as varied as the city's denizens. Get louche in plush lounges, hang with the barflies at a local dive, or sip superb cocktails alongside the chic and sleek set. Everything's open 'til late, so you can take your time.

dj bars

☆ ALPHABET LOUNGE
♭A12

The best the Village has to offer: plush banquettes, monster-sized martinis, a rotating roster of DJs spinning house and drum 'n' bass, and an address so far east that no drunken frat boys can find it. Best of all: no bouncers or velvet ropes – just lotsa groove.

104 Avenue C, East Village ☎ 780-0202 Ⓜ L to 1st Ave; 6 to Astor Pl

☆ BABY JUPITER
♭C12

A bar, club, performance space, and restaurant all squeezed into one, Baby Jupiter is always packed. Their popular club nights change frequently, so call ahead to confirm scheduling. Perfect for cheap dates and indecisive groups.

170 Orchard Street, LES ☎ 982-2229 Ⓜ F to 2nd Ave

☆ BARAZA
♭F10

Can't afford that tropical vacation? Take a trip to this Alphabet City bar where DJs spin salsa and samba, bartenders serve *mojitos* and *caipirinhas* and the average duration of relationships formed on the premises is ten days.

133 Avenue C, East Village ☎ 539-0811 Ⓜ L to 1st Ave

☆ BOTANICA
♭D11

Sick of the megaclubs? Come to Botanica for jungle, dub and drum 'n' bass spun by top DJs in a cozy basement lounge. Cheap drinks and a monthly surf music party too.

47 E Houston Street, Noho ☎ 343-7251 Ⓜ B•D•F•Q to Broadway-Lafayette St

Butta Cup Lounge
♭off map

Features hip-hop, a comfy lounge upstairs and African statuettes dotted around.

271 Adelphi Street, Fort Greene ☎ 1-718-522-1669 Ⓜ G to Fulton St

Double Happiness 〽C12
Excellent DJs are a fixture at this former Mafia-controlled gay social club transformed into a sleek subterranean lounge.
173 Mott Street, Noho ☎ 941-1282 Ⓜ J•M to Bowery

Drinkland 〽A12
A favourite destination for fans of electronica and breakbeats.
339 E 10th Street, East Village ☎ 228-2435 Ⓜ 6 to Astor Pl

Good World Bar & Grill 〽D12
This highly popular bar/restaurant is basic but inviting, with laid-back tunes and a garden.
3 Orchard Street, LES ☎ 925-9975 Ⓜ F•J•M•Z to Delancy St-Essex St

Guernica 〽F10
An eclectic enthusiastic bunch party down in this dark basement bar (complete with blue waterfall). It's a happening scene and there's another bar upstairs – plus a restaurant too.
25 Avenue B, East Village ☎ 674-0984 Ⓜ L to 1st Ave

☆ HALO 〽A11
Wanna hang out with Puffy, Leo, and the rest of the fabulous ones at this white-hot, basement-level lounge? Get in line... behind the velvet rope and flash your smile (and your Prada) at the doorman. Once you're in, order some $100 champagne and take time to revel in your own fabulousness.
49 Grove Street, West Village ☎ 243-8885 Ⓜ 1•9 to Christopher St

Ice Bar 〽F11
Weekends tend to get packed at the Ice Bar, one of the hottest tickets in town, with its all white interior, sexy crowd, and wizard DJs.
528 Canal Street, Tribeca ☎ 226-2602 Ⓜ 1•9 to Canal St

One 51 〽D8
This art deco-inspired bar is chic and drinks are appropriately pricey. There's a dancefloor at the back, but the upstairs lounge provides a haven for those who like to talk rather than get their groove on.
151 E 51st Street, Midtown ☎ 753-1144 Ⓜ 6 to 51st St

☆ ORCHARD BAR 〽C12
DJs spin all forms of electronica nightly in an atmosphere reminiscent of a terrarium. From the foliage-filled glass tanks to the apples suspended in jars, an unnatural green glow pervades everything in the room – including visitors, who often take excessive advantage of the bar's cheapish drinks.
200 Orchard Street, LES ☎ 673-5350 Ⓜ F to 2nd Ave

☆ **SWEET & VICIOUS** *♭C12*

The best time to enjoy this sleek, sexy lounge is on a Sunday night, when the weekend crowds have dissipated, DJs spin break beats and you can linger over your raki. Come summer, the garden is an urban oasis.

5 Spring Street, Noho ☎ 334-7915 Ⓜ 6 to Spring St

cocktail & champagne bars

Black & White *♭F10*

The cocktails are pretty fine, though this cozy bar/restaurant can get real noisy when the dinner crowd stop by.

86 E 10th Street, East Village ☎ 253-0246 Ⓜ L to 1st Ave

Bongo *♭D9*

Bongo's style is bobby sock's retro, a paean to the 50s/60s and popular with Chelsea's arty types, as well as cocktail addicts. A seafood menu is also available

299 10th Avenue, Chelsea ☎ 947-3654 Ⓜ C•E to 23rd St

☆ **BUBBLE LOUNGE** *♭F11*

The ideal place for popping your cork in a crowd. Exceptional champagnes, tempting appetizers and enough platinum cards to buy a small Central American nation can all be found at the Bubble Lounge. Wear this season's Gucci to fit in.

228 W Broadway, Tribeca ☎ 431-3433 Ⓜ 1•9 to Franklin St

Clementine *♭B11*

A swank vibe can be found here – resplendent cocktails (and inventive American fusion dishes) are available in the art deco lounge until 3am.

1 Fifth Avenue, West Village ☎ 253-0003 Ⓜ N•R to 8th St NYU

Dylan Prime *♭F11*

A recent arrival, where a sophisticated set come to savour excellently mixed cocktails. (Meaty dining options are also available.)

62 Laight Street, Tribeca ☎ 334-2274 Ⓜ 1•9 to Canal St

The Galaxy *♭E10*

A bar and a fusion restaurant. The house cocktails – much like its planetarium-chic decor – are both imaginative and palatable, and it makes an ideal stop en route to or from a concert at Irving Plaza.

15 Irving Place, Gramercy Park ☎ 777-3631
Ⓜ L•M•R•4•5•6 to 14th St-Union Sq

Junno's *♯C11*
An intimate Korean-French bar that serves excellent sushi alongside creative house cocktails.
64 Downing Street, West Village ☎ 627-7995 Ⓜ 1•9 to Houston St

Lot 61 *♯D9*
Located in a giant converted industrial space, it serves an array of cocktails and international tapas. Visit after gallery openings when local artists stop by to toast their new opuses.
550 W 21st Street, Chelsea ☎ 243-6555 Ⓜ C•E to 23rd St

Metrazur *♯E8*
Besides a fantastic view onto the commuters below, Metrazur offers cocktails and very classy bar snacks such as lobster spring rolls.
Grand Central Station, 42nd Street, Midtown ☎ 687-4600 Ⓜ 4•5•6•7 to Grand Central-42nd St

Potion Lounge *♯C5*
Feels more Downtown than Uptown, and is known for its coloured layered 'potion' cocktails.
370 Columbus Avenue, UWS ☎ 721-4386 Ⓜ 1•9 to 79th St

Void *♯F11*
A semi-secluded cyber bar that features tables-cum-web browsers, cult-film screenings and cocktails.
16 Mercer Street, Soho ☎ 941-6492 Ⓜ N•R to Canal St

neighbourhood bars

Bellevue Bar *♯F7*
A good place to fortify yourself with a beer.
538 Ninth Avenue, Midtown ☎ 695-5507 Ⓜ A•C•E to 42nd St-Port Authority Bus Terminal

Brooklyn Ale House *♯off map*
A parade of serious beer including some made at the local Brooklyn Brewery.
103 Berry Street, Williamsburg ☎ 1-718-302-9811 Ⓜ L to Bedford Ave

Brooklyn Moon Café *♯off map*
A lively scene resides at this intimate café, where the chatty crowd gets big at the Friday open-mic sessions.
745 Fulton Street, Fort Greene ☎ 1-718-243-0424 Ⓜ G to Fulton St

☆ CHUMLEY'S
♫A11

A former speakeasy with two secret entrances, Chumley's was once a literary hang-out for the likes of John Reed, Eugene O'Neill, John Dos Passos, TS Eliot, and many others. Today, in this last remaining vestige of New York's prohibition era, there's a friendly neighbourhood crowd; a choice of over 25 beers on tap; and a varied steak and pasta menu.

86 Bedford Street, West Village ☎ **675-4449** Ⓜ **1•9 to Christopher St**

Enid's
♫off map

A drinking outpost worth the trek. This bar is huge, with well-priced brews, comfy furniture, good Southern food, a pinball machine and a knowing crowd.

560 Manhattan Avenue, Williamsburg ☎ **1-718-349-3859** Ⓜ **L to Bedford Ave**

Fall Café
♫off map

A place to find Brooklyn's true bohemians – a haven of big sofas, little tables, cool music, art on the walls, and artistic types dawdling over chilli, sandwiches and coffee.

307 Smith Street, Carroll Gardens ☎ **1-718-403-0230** Ⓜ **F•G to Carroll St**

Liquor Store
♫F11

A friendly local, featuring wall-to-wall windows – perfect for people-watching or just settling in with a pint and the paper.

235 White Street, Tribeca ☎ **226-7121** Ⓜ **1•9 to Franklin St**

M&R
♫C12

A neighbourhood staple, and mellow alternative to nearby Rialto. This joint is ground-zero for Nolita hipsters. Superb margaritas served in two-and-a-half glass-sized shakers are a big draw.

239 Elizabeth Street, Noho ☎ **632-6376** Ⓜ **F to 2nd Ave; 6 to Spring St**

Mars
♫C12

One of the finest East Village bars. Cheap drinks and borderline personalities.

25 E 1st Street, East Village ☎ **473-9842** Ⓜ **F to 2nd Ave**

Marylou's
♫A11

A few notable names also hang out in this West Village institution. This joint is always packed with regulars, and everyone seems to know everyone else.

21 W 9th Street, West Village ☎ **533-0012** Ⓜ **A•B•C•D•E•F•Q to W 4th St-Washington Sq**

Night Café ♯C3
Favourite of the edgier UWS set. Expect a competitive pool table, and a number of Nietzsche fans.
938 Amsterdam Avenue, UWS ☎ 864-8889 Ⓜ 1•9 to 103rd St

O'Reilley's Pub ♯A10
Young Irish expats – and anyone fond of whisky and beer – sing along with the jukebox, seduce local lasses and generally have a raucous good time.
56 W 31st Street, Midtown ☎ 684-4244 Ⓜ 6 to 33rd St

Pete's Tavern ♯E10
Boasting original tin ceilings, an ancient oak bar and, in some cases, what look like original bartenders, this friendly neighbourhood institution is still going strong after a century of business. Expect old-fashioned cocktails and classic pub grub.
129 E 18th Street, Gramercy Park ☎ 473-7676 Ⓜ L•M•R•4•5•6 to 14th St-Union Sq

PJ Hanley's ♯off map
This atmospheric saloon is a dark, comfy 100-year-old place with an ornate bar, frequented by plumbers and bond-traders alike.
449 Court Street, Carroll Gardens ☎ 1-718-834-8223 Ⓜ F•G to Carroll St

☆ POUR HOUSE ♯off map
Unlike many of its sleek Williamsburg neighbours, Pour House is not a place to 'see and be scene'. It is, however, a laid-back, lively local bar where neighbours young and old toss back brews, play pinball, and wonder why the bar down the street charges $6 for a beer.
790 Metropolitan Avenue, Williamsburg ☎ 1-718-599-0697 Ⓜ L to Graham Ave

☆ RAOUL'S ♯D11
There may be no better end to the week than a glass of wine and a steak at Raoul's. Reservations are a must in the dining room, but you may prefer to eat at the bar where after-work drinkers gather to soak up the pub-like atmosphere – although this gets crowded too.
180 Prince Street, Soho ☎ 966-3518 Ⓜ N•R to Prince St

Sophie's ♯C12
Offers the requisite cheap drinks, video games and a good chance of scoring a one-night stand. Also has a competitive pool table.
507 E 5th Street, East Village ☎ no phone Ⓜ F to 2nd Ave

Spring Lounge (aka The Shark Bar) ♭C12
Considerably more gentrified, but a few older locals still call it home.
48 Spring Street, Noho ☎ 965-1774 Ⓜ 6 to Spring St

Teddy's ♭off map
A perennial favourite with its majestic wooden bar and big windows that are opened in good weather.
96 Berry Street, Williamsburg ☎ 1-718-384-9787 Ⓜ L to Bedford Ave

Xth Ave Lounge ♭F7
Mix with budding thespians, writers and other rent-challenged types.
642 Tenth Avenue, Midtown ☎ 245-9088 Ⓜ A•C•E to 42nd St-Port Authority Bus Terminal

2A ♭C12
Indie-rock stars and rockabilly kids love this bi-level bar with views onto Avenue A, and a mish-mash of comfy sofas upstairs.
25 Avenue A, East Village ☎ no phone Ⓜ F to 2nd Ave

Village Idiot ♭F9
A bar to call home. With a jukebox that plays country & western music, patrons who spontaneously two-step, and some of the cheapest beer in town, it feels more like Nashville than 14th Street.
355 W 14th Street, Chelsea ☎ 989-7334 Ⓜ A•C•E to 14th St

Zapatas Manoletas ♭off map
A fantastic bar filled with bull-fighting posters and glittery tropical murals. Patrons are partial to salsa and the crowd tends to be older.
1218 St Nicholas Avenue, Harlem ☎ 923-9769 Ⓜ 1•9 to 137th St-City College

bars with live music

Café Carlyle ♭C6
Cabaret queens will not want to miss this glamorous joint where singer-pianist and enduring favourite Bobby Short is usually in residence. Eartha Kitt, Barry Manilow, and other legends perform here regularly.
Carlyle Hotel, 981 Madison Avenue, UES ☎ 744-1600 Ⓜ 6 to 77th St

Café Largo ♭off map
A newer bar and restaurant caters to an early-evening crowd, with live jazz performances starting at 8pm, and lazy jazz brunches served on Sundays.
3387 Broadway, Harlem ☎ 862-8142 Ⓜ 1•9 to 137th St-City College

☆ CIEL ROUGE

More like Weimar Berlin than modern-day Chelsea, Ciel Rouge serves up sexy torch singers crooning at the piano and exceptional cocktails in its plush, decadent lounge. When no one's performing, the CD player is partial to opera arias and Marlene Dietrich. Its yards of red velvet and chiffon are sure to bring out the romantic in you. Gorgeous garden, too.

176 Seventh Avenue, Chelsea ☎ 929-5542 Ⓜ 1•9 to 23rd St

☆ FEINSTEIN'S AT THE REGENCY ♯B8

Life is a cabaret, old chum – especially in this oh-so-swank Park Avenue club, where songbirds like Rosemary Clooney serenade stars, society mavens and anyone else who can afford the cover charge. It's pricey, but the lavish setting and attentive staff will make you feel like royalty.

540 Park Avenue, UES ☎ 759-4100 Ⓜ 4•5•6 to 59th St; N•R to Lexington Ave

Fez ♯A12

A relaxed, fun, Moroccan-inspired lounge under the trendy Time Café (serving creative American food), where drag acts and an eclectic roster of musicians (including the Mingus Big Band) can be seen at deliciously close quarters.

380 Lafayette Street, Noho ☎ 533-2680 Ⓜ 6 to Bleecker St

Japas 55 ♯B7

Part bar, part sushi restaurant, Japas features private karaoke booths where you can humiliate yourself in front of up to 20 friends, or do a duet in a space for two.

253 W 55th Street, Midtown ☎ 765-1210 Ⓜ N•R to 57th St

☆ JOE'S PUB ♯A12

Built into the Public Theater, Joe's Pub has remained one of New York's hottest nightspots since its arrival stirred up the Noho scene. It is both an elegantly modern lounge and an intimate performance space with inebriated models performing unintentionally between sets.

425 Lafayette Street, Noho ☎ 539-8770 Ⓜ 6 to Astor Pl

Knitting Factory's Tap Bar ♯F11

A young scene, where 18 beers are offered on tap. Free, live music ranges from funk to bizarre, experimental acts (11pm–2am nightly). John Cale, Yoko Ono, and Lou Reed, among others, work out their new material here.

74 Leonard Street, Tribeca ☎ 219-3055 Ⓜ 1•9 to Franklin St

☆ LAKESIDE LOUNGE ♯F10

Catch some of New York's best indie bands before they hit the charts. A few big names play here as well, and, on nights when no one performs, you'll find plenty of out-of-work musicians slumped over their beers.

162–164 Avenue B, East Village ☎ 529-8463 Ⓜ L to 1st Ave

Lenox Lounge ♯D1

Attracting a younger crowd thanks to aggressive party promoters, DJs, and superb live jazz, this Harlem institution starts to fill up at 11pm.

288 Lenox Avenue, Harlem ☎ 427-0253 Ⓜ 2•3 to 125th St

Londel's ♯A1

A friendly, unintimidating joint that draws a healthy mix of the old school locals as well as new additions to the neighbourhood. Catch some live jazz on weekends.

2620 Eighth Avenue, Harlem ☎ 234-6114 Ⓜ B•C to 135th St

Primorski ♯off map

A bar/restaurant/club with good food and a small dance floor.

282B Brighton Beach Avenue, Brooklyn ☎ 1-718-891-3111 Ⓜ D•Q to Brighton Beach

St Nick's Pub ♯off map

This shoebox-sized pub is one of the oldest in Harlem. Jazz musicians perform here all week, and Monday nights feature saxophonist Patience Higgins jamming with the Sugar Hill Jazz Quartet.

773 St Nicolas Avenue, Harlem ☎ 283-9728 Ⓜ A•B•C•D to 145th St

☆ SLIPPER ROOM ♯D12

An opulent one-stop venue that's good for catching crazed cabaret acts and sipping exotic cocktails. On Tuesdays, Lil' lady of nightlife Penelope Tuesdae gets together with drag king Murray Hill to inject some burlesque, music, and comedy into New York (shows start at 11pm & 12.30am). Dress to impress and party with an interesting crowd of locals and drag luminaries.

167 Orchard Street, LES ☎ 253-7246 Ⓜ F•J•M•Z to Delancy St-Essex St

☆ STINGER CLUB ♯off map

Looking for a great martini, a game of pool, or a half dozen abstract-impressionist sculptors? You'll find 'em all just off the beaten Bedford Avenue track. This trendy Brooklyn haunt is a seedy, red-lit, occasionally raucous tavern renowned for its cheap beers, fabulous jukebox, and even more fabulous clientele. It's all in the name of art, baby.

241 Grand Street, Williamsburg ☎ 1-718-218-6662 Ⓜ J•M•Z to Marcy Ave

Tillie's of Brooklyn   ⚲off map
An arty coffee bar with jazz on the weekends (and occasional sightings of actress Rosie Perez who lives locally).
248 DeKalb Avenue, Fort Greene ☎ 1-718-783-6140 Ⓜ G to Fulton St

☆ TONIC   ⚲D12
Ever had a drink in a giant wine barrel? This former Kosher wine shop now houses a performance space, an alternative press, and a basement bar featuring oversized casks that have been converted into miniature private rooms, complete with seating. Movies shown on Mondays.
107 Norfolk Street, LES ☎ 358-7504 Ⓜ F•J•M•Z to Delancey St-Essex St

☆ WINNIE'S   ⚲E12
Tucked away on a side street in Chinatown, Winnie's caters to both Asian and non-Asian karaoke fans. A makeshift stage inspires the seasoned songsters to ham it up. This is helped along with copious quantities of Tsing Tao beer to encourage raucous novices to screech at the bar. A lively, boisterous crowd adds to the fun.
104 Bayard Street, Chinatown ☎ 732-2384 Ⓜ J•M•N•R•Z•6 to Canal St

big-deal bars

☆ BAR 89   ⚲D11
Bar 89 was built for bull-market imbibing. If 40-ft ceilings, co-ed bathrooms with see-through doors, and bottomless martinis aren't enough to make you feel like a master of the universe, steal one of the trophy girlfriends sitting at the banquettes.
89 Mercer Street, Soho ☎ 274-0989 Ⓜ N•R to Prince St

Bemelman's Bar   ⚲C6
A Carlyle Hotel classic, offering all the swank of Café Carlyle without the steep tab. Piano players perform nightly.
Carlyle Hotel, 981 Madison Avenue, UES ☎ 744-1600 Ⓜ 6 to 77th St

☆ ELAINE'S   ⚲B6
This Upper East Side establishment has managed to maintain a loyal local clientele and attract enough swells and glitterati to keep the gossip columnists busy. And yes, Billy Joel did write a song about it. Dress up for this chic Italian with fresco-like wall paintings and literary parties galore. It can be intimidating, but act like you belong and you'll do just fine.
1703 Second Avenue, UES ☎ 534-8103 Ⓜ 4•5•6 to 86th St

bars

☆ GRAND BAR
ϸF11

Barely removed from the bustle of Soho, the Grand Bar is ideal for both stylish midday drinks and comfortable nightcaps *à deux*: just don't expect too much privacy at weekends when footsore shoppers and cultured-out gallery-goers take over.

Soho Grand Hotel, 310 W Broadway, Soho ☎ 965-3000 Ⓜ A•C•E to Canal St

☆ THE GREATEST BAR ON EARTH
ϸB13

The view from here is spectacular. Bring your friends, order a round of classic cocktails and stick someone else with the tab. After 10 in the evening, the Wall Street crowd goes home and the kids come out for swing music and Sidecars. Be sure to visit on Wednesdays, when Lucien the Loungecore DJ spins kooky soundtracks and other lounge music staples.

107th Floor, 1 World Trade Center, Lower Manhattan ☎ 524-7011 Ⓜ N•R•1•9 to Cortlandt St; 2•3 to Park Pl; A•C•E to Chambers St

☆ HARRY CIPRIANI
ϸA8

Nostalgic for Italy? Don understated designer clothing and head for Harry Cipriani, where bartenders pour the same Bellinis (prosecco and peach purée) made famous at Harry's Bar in Venice. If power lunches frighten you, request your midday meal at the bar. Either way, make sure you have a generous credit line. (The downtown outpost of Harry's is worth a visit for its rooftop garden.)

781 Fifth Avenue, UES ☎ 753-5566 Ⓜ N•R to 5th Ave

☆ LUSH
ϸB13

When you crave luxury, head to Lush, a favourite of dotcom moguls, stockbrokers, and Tribeca film execs. The velvet banquettes are sumptuous; the specialty cocktails are spectacular; and everyone looks good beneath the amber lights. If you don't like crowds, find yourself a private nook – and someone to share it with.

110 Duane Street, Tribeca ☎ 212-766-1275 Ⓜ A•C to Chambers St

Moomba
ϸA11

Once past the bouncers with way too much attitude, you can join celebs sipping pricey cocktails. But their numbers are steadily dwindling and many have jumped ship.

133 Seventh Avenue S, West Village ☎ 989-1414 Ⓜ 1•9 to Christopher St

☆ 357
ϸD11

A resolutely swanky champagne lounge serving both bubbly and booze by the bottle or glass. The crowd is equal parts downtown hipster and well-heeled Soho-ite. Regular club nights – call ahead for DJ information.

357 W Broadway, Soho ☎ 965-1491 Ⓜ N•R to Prince St

☆ TOP OF THE TOWER   *♭D8*

Top of the Tower is the epitome of old New York elegance. The views from this art deco hotel bar – located on the 26th floor – are stunning. Ancient waiters serve classic cocktails and a piano player performs nightly.
Beekman Tower Hotel, 3 Mitchell Place, Midtown ☎ 355-7300
Ⓜ E•6 to 51st St

Veruka   *♭C12*

The door policy at this super-trendy bar may be the area's strictest, though women dressed in Gucci and Prada fare well, and models are a shoo-in.
525 Broome Street, Soho ☎ 625-1717 Ⓜ 6 to Spring St; C•E to Spring St

Wet Bar   *♭E8*

A roomy, red-walled place with a velvet rope and private nooks for getting up to no good in. No wonder it's gained a reputation as a pick-up spot.
W Court Hotel, 130 E 39th Street, Midtown ☎ 726-9500
Ⓜ 4•5•6•7 to Grand Central-42nd St

Whiskey Park   *♭B7*

Housed in the Trump Parc building – that's all you need to know.
Trump Parc, 100 Central Park S, Midtown ☎ 307-9222 Ⓜ B•Q to 57th St

Whiskey Blue   *♭D8*

This bar in the W New York hotel attracts a bar-to-boudoir crowd (especially on Thursdays), Hamptons-haunting ladies, and wealthy sugar daddies.
W New York, 541 Lexington Avenue, Midtown ☎ 407-294 Ⓜ 6 to 51st St

themes & schemes

Bongo   *♭D9*

Bobby sock's retro, a paean to the 50s/60s and popular with Chelsea's arty types, as well as cocktail addicts. A seafood menu is also available.
299 10th Avenue, Chelsea, ☎ 947-3654 Ⓜ C•E to 23rd St

Café Noir   *♭F11*

This sexy, smoker-friendly, Moroccan themed bar-restaurant is a good option for the attitude-weary.
32 Grand Street, Soho ☎ 431-7910 Ⓜ 1•9 to Canal St; A•C•E to Canal St

☆ DECIBEL

♭A12

Sample the sake at Decibel and you'll never settle for a flavourless flask of rice wine again. An impressive selection of premium sakés, mixed saké cocktails, and Japanese munchies (hot peas, shrimp crackers) are offered at the bar, while full meals are served at the tables.

240 E 9th Street, East Village ☎ 979-2733 Ⓜ 6 to Astor Pl

Denial

♭F11

If you can't abandon your posse, head to this dark, sensual sake bar where your social pedigree is, thankfully, irrelevant.

46 Grand Street, Soho ☎ 925-9449 Ⓜ A•C•E to Canal St

☆ GOOD WORLD BAR & GRILL

♭F12

New York's only Swedish-themed bar serves up more than 60 beers, tasty bar snacks like cured herring and meatballs, and a laid-back crowd of hotties so hip they can actually find this way out-of-the-way hot spot.

3 Orchard Street, LES ☎ 925-9975 Ⓜ F to East Broadway

Hogs & Heifers

♭F9

A resolutely straight meat market, good for late-night boozing. Ostensibly a biker bar with men in leather vests arriving on Harley-Davidsons, the scene is more kitsch than threatening, and it also attracts a fair number of bright young media moguls. The bar is most notorious for its collection of bras displayed behind the bar – Drew Barrymore once whipped off her brassiere here. A wild, raucous night is guaranteed.

859 Washington Street, Chelsea ☎ 929-0655 Ⓜ A•C•E to 14th St

Idlewild

♭C12

For a freaky theme bar, hit Idlewild with a lounge designed to look just like an airplane's cabin. Lots of regular parties keep the joint jumping.

145 E Houston Street, LES ☎ 477-5005 Ⓜ F to 2nd Ave

Joe's Bar

♭C12

A must for country and western aficionados. No live music here, but the jukebox could have easily been stolen from a Texas roadhouse.

520 E 6th Street, East Village ☎ no phone Ⓜ F to 2nd Ave

☆ KGB

♭A12

Don't be fooled by the commie-chic decor. Commercially successful authors read here regularly, as do a number of the literary world's brightest young stars. A haven for aspiring literati and their devotees.

85 E 4th Street, East Village ☎ 505-3360 Ⓜ 6 to Astor Pl

☆ KUSH ♫C12
Flop on a pillow-strewn couch, smoke a hookah, and make believe you're in Marrakech. Kush brings the Middle East to the Lower East Side every Tuesday night with belly dancers, henna hand-painting, and tarot card readings. Other nights feature live jazz or DJs but the vibe's still mellow.
183 Orchard Street, LES ☎ 677-7328 Ⓜ F to 2nd Ave

☆LEI BAR ♫A12
Nestled in the basement of Niagara, this tiny East Village tiki bar-within-a-bar boasts a DJ spinning surf-movie soundtracks and mambo as well as a bamboo-lined bar serving a delectable array of frozen tropical cocktails and kitsch drinks garnished with fruit kebabs and paper umbrellas.
112 Avenue A, East Village ☎ 420-9517 Ⓜ 6 to Astor Pl

Ñ ♫C12
Room to move is not an option at this sexy slip of a tapas bar with potent sangria and at least two people waiting for each seat at the bar.
33 Crosby Street, Noho ☎ 219-8856 Ⓜ 6 to Spring St

☆ THE RUSSIAN SAMOVAR ♫D7
Idle Russian beauties line the bar; a piano tinkles in the background; dozens of infused vodkas beckon to be sampled: the Cold War may be over, but intrigue lingers on at this gaudy and elegant Theater District bar and restaurant. Bar snacks include boiled potatoes and black bread!
56 W 52nd Street, Midtown ☎ 757-0168 Ⓜ 1•9 to 50th St

Serena ♫D9
An atmospheric, popular Moroccan-themed boîte in the basement of the famed Chelsea hotel. Skip the front bar and head straight to the back bar for a warmer welcome.
222 W 23rd Street, Chelsea ☎ 255-4646 Ⓜ 1•9 to 23rd St

Subway Inn ♫B8
Easily one of UES's most beloved theme bars. The booze is cheap and everybody is welcome.
**143 E 60th Street, UES ☎ 223-8929 Ⓜ N•R to 5th Ave;
N•R to Lexington Ave**

☆ SWINE ON NINE ♫D7
The most garishly entertaining paean to pigs man has ever known. Pig murals, drawings and figurines line the walls, and a giant besuited boar greets visitors at the door. A dive at heart, Swine offers dirt-cheap drinks, free chicken soup and a complimentary pink porcelain piggy bank for ladies.
693 Ninth Avenue, Midtown ☎ 397-8356 Ⓜ C•E to 50th St

☆ VOID   ♩F11
Dark, cavernous and striving for an air of deviance, Void has to be one of
New York's best cyber bars, with film screenings every Wednesday, and
electronica every Tuesday and Thursday, while punters surf the Web.
16 Mercer Street, Soho ☎ 941-6492 Ⓜ N•R to Canal St

Welcome to the Johnsons'   ♩D12
This fun bar is fitted out to resemble the typical mid-70s living room,
complete with plastic-covered furniture.
123 Rivington Street, LES ☎ 420-9911 Ⓜ F•J•M•Z to Delancy St-Essex St

great dives

Dive Bar   ♩E3
Located a safe 20 blocks south of Columbia, this is one of the few
tolerable neighbourhood joints – if you don't mind the cigar smoke.
732 Amsterdam Avenue, UWS ☎ 749-4358 Ⓜ 1•2•3•9 to 96th St

☆ MARE CHIARO   ♩C12
The quintessential Italian dive bar. Once a popular stop for visiting
celebrities (photos of which proudly line the walls), then a favourite
haunt of downtown literati, this joint is now seeing increased traffic
from Nolita's fashionable new residents. Avoid weekends, when cigar-
chomping bridge-and-tunnel types pour in.
176 Mulberry Street, Nolita ☎ 226-9345 Ⓜ 6 to Spring St

☆ MAX FISH   ♩C12
The best dive bar in the Lower East Side is packed every evening with
indie-rockers, students, artists, and locals. Long since discovered by the
outside world, Max Fish has managed to retain its edge without scaring
off new visitors; the pool table, however, remains viciously competitive.
178 Ludlow Street, LES ☎ 529-3959 Ⓜ F to 2nd Ave

Milano's   ♩D11
For a taste of the old neighbourhood, visit this shoebox-sized den where
old men start nodding off at 3pm and Jimmy Rosselli tunes remain a
jukebox favourite.
1 E Houston Street, Noho ☎ no phone Ⓜ B•D•F•Q to Broadway-Lafayette St

☆ NANCY WHISKEY PUB   ♩F11
A dive bar in Tribeca, Nancy Whiskey Pub is the real thing with a motley
clientele, high-stakes shuffleboard tournaments, and a bartender who
steals sips of your beer when you aren't looking.
1 Lispenard Street, Tribeca ☎ 226-9943 Ⓜ A•C•E to Canal St

169 Bar ♭F12
Unpretentious, basic dive with an underground feel that's playing host to exellent, music-orientated parties.
169 E Broadway, LES ☎ 473-8866 Ⓜ F to East Broadway

☆ RUDY'S ♭F7
The $3.00 pitchers and free hotdogs are legendary, but the real reason everyone loves this dingy dive is the eclectic crowd. Models, mobsters, and local drunks share rickety tables, overflowing shots, and quarters for the juke. A great happy hour and heaps of authenticity add to its appeal. If you don't leave with a story – and a hangover – you're doing something wrong.
627 Ninth Avenue, Midtown ☎ 212-974-9169 Ⓜ A•C•E to 42nd St

☆ SIBERIA ♭D7
Located in a subway station (and Russian only in decor) this joint is a welcome break from the theme palaces taking over Times Square. The bar is tiny, the proprietor is gregarious, and patrons are encouraged to cut loose, often with complimentary shots of chilled vodka. Not many dive bars can shut off your shy side like Siberia. Great jukebox, too.
Downtown 1•9 Subway Station, 1627 Broadway, Midtown ☎ 333-4141 Ⓜ 1•9 to 50th St

Smoke ♭C3
This smoky jazz dive attracts Columbia students and a mellow crowd.
2751 Broadway, UWS ☎ 316-3737 Ⓜ 1•9 to 103rd St

Stinger Club
The extremely partisan Williamsburgian bar pack all agree – this is a hit. Off the beaten Bedford Avenue track, this place is an appropriately seedy home to cheap beer, live bands and red lights.
241 Grand Street, Williamsburg ☎ 1-718-218-6662 Ⓜ L to Bedford Ave

288 ♭A12
Prefered by Nolita's younger dive denizens, 288 (aka Tom & Jerry's) is great for beer but a martini might disappoint.
288 Elizabeth Street, Noho ☎ 334-8429 Ⓜ 6 to Bleecker St

☆ ANGEL'S SHARE
♭A12

Don't come in a group: well-concealed Angel's Share enforces a strict four-person limit per group, making it most suitable for first-time dates, social recluses, or a tryst. The biggest draw here is the Japanese bartenders, renowned for mixing marvellous cocktails such as lychee daiquiries with expert precision.

8 Stuyvesant Street, East Village ☎ 777-5415 Ⓜ 6 to Astor Pl

☆ BLUE BAR
♭F7

The rarefied, literary atmosphere of the historic Algonquin Hotel provides the setting for this friendly, low-key bar in the heart of Manhattan. Non-guests are warmly welcomed and the loquacious bartenders will brew you a warming Irish coffee on cold winter days.

59 W 44th Street, Midtown ☎ 840-6800 Ⓜ B•D•F•Q to 42nd St

Velvet
♭C12

If you need space, head straight here, where business has yet to boom. Get a drink in the restaurant's romantic, antique-furnished lounge bar.

223 Mulberry Street, Noho ☎ 965-0439 Ⓜ 6 to Spring St

Von
♭A12

A laid-back bar without attitude in a neighbourhood that's renowned for its trendiness. You can actually hear yourself speak in here, the bar staff are all lookers, and you almost always get into drunken conversation with some artist dude at the bar.

3 Bleecker Street, Noho ☎ 473-3039 Ⓜ 6 to Bleecker St

lounge bars

Bond St
♭A12

Bond St's sleek and minimalist basement lounge offers a modified version of the restaurant's menu, sakétinis and young, gorgeous girleens nibbling sushi.

6 Bond Street, Noho ☎ 777-2500 Ⓜ 6 to Bleecker St

Evelyn Lounge
♭C5

A labyrinthine bar-lounge with a door policy, comfy sofas, separate cigar bar and a smoky, low-lit atmosphere.

380 Columbus Avenue, UWS ☎ 724-5145 Ⓜ 1•9 to 79th St

Odessa
♭F10

A former Eastern European diner that was transformed into a bar when the owners relocated the diner to a larger space next door. (The bar kitchen still serves diner fare 'til midnight.)

117 Avenue A, East Village ☎ 253-1470 Ⓜ L to 1st Ave

Quench
♭off map

A new lounge-bar with a super-slick look, an impressive wine list, beers on tap, and nicely inventive cocktails.

282 Smith Street, Carroll Gardens ☎ 1-718-875-1500 Ⓜ F•G to Carroll St

Restaurant 147's
♭F9

This basement lounge (designed by Christopher Ciccone, Madonna's brother) has returned some of the heat to this former hot spot – another place to go for a pretty cocktail.

147 W 15th Street, Chelsea ☎ 929-5000 Ⓜ L to 8th Ave; A•C•E to 14th St

Rhône
♭F9

Focuses more on wine: no less than 26 wines are available by the glass and surprise, surprise, come from the Rhône valley. Relaxed and stylishy slick.

**63 Gansevoort Street, Gramercy Park ☎ 367-8440
Ⓜ A•C•E to 14th St; L to 8th Ave**

Sway
♭D11

A hot Moroccan lounge frequented by musicians and mannequins. Thursday nights are best, but avoid weekends, when the crowd pressing the door is impenetrable.

305 Spring Street, Soho ☎ 620-5220 Ⓜ C•E to Spring St

sports bars

Coogan's
♭off map

A spacious Irish sports bar. Large-screen TVs make it a local favourite during any play-offs.

**4015 Broadway, Harlem ☎ 928-1234
Ⓜ A•C•1•9 to 168th St-Washington Heights**

ESPN Zone
♭F7

The kind of big, brash, commercial sports bars that Americans know how to do well. The big screen is dedicated to whichever game the management thinks is of most interest to customers. Also has vast space dedicated to interactive games and attractions.

1472 Broadway, Midtown ☎ 921-3776 Ⓜ N•R•S•1•9•2•3•7 to 42nd St-Times Sq

bars

Jimmy's Corner Bar   ✲F7
A sport's bar – just like they used to be.... a small, neighbourhood bar that's been around for almost 30 years, with just 4 regular sized TVs. The owner is a former boxing trainer, so this is a great place to watch a bout.
140 W 44th Street, Midtown ☎ **221-9510**
Ⓜ **N•R•S•1•9•2•3•7 to 42nd St-Times Sq**

Malachy's Donegal Inn   ✲C5
Loud, local sports fans gather round the big-screen TV for games, and their shouting is only rivalled by the jukebox. Perfect for wolfing down a burger and swilling a beer or two.
103 W 72nd Street, UWS ☎ **874-4268** Ⓜ **1•2•3•9 to 72nd St**

clubs

Despite Mayor Giuliani's 'Quality of Life' laws putting a stranglehold on New York nightlife, club promotors still cook up the new, the retro and the extravagant and dish it out at venues all over the city. The club beat goes on, even if at some of the city's lounges, dancing isn't strictly allowed...

Angel *D12*
With low-level lighting, plush seating for slummers and regular roster of DJs.
174 Orchard Street, LES ☎ 780-0313 🅼 F•J•M•Z to Delancy St-Essex St

☆ Baktun *F9*
Music comes first at this sleek, cozy and truly unique lounge, with staple nights providing different types of dance or electronic music. Creative party promotions, video projections, modest bar prices and friendly staff make it a diamond in the rough. Direct Drive on Saturday nights provides a much-needed night of drum 'n' bass with an unbelievable line up of DJs: Seoul, Seen, and Reid Speed are among the residents, and guests drop in on occasion. Enjoy it hard and fast in this high-tech, yet warm and intimate, atmosphere.
418 W 14th Street, Chelsea ☎ 206-1590 🅼 A•C•E to 14th St; L to 8th Ave

☆ Fun *F12*
Party people have a great time at Fun, a vast space under the Manhattan Bridge, where the music comes in hip-hop, funk, reggae and house colours. Suited doormen meet and greet at the entrance, but there are no guest lists nor cover charges! The drinks are pricey but that's all you'll have to pay for. You'll need a sense of humour to pay a visit, though: the sinks in the bathrooms have surveillance monitors (so guys can spy on girls, and vice versa).
130 Madison Street, LES ☎ 964-0303 🅼 F to East Broadway

☆ Limelight *C10*
The controversy surrounding owner Peter Gatien's involvement with drug rings and murder has made his club a must-see for the curious. By day, Limelight presents art shows and theatre; by night, it's home to themed parties. Hard house is usually featured on the main floor, while hip-hop and pop are elsewhere. The huge, thumping fiestas allow you to appreciate how they can charge top whack admission.
660 Sixth Avenue, Chelsea ☎ 807-7780 🅼 F•N•R to 23rd St

☆ Nell's
♭F9

Having hit on the recipe for success way back, Nell's has changed little over the years. Upstairs, a lush bar has a DJ playing between live R&B sets, while downstairs pulsates to a classic dance mix. It's renowned for a picky door policy so come well-dressed (and men come with a woman). Particularly popular is Voices (Tue) where amateur songbirds and the occasional celeb-birdie perch on the open mic.

246 W 14th Street, West Village ☎ 675-1567 Ⓜ A•C•E to 14th St; L to 8th Ave

Rasputin
♭off map

Glamorous nightclub full of Russians hell-bent on partying. Best to book way in advance.

2670 Coney Island Avenue, Brighton Beach ☎ 1-718-332-9187 Ⓜ D to Neck Rd

☆ Shine
♭F11

A rock 'n' roll venue transformed into a party paradise, Shine radiates good clean fun. There are cushy couches and a mini-stage hosting everything from dance and drag to burlesque and comedy. Promoters bring all sorts of special events and parties. Home Cookin' hip-hop party (Wed). Giant Step returns with their musically innovative club night on Mondays and it now features Chicago house producer Ron Trent as resident. The funky, Afro-infused, danceable tunes allow early-week scenesters and record industry schmoozers to party hearty.

285 W Broadway, Tribeca ☎ 941-0900 Ⓜ A•C•E•1•9 to Canal St

☆ Spa
♭E10

After being The Grand, System, and Key Club, the Spa incarnation at this address is the most glamorous. Its white decor is accented with 'spa' touches, such as sauna-like bathrooms, and a tanning bed above the dancefloor. But the sound system has been neglected. Great if you don't mind paying top dollar for a cocktail in a plastic cup for a chance to see and be seen.

76 E 13th Street, East Village ☎ 388-1060 Ⓜ N•R•L•4•5•6 to 14th St-Union Sq

Tribeca Blues
♭B13

DJs spin hip-hop, funk and soul at actor Michael Rapaport's dark and atmospheric bar and club. With its large, promoter-driven parties, the club has a secure future.

16 Warren Street, Tribeca ☎ 766-1070 Ⓜ A•C to Chambers St

☆ **Tunnel** *♭off map*

Thousands of people from all walks of life converge at this megaclub. Every area – even the bathroom – has its own bar and sound system; so weave in and out through hard house, 80s pop, hip-hop, and deep house. Admission's expensive, but there's more than enough bang for the buck with smash hit nights and special events. Dress up; and men, come with a woman.

220 Twelveth Avenue, Chelsea ☎ **695-4682** Ⓜ **C•E to 23rd St**

☆ **Vinyl** *♭F11*

This hallowed patch of land is the birthplace of legendary clubs of old: Area, Quick, and Shelter. Now known as Vinyl, it's dance heaven, still carving out a giant reputation. Deep house lovers let rip on the dancefloor as internationally renown DJ/producer 'Little Louie' Vega lets loose on the booming system. On Saturday, Shelter attracts older souls as well as younger house disciples. The original DJ Timmy Regisford keeps the underground crowd dancing, twirling, and flipping to the classics non-stop until 9am. Body & Soul on Sunday is probably the best-known dance party in NYC, attracting house heads from the world over. Doors open at 3pm, and it's packed by 6pm. Residents François K, Joe Claussell, and Danny Krivit take dancers on a journey in house, world beat, soul et al.

6 Hubert Street, Tribeca ☎ **343-1379** Ⓜ **A•C•E to Canal St; 1•9 to Franklin St**

practical information

Magazines such as Paper and Time Out feature nightclub listings, as do free publications like Flyer NYC, NYPress, HX, Next and Wipe, found on street corners and in record and clubby clothes stores.

Club Nights move from venue to venue frequently, so it's best to call ahead.

☞ Some clubs have specific dress codes. Many have a 'no sneakers or jeans' policy and a few clubs will refuse entry to men not accompanied by a woman.

💲 Most clubs will only accept a credit card for a large bar tab.

◑ The majority of clubs open at 10pm and fill up around 1am. According to NYC law, all clubs must stop serving alcohol at 4am, so most of them close down at that time.

gay scene

Gotham City has plenty to tempt followers of all persuasions. Greenwich Village might be where it all started, but these days Chelsea and the East Village have the hottest scenes.

bars & cafés

☆ BAR D'O
C11

New York's premiere venue for drag entertainment just keeps getting better. Intimate and glamorous, it attracts a devoted following thanks to weekly performances by downtown legends Raven O and Joey Arias.

29 Bedford Street, West Village ☎ 627-1580 Ⓜ 1•9 to Houston St

Big Cup
D9

A fundamentally gay hangout, serving (yes) big cups of coffee along with muffins, pastries and sandwiches. The decor is droll and the atmosphere conducive to comfortable – and sober – cruising.

228 Eighth Avenue, Chelsea ☎ 206-0059 Ⓜ C•E to 23rd St $

☆ CHASE
B7

Buff boys in DKNY mix and mingle. During peak hours, it gets stuffy in the front room, but we hear it's even hotter in the back lounge.

255 W 55th Street, Midtown ☎ 333-3400 Ⓜ A•B•C•D•1•9 to 59th St-Columbus Circle

☆ THE COCK
off map

East Village's hottest gay bar. Homo heart-throb Mario Diaz and a gaggle of go-go dancers are on hand, while DJs spin classic rock 'n' roll. Foxy on Saturday is a quirky night, where between dancing and drinking, patrons are invited to strut their stuff on stage – and win $100. Judged by the crowd, contestants do dastardly deeds ranging from acrobatics to anal probing.

188 Avenue A, East Village ☎ 777-6254 Ⓜ L to 1st Ave

☆ DICK'S
F10

Famed for its cheap booze and superb jukebox, Dick's is one of Manhattan's best-loved gay dives. $2 shots and a few Morrissey singles should lower your inhibition. Cruising strongly encouraged.

192 Second Avenue, East Village ☎ 475-2071 Ⓜ L to 1st Ave

☆ A DIFFERENT LIGHT
♀D9

The café at this, the city's largest gay and lesbian bookshop which has books on all aspects of gay interest, is a fine place to meet some new friends. There's also a gift store (if you really click), plus nightly readings and other events, which have turned this place into a veritable community centre.

151 W 19th Street, Chelsea ☎ 989-4850 Ⓜ F•1•2• 3•9 to 14th St; L to 6th Ave

G
♀F9

The place for serious gay cruising. The lounge's circular bar aids mass flirtation. Plus, boys on the wagon can take advantage of the juice bar.

225 W 19th Street, Chelsea ☎ 929-1085 Ⓜ 1•9 to 18th St

Henrietta Hudson
♀C11

A neighbourhood girl bar, is more about cruising than boozing, though there's still plenty of the latter.

438 Hudson Street, West Village ☎ 924-3347 Ⓜ 1•9 to Houston St

☆ MEOW MIX
♀C12

The only lesbian bar in the Lower East Side offers live music seven nights a week and enough hard-rocking girls to keep the party going all night.

269 E Houston Street, LES ☎ 254-0688 Ⓜ F to 2nd Ave

☆ NOWBAR
♀C11

Those looking for the company of pre- or post-op transsexuals, or even transvestites, need only to visit this bar. Friday is Trannie Chaser – NY's only transexual promoter Glorya Wholsome has made a perfect place for Trannies and their Chasers to meet and cavort. Men of all shapes and sizes woo the 'ladies' downstairs, while in the upstairs 'lap dance' lounge, they go that bit further.

22 Seventh Avenue S, West Village ☎ 293-0323 Ⓜ 1•9 to Houston St

Regents
♀ C8

A quiet focal point for the older gay male community, Casually but neatly dressed gentlemen gather round the piano to sing show tunes and standards. A heart-warming gem, refreshingly free of young hustlers.

317 E 53rd Street, Midtown ☎ 593-3091 Ⓜ E•F to 5th Ave

Saints
♀B3

A hetero-friendly gay bar frequented by Columbia University students and anyone wishing to cruise them.

992 Amsterdam Avenue, UWS ☎ 222-2431 Ⓜ B•C to Cathedral Pkwy

Wonder Bar ♯A12

One of the rare gay nightspots that welcomes straight friends without putting a damper on cruising. Excellent DJs keep the crowd happy, but some of the boys still pine for the old porn videos and curtained back room.
505 E 6th Street, East Village ☎ 777-9105 Ⓜ 6 to Astor Pl

clubs

☆ **HELL** ♯F9

DJs spinning 70s and early 80s disco get the crowd moving on the dance floor, and Hell's potent house martinis keep lazy loungers blissful.
55 Gansevoort Street, Chelsea ☎ 727-1666 Ⓜ A•C•E to 14th St; L to 8th Ave

Splash ♯F9

Two floors of boozing, cruising, DJs and dancing. Sin City lives.
50 W 17th Street, Gramercy Park ☎ 691-0073 Ⓜ L to 6th Ave; F to 14th St

☆ **TWILO** ♯D9

The dancefloor dominates and psychedelic globes hang from the ceiling. Movies are screened on the walls, making this club feel rich, yet frivolous. Anyone who enjoys a big club experience will love Twilo on Fridays. Fab DJs like Sasha, Digweed, and Carl Cox tweak the state-of-the-art sound system for a sea of hard-house revellers. High-tech visuals and occasional art installations enhance the fun.
530 W 27th Street, Chelsea ☎ 268-1600 Ⓜ C•E to 23rd St; 1•9 to 28th St

For the latest lowdown on what's hot and what's not, check out:
www.gaynyc.com; www.gay-newyork.com; and
www.papermag.com/guide/gay.

entertainment

New York, the USA's undisputed cultural capital, throws up an infinite number of top-notch amusements on any given night. The only problem is how to choose between them...

listings magazines & the free press

Time Out New York has made a comfortable niche for itself in the market of weekly listings mags, which include the more conservative *New Yorker* and yuppie-ish *New York Magazine*. *The Village Voice*, a long-standing liberal mouthpiece, has declined recently, partly due to competition from the equally liberal listings mag, *The New York Press*. There's also the monthly *Paper*, though it's a little old hat nowadays. Free specialty publications such as *NYC* with up-to-date club gossip, and *Literal Latte*, a café-society rag, have become omnipresent in public spaces.

the papers

Perhaps with the exception of *The Washington Post*, the *New York Times* is the most well respected paper in America; it prides itself on its world news analysis and, despite its stuffy tone and appearance, is a comprehensive read. The Sunday version weighs in like a set of encyclopedias. As far as tabloids go, the *Daily News* and *New York Post* can't touch the down-and-dirty tactics of the British rat-pack but, with Rupert Murdoch at the helm of the *Post*, it can't be long in coming. As for the top financial paper, the *Wall Street Journal*: no WSJ...no comment.

radio

New York is well endowed with 24-hour radio stations, featuring all manner of music and talk shows. FM stations are your best bet but AM stations can also entertain, if not inform. Hot 97 (WBLS, 97.1 FM) provides the essential hip-hop accompaniment to a New York day, while K-Rock (WXRK, 92.3 FM) is shock-jock Howard Stern's personal soapbox every morning. WBGO (88.3 FM) is a round-the-clock jazz station, and the station of choice for rock 'n' roll classics is WNEW (102.7 FM). What you'll hear in most cabs is WKTU (103.5 FM) – pumped-up versions of mainstream house anthems. College radio stations showcase big name DJs at weekends to get you in the party spirit. Non-music alternatives are WNYC (820 AM), a member station of National Public Radio or WBAI (99.5 FM), both of which have public-forum type news discussions and good coverage of politics.

television

Americans are a nation of TV junkies and New Yorkers, no matter how cosmopolitan they seem, are no exception. There are 70-odd channels to be had if you have cable and around a dozen if you don't, but for the visitor the novelty soon wears off. Exceptions to the rule are channels 13, 21 and 31, which are given over to public broadcasting and have higher quality programming. Channel 11 screens re-runs of Friends, Seinfeld and Cheers every night, and NBC shows the phenomenally successful ER. Channel 21 also shows BBC world news every night at 11.30pm. The main television news slot is 10pm on terrestrial channels, but there are plenty of all-news-all-the-time cable channels: MSNBC (15), CNN (10), Fox News (46) and, for good local info, New York News One (1). Don't forget to have a quick flick past the public access channels for freak-show-style laughs.

websites

w www.newyork.citysearch.com has up-to-the-minute info on events; **w** www.clubnyc.com is nightlife oriented; **w** www.sidewalk.com is Microsoft's comprehensive listings and information network, covering everything from restaurant reviews to club listings. The internet can also be a good option to book tickets. Try **w** www.ticketmaster.com or **w** www.nytoday.com.

If these don't help you out, **w** www.nynetwork.com has a listing of all New York websites. If your hotel doesn't have internet access, try the terminals at the New York Public Library for free access, or one of the city's cyber cafés:

Cyber café
273 Lafayette Street (at Prince St) ☎ 334-5140
Internet café
82 E 3rd Street (bet. First & Second Aves) ☎ 614-0747
Void
16 Mercer St (at Howard St) ☎ 941-6492

theatre

For credit card booking for all the Broadway theatres, ring Ticketmaster ☎ 307-7171 or Telecharge ☎ 239-6200. Each makes a small surcharge for telephone reservations; tickets can then be picked up at the box office (show your credit card as proof of identity). You can also buy tickets over the internet [→websites] or directly from the theatre box offices. There are often special discounts for those with disabilities (Telecharge wheelchair hotline ☎ 239-6280). On the day of the performance, you can get half-price tickets to both Broadway and Off-Broadway shows at the TKTS booths in Times Square (at 47th St) and at the World Trade Center (often less busy). Lines are long, but move quickly. These tickets cannot be purchased by phone or with a credit card (cash only).

○ Broadway theatres are dark on Monday, and many shows are closed Sunday night as well. The main ones usually have Wednesday, Saturday and Sunday matinees. Performances generally start at 8pm (matinees 2pm Wed & Sat; 3pm Sun).

♠ Phone the venues direct to get the low-down on seating. Many Broadway theatres now carry infra-red hearing enhancement (headsets available on request).

☒ Expect to pay $75 and up for big Broadway shows; tickets for Off-Broadway shows are usually $25–$40, and Off-Off Broadway tickets are roughly $15–$25.

❶ Friday and Sunday papers tend to have the most theatre coverage – critics on the *New York Times* and the *New Yorker* are especially well respected. Check also the weekly magazines [→listings magazines]. New York City Onstage ☎ 768-1818 gives recorded information on shows and Playbill's website, **w** www.playbill.com, has the low-down on what's on, plus seating plans for the main theatres.

cabaret

To book tickets, contact venues directly.

○ Most cabaret performances are Tuesday–Saturday, with a few smaller shows on Sundays and Mondays. Except for the big extravaganzas, almost all theatres are dark on Mondays, so you might find a singer from a Broadway musical doing a one-night-only event at a cabaret venue.

♠ Reservations are highly recommended for shows with very big names and it's a good idea to call ahead for seats for smaller shows. ☒ Most venues have a cover charge and a one- to two-drink minimum. Restaurants offering entertainment sometimes require guests to dine at earlier shows, so it's best to ask when making a reservation. Cover charges range from $10 to $50 at more high-end spaces. Most smaller clubs take only cash, but the larger venues take credit cards.

❶ *In Theater*, *Back Stage*, the *New York Times*, the *New York Daily News* and the *New York Post* often review performances, but you might have to hunt to find cabaret coverage among the other entertainment news. [→listings magazines; websites].

comedy

Reserve seats by calling the club. Be sure to book a day or two in advance, especially for weekend shows or those with big-name headliners. Most take major credit cards apart from Dangerfield's.

○ Comedy in New York never takes a vacation – clubs run shows year round. Typical weekday shows (Sun–Thu) run continuously from 9pm–midnight. Weekend shows (Fri & Sat) are more structured, with shows at 8pm, 10pm and 12.30am. The later the show, the racier the material gets.

♠ Reservations don't guarantee a seat: seating is first come, first served, so get there at least half an hour before show time.

§ Cover charges range from $5–$25 and almost all clubs have a two-drink minimum, with prices ranging from $3 (non-alcoholic drinks) to $8 (mixed drinks).

❶ For recorded listings detailing the week's lineups, the best bet is to call the club direct [→listings magazines].

cinema

It's best to buy or book tickets in advance, and you can do this for most cinemas via the credit-card reservation at ☎ 777-FILM (3456) – they charge a booking fee of $2 per ticket. The service is very easy to operate and it also gives preview information.

☾ New films generally open on Fridays. Screening times vary, but usually start around 10am and run 'til around midnight (there are many more midnight shows at the weekends). In general, movies have only a few trailers and maybe an ad preceding them, so don't assume there's masses of time to spare after the official programme start time.

♠ Automated booking services so the early bird gets the best seats.

§ Ticket prices are currently about $9, and slightly less for the smaller, artier theatres.

❶ On the net, check out: **w** www.nytoday.com/movies. The *New York Times* and *New York Observer* both run regular film reviews [→listings magazines].

Tickets for the Lincoln Center venues can only be booked through agencies, with a surcharge of $4.80 to $5.50 per ticket. Call Centercharge ☎ 721-6500 for Alice Tully Hall and Avery Fisher Hall; CarnegieCharge ☎ 247-7800 for Carnegie Hall; and ☎ 362-6000 for the Metropolitan Opera. Tickets for other main venues, like the BAM, can be booked through Ticketmaster ☎ 307-7171 (surcharges vary by venue) or by calling the venues direct.

♈ Nowadays, even at the Met, anything and everything goes, from jeans to tuxedos.

☾ The Metropolitan Opera plays from October to April. Evening performances generally begin at 8pm (occasionally, at 7 or 7.30pm), but Sunday performances and recitals are sometimes earlier. There are no Sunday performances at the Met.

♠ Binoculars are useful in the Lincoln Center's huge auditoria. Sitting at the top of the Met isn't necessarily a liability – the acoustics are great.

§ Tickets are usually $10–$180. At the Met, standing-room tickets for the week go on sale the preceding Saturday morning; people line up before dawn to procure the $12 spots. At music schools, performances are often free.

❶ Performances are reviewed in most of the daily papers a couple of days after the event. *The New York Times* is the most respected but the critics on the *New York Post* and *Newsday* are usually spot on [→listings magazines].

Some of the larger companies sell through ticket agencies such as Ticketmaster ☎ 307-7171. The TKTS booth (at Times Square and the World Trade Center) sometimes has dance tickets for City Center or Joyce performances. Tickets can only be purchased on the day, and they don't accept credit cards. Smaller venues have their own box office and booking system and there's often no assigned seating: first come, first served.

☾ Most companies' seasons last only a week or two so you have to be on the ball to get tickets. Show times vary but there are often weekend matinees.

♠ Binoculars are useful at the Met and the New York State Theater.

☷ Ticket prices are $10–$200 .

❶ Although all the main papers review dance, the *NY Times* is the best bet. But it's the luck of the draw as to which day reviews will run [→listings magazines].

poetry

Tickets are usually available on the door but you'll need to book ahead for major performance poets or the big poetry slams.

☾ Times of shows vary (check with the venue) but they can start as early as 5pm and as late as 11pm.

☷ Prices vary from free admission to $5–$15 for special events.

❶ The *Village Voice* features the Poetry Calendar of New York council. Keep an eye out for flyers in cafés or bookshops [→listings magazines].

music

You can get tickets from venues in advance, but the main purveyor is Ticketmaster ☎ 307-7171, which can also be accessed on the internet [→websites]. As everywhere, good shows get sold out quickly but the desperate can join the tradition of being ripped off by ticket scalpers outside.

☾ There are gigs nightly but many more on Friday and Saturday nights. Most start between 8/9pm. Big names will often have a support band, which will start earlier.

♠ Larger venues tend to be seated and smaller ones seats only.

☷ Tickets for the big names are around $40–$50. Otherwise, reckon on paying $8–$20.

❶ Up-to-date scoop can also be gleaned from Funkmaster Flex's nightly radio show on 96 Kiss FM. Hip happenings can be discovered by making enquiries at places like Earwax Records, 204 Bedford Ave (bet. N 5th & 6th Sts) ☎ 1-718-218-9608. Trail the underground scene on the web at sites like **w** www.supa.com and check the weekly papers [→listings magazines].

events

A year's worth of events and happenings in and around the Big Apple...

Summer

Bryant Park ♯E8
Come here for free Cinema Paradiso-esque outdoor screenings of old movies.
Sixth Avenue, Midtown ☎ 983-4142 Ⓜ N•R•1•2•3•7•9 to 42nd St-Times Sq ◖ *every Monday, June–August*

Central Park Summerstage ♯F5–E6
Weekend afternoon concerts feature big name music acts such as Roy Ayres and James Brown. Spoken word and dance recitals on week nights – see listings mags for details.
Rumsey Field, mid-park ☎ 360-2777 Ⓜ 6 to 68th St-Hunter College; 6 to 77th St; 1•2•3•9 to 72nd St ◖ *June–August*

Guinness Fleadh ♯off map
A Celtic fun-fest weekend with rivers of the black stuff and Irish sounds.
East and Harlem Rivers, Randall's Island (bet. 96th & 106 Sts) ☎ 307-7171 Ⓜ M35 bus to Randall's Island ◖ *June*

Mermaid Day Parade ♯off map
King Neptune chomping on a hot dog while dozens of mermaids and other fairy-tale creatures cavort on the boardwalk at Coney Island make for a real off-beat experience.
From Steeplechase Park to Boardwalk (at 8th St), Coney Island ☎ 1-718-372-5159 Ⓜ B•D•F•N to Stillwell Ave-Coney Island ◖ *end June*

Shakespeare in the Park ♯F5–E6
Every season the Delacorte Theater in Central Park shows two plays: one by Shakespeare and one American classic.
Delacorte Theater, mid-Central Park ☎ 539-8500 Ⓜ 6 to 68th St-Hunter College; 6 to 77th St; 1•2•3•9 to 72nd St ◖ *late June–late August*

Washington Square Music Festival ♯B11
Continuing a long-running Greenwich Village tradition of a civilized night out, this festival provides chamber music for an appreciative audience.
Washington Square, West Village ☎ 431-1088 Ⓜ A•B•C•D•E•F•Q to W 4th St-Washington Sq ◖ *July–August*

Macy's Fourth of July Fireworks $off map
When 14,000 aerial shells and special effects explode over the East River. The hour-long extravaganza ends with a rousing rendition of 'The Star Spangled Banner'.
East River; for the best view get down to FDR Drive (bet. 14th & 51st Sts)
☎ 494-4495 Ⓜ L to 1st Ave; 4•5•6•7 to Grand Central-42nd St; 6 to 51st St
Ⓘ *Independence Day*

Lincoln Center Festival $E5
This festival's programme features theatre, classical music and opera, and dance companies such as Merce Cunningham's and the Stuttgart Ballet.
Lincoln Center, UWS ☎ 875-5127 Ⓜ 1•9 to 66th St-Lincoln Center Ⓘ *July*

Celebrate Brooklyn $off map
This free weekend concert series offers African Music, Soul, and silent movies with the score performed by a full live orchestra.
Prospect Park, Flatbush Avenue (at Grand Army Plaza), Brooklyn
☎ 1-718-855-7882 Ⓜ 2•3•4 to Grand Army Plaza Ⓘ *July–August*

Harlem Week $maps 1–2
The highlight of this uptown extravaganza is the street festival on Fifth Avenue between 125th and 135th Streets with live jazz, gospel and R&B.
Throughout Harlem ☎ 862-8477 Ⓜ 2•3 to 125th St; 2•3 135th St
Ⓘ *early–mid-August*

Autumn

US Open Tennis Tournament $off map
Pete Sampras, Stefi Graf, and Monica Seles have all strutted their stuff here, at one of the most demanding tennis tournaments on the world circuit.
USTA Tennis Center, Flushing, Queens ☎ 1-718-760-6200
Ⓜ 7 to Willets Point-Shea Stadium Ⓘ *end August–early September*

Feast of San Gennaro $C12–E12
Spicy Italian sausages, fairground games and pumping house music. Crowds flock from the outer boroughs for this raucous 10-day street party.
Mulberry Street, from Houston to Canal Streets, Nolita ☎ 764-6330
Ⓜ B•D•F•Q to Broadway-Lafayette St; 6 to Bleecker St; N•R to Prince St;
J•M•Z•6 to Canal St Ⓘ *mid-September*

Wigstock
♯E9

As the name implies, it's all about hair – and stilettos and frocks, with a salubrious stage show hosted by the reigning drag queen. See listings mags or call the Lesbian & Gay Center for details.

Pier 54, West Side Highway, West Village ☎ 620-7310 (Lesbian & Gay Center) Ⓜ 1•9 to Christopher St ◑ Labor Day weekend

West Indian-American Day Carnival
♯off map

Not on the scale of London's Notting Hill but excellent beef patties, jerk chicken, and many sound systems make for a carnival spirit nonetheless.

Eastern Parkway, Brooklyn ☎ 1-718-467-1797 Ⓜ 2•3 to Grand Army Plaza ◑ Labor Day

New York Film Festival
♯E5

A wide range of new films from established directors debut before a critical audience. Tickets sell out fast in this film-crazed community.

Alice Tully Hall, Lincoln Center, Columbus Avenue (bet. 62nd & 66th Sts), UWS ☎ 875-5610 Ⓜ 1•9 to 66th St-Lincoln Center ◑ end September–mid-October

Hispanic Day Parade
♯E8–C6

Thousands of flag-waving New Yorkers line Fifth Avenue to salute a parade of floats and dancers representing the Hispanic nations.

Fifth Avenue, from 44th to 72nd Streets, Midtown & UES ☎ 864-0715 Ⓜ B•D•F•Q to 47th-50th Sts-Rockefeller Center; any stops on 4•5•6 from 42nd St-Grand Central to 77th St ◑ early October

Columbus Day Parade
♯E8–C6

The official celebration of Columbus's so-called 'discovery' of America with an Italian-oriented show of floats and military marching bands.

Fifth Avenue, from 44th to 72nd Streets, Midtown & UES ☎ 249-9923 Ⓜ B•D•F•Q to 47th-50th Sts-Rockefeller Center; any stops on 4•5•6 from Grand Central-42nd St to 77th St ◑ early October

Rangers Ice Hockey Season
♯B9

NYC is big on local sports – the Rangers are home grown heroes and have a huge following.

Madison Square Garden (bet. W 33rd St & Seventh Ave), Midtown ☎ 465-6741 Ⓜ A•C•E•1•2•3•9 to 34th St-Penn Station ◑ October–April

Greenwich Village Halloween Parade *maps 11 & 9*

An orgy of freaks, ghouls and outlandish costumes. Gay New Yorkers guarantee a totally uninhibited, high-spirited affair.

Sixth Avenue, from Spring to 21st Streets ☎ 1-914-758-5519 Ⓜ C•E to Spring St; A•B•C•D•E• F•Q to W 4th St-Washington Sq; 1•9 to 18th St ◑ *31 October*

Winter

New York City Marathon *across town*

Combine cheering on the stragglers with a beautiful day in Central Park – or, if it's your thing, sign up! Best views are usually from within Central Park.

Verazzano Bridge on Staten Island (start); Tavern on the Green, W 67th St (finish) ☎ 860-4455 (for details of route) Ⓜ 1•2•3•9 to 72nd St (finish) ◑ *end October/early November*

'Knicks' Basketball Season *B9*

New Yorkers are a loyal bunch and despite the Knicks' patchy track record, diehard fans like Spike Lee and Woody Allen, who are at every home game, keep on cheering and hoping.

Madison Square Garden (bet. W 33rd St & Seventh Ave), Midtown ☎ 465-6741 Ⓜ A•C•E•1•2•3•9 to 34th St-Penn Station ◑ *November–April*

Macy's Thanksgiving Day Parade *C5–E5, B7–F7 & B9*

Balloons of suitably skyscraper proportions are inflated in Central Park the day before and paraded on Thanksgiving Day – this pre-turkey spectacular is unmissable.

From Central Park W (at 77th St), down Broadway and finishing at Herald Square ☎ 494-4495 Ⓜ 1•2•3•9 to 72nd St (start); B•D•F•N•Q•R to 34th St-Herald Sq (finish) ◑ *Thanksgiving Day*

Lighting the Rockefeller Center Christmas Tree *D7*

Traditional and kitschy with twinkling lights, Christmas carollers and throngs of shopping-bag-toting tourists.

47th to 50th Streets (at Sixth Ave), Midtown ☎ 632-3975 Ⓜ B•D•F•Q to 47th-50th Sts-Rockefeller Center ◑ *early December*

'Dropping the Ball' *F7*

You thought the subway at rush hour was crowded? A generally well-mannered crowd counts down to the New Year.

Times Square, Midtown ☎ 922-9393 Ⓜ N•R•1•2•3•7•9 to 42nd St-Times Sq ◑ *New Year's Eve*

Midnight Footrace in Central Park *♯C5*
A festive race around the park, and plenty of champagne when you make
it to the finishing line. Good healthy fun.
Tavern on the Green, Central Park ☎ 860-4455 Ⓜ 1•2•3•9 to 72nd St
◐ *New Year's Eve*

Altogether Different Dance Festival *♯D9*
Now in its 16th year, this festival features choreographers working in
novel directions.
Joyce Theater, 175 Eighth Avenue, Chelsea ☎ 242-0800 Ⓜ 1•9 to 18th St
◐ *January*

Tax Free Week! *♯across town*
No tax on all retail items twice a year – it certainly takes the sting out
of shopping.
☎ 788-3000 (mayor's office) ◐ *mid-January & September*

Martin Luther King Jr Day *♯maps 6 & 8*
A solemn tribute to Dr King, the parade also serves as a memorial to all
black soldiers who have fought for America.
**Fifth Avenue (bet. 60th & 68th Streets), UES ☎ 374-5176 Ⓜ 4•5•6 to 59th St
(start); 6 to 68th St-Hunter College (finish)** ◐ *late January*

Chinese New Year *♯maps 11–12*
Strict enforcement of the firecracker ban has dampened this manic
celebration, but dragons still dance around Chinatown.
Chinatown ☎ 373-1800 Ⓜ J•M•N•R•Z•6 to Canal St
◐ *February*

Spring

St Patrick's Day Parade *♯maps 6 & 8*
The city's Irish contingent turns out to parade (and drink) in celebration
of their cultural heritage: a rowdy day-out.
**Fifth Avenue, from 44th to 86th Streets, then east to Third Ave
☎ 1-718-357-7532 Ⓜ 7 to 5th Ave; any stop on Sixth Ave, from 51st to 86th
Streets** ◐ *17 March*

MoMA's New Directors/New Films Festival *♯C8*
This celluloid jamboree shows the works of film-makers who are about to
hit the big time.
**11 53rd Street (bet. Fifth & Sixth Aves), Midtown ☎ 708-9480
Ⓜ E•F to Fifth Ave** ◐ *March*

New York Underground Film Festival ♯*A12*
A young, downtown audience critiques over 120 new movies. Brit films have also been showcased since 1999.
Anthology Film Archives, Second Avenue (at 3rd St), LES ☎ 925-3440
Ⓜ F to 2nd Ave ◑ *March*

Easter Sunday Parade ♯*A8–C8*
Pet dogs dressed up as Easter bunnies, kiddies in bonnets, and eggs galore.
Fifth Avenue (bet. 49th & 57th Sts), Midtown ☎ 484-1222 Ⓜ B•D•F•Q to
47th-50th Sts-Rockefeller Center; E•F to 5th Ave ◑ *Easter Sunday*

Yankees & Mets Baseball Season ♯*off map*
Tickets are easy to come by, unlike basketball games. The Yankees are team winners and have a huge home following.
Mets: Shea Stadium, 126th St (at Roosevelt Ave), Queens ☎ 1-718-507-8499
Ⓜ 7 to Willets Point-Shea Stadium
Yankees: Yankee Stadium, 161st St & River Ave, Bronx ☎ 1-718-293-6000
Ⓜ C•D•4 to 161st St-Yankee Stadium ◑ *April–October*

Spring Festival ♯*off map*
Stalls selling home-baked goods rub shoulders with carnival games and bouncy castles, and sound systems get everyone dancing in the streets.
Broadway (bet. 110th & 118th Streets), Morningside Heights ☎ 764-6330
Ⓜ 1•9 to Cathedral Pkwy (110th St) ◑ *April*

Bike New York: The Great Five Boro Bike Tour ♯*off map*
The largest mass bike ride passes through Manhattan, the Bronx, Queens, Brooklyn, and Staten Island, covering 42 miles in a single day.
Battery Park (start); Staten Island (finish) ☎ 932-2453 (for details of route)
◑ *early May*

Memorial Day Parade ♯*maps 8 & 6*
Old soldiers are remembered by their comrades in arms. The city is eerily quiet when the minute of silence is observed.
Fifth Avenue, from 44th to 72nd Street ☎ 374-5176 Ⓜ B•D•F•Q to 47th-
50th Sts-Rockefeller Center; any stops on 4•5•6 from Grand Central-
42nd St to 77th St ◑ *end May*

sights, museums & galleries

Immigrants from all over the world have contributed to the palimpsest that is New York: a heritage exemplified by the city's mosaic of museums and cultural institutions.

landmarks

Brooklyn Bridge   *♭B14*
When this 1596-ft bridge (the first to employ steel-wire suspension) was unveiled in 1883, it was the world's longest. The Williamsburg Bridge beat it by 4ft 20 years later, but the walkway of one of New York's most visible landmarks still commands unrivalled views. Catch the Brooklyn Bridge live camera at **w** www.romdog.com/bridge/brooklyn.html
Lower Manhattan Ⓜ 4•5•6 to Brooklyn Bridge-City Hall; A•C to High St

Chrysler Building   *♭F8*
Unmistakable in the Midtown skyline, the 77-storey art deco skyscraper was built as a celebration of the motor car's rise to success in the 1930s. Exterior details are based on car motifs like the gargoyles modelled as hood ornaments; inside, Edward Trumball's ceiling mural glows above the red marble lobby.
405 Lexington Avenue, Midtown Ⓜ 4•5•6•7 to Grand Central-42nd St

City Hall   *♭B13*
A prime example of Federal architecture, this has been home to the mayor and seat of NYC government since 1812. It's also the traditional finishing point of tickertape parades along Broadway. The apple trees in the park opposite were used as gallows by the British before Independence.
City Hall Park, Lower Manhattan Ⓜ N•R to City Hall;
4•5•6 to Brooklyn Bridge-City Hall; 2•3 to Park Place

Flatiron Building   *♭C10*
NYC's first skyscraper, this building got its shape and name from its plot at the intersection of Broadway, Fifth Avenue, and 23rd Street. The site was a favourite with turn-of-the-century voyeurs as swirling drafts raised women's skirts: policemen who chased them away gave rise to the expression '23 skidoo'.
175 Fifth Avenue, Flatiron District Ⓜ N•R to 23rd St

The MetLife Building   *♭E8*
Built for Pan Am in 1963 by a team of architects which included Bauhaus founder Walter Gropius, and now owned by Metropolitan Life Insurance

Company, this may be the most hated building in the city. Not only does it block the Fifth Avenue view, but it glowers over Grand Central Station.
200 Park Avenue, Midtown Ⓜ **4•5•6•7 to Grand Central-42nd St**

Radio City Music Hall
⚲C8

Part of the Rockefeller Center, and resplendent in its art deco finery, cascading chandeliers (the world's largest) and sweeping staircases, Radio City defines the opulence of 1930's New York. As well as the resident Rockettes, acts as varied as Barry Manilow and Riverdance have shared the stage in its vast auditorium.
Sixth Avenue, Midtown Ⓜ **B•D•F•Q to 47th–50th Sts-Rockefeller Center**

Rockefeller Center
⚲C8

JD Rockefeller Jr, the benevolent billionaire, created many jobs during the Depression with the construction of this monument to business – a gift to his city. Mitsubishi is now the major shareholder of the complex, which boasts 19 buildings, 40 restaurants, and one of NYC's best seasonal ice rinks.
Sixth Avenue, Midtown Ⓜ **B•D•F•Q to 47th–50th Sts-Rockefeller Center**

St John the Divine
⚲A3

Though the building of this cathedral began in 1892, it is still unfinished to this day. If it is ever completed, this cathedral church will be the largest in the world (work in progress can be seen in the stoneyard). The annual October 'animal blessing' sees a parade of New Yorkers and their pets, in line for benediction.
Amsterdam Avenue (at 110th St), Harlem Ⓜ **B•C to Cathedral Pkwy**

St Patrick's Cathedral
⚲C8

Once set in rolling hills, the largest Roman Catholic church in the USA, and the seat of the archdiocese of New York, now resides in the shadows of Midtown's skyscrapers. The relief-figure on the central doors is Anne Seton – the first American-born saint.
Fifth Avenue (at 50th St), Midtown Ⓜ **E•F to 5th Ave**

Strawberry Fields & the Dakota Building
⚲D5

Tucked in Central Park, a leafy shrine commemorates the life of John Lennon who was killed outside his home in the Dakota building opposite. NYC's first luxury apartments (built in 1884) were so far from the city that 'society' named them Dakota after Indian territory in the Wild West.
Central Park West, UWS Ⓜ **1•2•3•9 to 72nd St**

Times Square
⚲F7

Once the heart of NY's Theater District, after the Depression this area declined and became the epitome of sleaze. Beneath the trademark neon

signs of this now spruced-up part of town, gawping out-of-towners shuffle by the fast-disappearing strip clubs. The place to be on New Year's Eve in the Big Apple.
Times Square, Midtown Ⓜ N•R•1•2•3•7•9 to Times Square-42nd St

Trump Tower ✂A8
Often called gauche, tacky and over-the-top, Donald Trump's erection stands tall; a tribute to the days when Dallas was considered chic. Above the atrium's shiny brass and pink marble five-storey waterfall are 20 floors of offices and ritzy apartments – most worth well over one million dollars.
725 Fifth Avenue, Midtown Ⓜ E•F to 5th Ave

UN Building ✂F8
Overlooking the East River, the three buildings (greatly influenced by Le Corbusier's design philosophy) that make up the United Nation's head-quarters are flanked by the flags of its 180-member nations. The site is actually an international zone and not part of US territory.
First Avenue, Midtown Ⓜ 4•5•6•7 to Grand Central-42nd St

Woolworth Building ✂B13
Until the sad demise of 'Woolies' in 1997, the 60-storey 'cathedral of commerce' was the headquarters of the five-and-dime store empire. A comical sculpture inside the building shows founder, Frank Woolworth counting the coins that made his fortune.
233 Broadway, Lower Manhattan Ⓜ 2•3 to Park Place

World Trade Center ✂D13
Some 50,000 workers occupy 12 million sq ft of office space in the five buildings of the World Trade Center. Its two stainless steel and glass towers, a quarter of a mile high, have transformed the Manhattan skyline. In 1993, six people died in a terrorist bombing that shook more than the foundations of the building.
West Street, Lower Manhattan Ⓜ C•E to World Trade Center;
1•9 to Cortlandt St

viewpoints

Brooklyn Heights Promenade ✂off map
Ⓜ 2•3 to Clark St; N•R to Court St

Empire State Building ✂A10
350 Fifth Avenue, Midtown ☎ 736-3100 💲 $6 ◑ 9.30am–midnight daily.
Ⓜ B•D•F•N•Q•R to 34th St-Herald Sq

Riverside Church Observatory ⚲off map
490 Riverside Drive, Morningside Heights ☎ 870-6700 💲$2
🌓 11am–4pm Tue–Sat; 12.30–4pm Sun. Ⓜ 1•9 to 116th St-Columbia Uni

Rooftop Sculpture Garden ⚲C8
Metropolitan Museum of Art, 1000 Fifth Avenue, Midtown ☎ 535-7710
💲 suggested $8 🌓 May–Nov: 10am–5.15pm Tue–Sun (to 8.30pm Fri &
Sat). Ⓜ E•F to 5th Ave

Roosevelt Island Tramway ⚲B8
Second Avenue & E 60th Street, UES ☎ 832-4543 💲 $1.50 🌓 6–2am
daily (to 3.30am Fri–Sat). Ⓜ 4•5•6 to 59th St

Staten Island Ferry ⚲E14
Battery Park ☎ 1-800-573-7469 💲 free 🌓 24 hrs daily.
Ⓜ 1•9 to Whitehall St

Subway ⚲off map
Ⓜ B•D•Q across the East River

World Trade Center Observation Deck ⚲D13
2 World Trade Center, West Street, Lower Manhattan ☎ 323-2340
💲 $8 🌓 9.30am–9.30pm daily (to 11.30pm Jul–Aug).
Ⓜ C•E to World Trade Center; 1•9 to Cortlandt St

The Rainbow Room ⚲C8
30 Rockefeller Plaza, W 50th Street, Midtown ☎ 632-5000
Ⓜ B•D•F•Q to 47th-50th Sts-Rockefeller Center

Top of the Tower ⚲D8
Beekman Tower, 3 Mitchell Place, Midtown ☎ 355-7300 Ⓜ 6 to 51st St

The View Lounge ⚲F8
Marriot Marquis, 1700 Broadway, Midtown ☎ 398-1900
Ⓜ N•R•S•1•2•3•7•9 to Times Square-42nd St

main attractions

☆ ELLIS ISLAND (MUSEUM OF IMMIGRATION) ⚲off map
Ellis Island stands as a testament to the millions of European immigrants
who dared to venture into the 'new world', forced from their homes because
of famine and political unrest. By 1892, the number of immigrants had
reached such a phenomenal level – one million a day at its peak – that a
huge complex was built on Ellis Island, comprising dormitories, a baggage

room, a registration room, and a hospital. Over the next 60 years, the station processed 17 million successful immigrants, mainly from Ireland, Germany, southern Italy, and the old Russian empire.

Some people say that recent renovations have resulted in an overly sanitized atmosphere. But seeing the personal testimonies, belongings, and photographs, and hearing voice-recordings of some immigrants, you can go some way to imagining their anguish and hope. It is even more poignant if you remember that just under half of all US citizens have ancestors who were registered at Ellis Island. The highlight is the beautiful Registry Hall, where each new arrival waited anxiously for medical and legal processing. The corny 30-min documentary film *Island of Hope, Island of Tears* (shown continuously in two theatres) offers some fascinating insights. ☎ 363-3200; 269-5755 (ferry information) ⑤ $7 ◑ *8.30am–3.45pm, every 30 min, daily (may change in winter)*. Ⓜ 4•5 to Bowling Green; 1•9 to South Ferry

☆ STATUE OF LIBERTY ♪*off map*

So thoroughly has Lady Liberty come to symbolize America and the values upheld by the American Constitution that it is easy to forget her European origins. A gift from the French people in 1886, the 151-ft-high statue was designed by sculptor Frédéric Auguste Bartholdi, together with Gustave Eiffel. The latter was the brain behind designing Liberty's flexible 'skeleton', which allows the statue some give during high winds. The separately designed pedestal – a formidable structure in its own right at 89 ft – now houses the museum and elevator (taking visitors as high as Liberty's feet). The climb to the top of the crown (the narrow, steep route up the torch is now prohibited for safety reasons) is the equivalent of a 22-storey trek, and is not for those who are claustrophobic or prone to vertigo.

In her right hand Liberty carries a burning torch, metaphorically lighting the way for millions of immigrants whose first sight of America was her awesome silhouette. The tablet in her left hand is inscribed with the date of Independence Day, 4 July 1776, and the broken shackles at her feet represent the end of slavery and escape from tyranny. To modern visitors, her comparatively diminutive size (now that she is dominated by the sky-scrapers of Manhattan) may well be a little disappointing.

Liberty Island ☎ 363-3200; 269-5755 (ferry information) ⑤ $7 ◑ *9.30am–3.15pm, every 30min, daily (may change in winter)*. Ⓜ 4•5 to Bowling Green; 1•9 to South Ferry

☆ EMPIRE STATE BUILDING ♪*A10*

Probably the best-known stack of bricks, cement and glass in New York. Aside from being the city's second highest building at 1450 ft, the Empire State holds a special place in the heart of New York: it was the secret meeting spot for a highly romantic rendezvous in *An Affair to Remember*,

Spiderman used to climb it at the beginning of every episode, and King Kong hung from the point at the top. Spectacular panoramic views – as far as 80 miles on a clear day – can be seen from two observatories: an outdoor one on the 86th floor and an enclosed glass one on the 102nd floor. There are no extra gimmicks, frills or thrills, though if that's what you crave, the Skyride on the 2nd floor simulates a flight over the city.

350 Fifth Avenue, Midtown ☎ 736-3100 ⬚ $11.50 ◑ 9.30am–midnight daily. Ⓜ B•D•F•N•Q•R to 34th St-Herald Sq; 6 to 33rd St

☆ GRAND CENTRAL STATION ⏴E8

Even New Yorkers are blown away by the transformation of Grand Central Station (officially Grand Central Terminal) following its recent facelift. The marble interior is now so clean it's almost translucent. Huge, sparkling chandeliers and 2500 lights – representing the constellations of a winter sky and set in the vaulted ceiling – light the main concourse. The vast wall of windows, recognizable from so many of Hollywood's best black-and-whites, lets the sun stream into the main hall in dusty shafts of light, illuminating the clock in the centre of the hall – *the* place to meet. Original brass fixtures and wrought-iron ticket-booth window grates have been put back in place with the same attention to detail that has gone into the whole restoration process. The downside with the renovation is that parts of the station have been transformed into a shopping mall.

For the authentic Grand Central encounter, however, descend through the confusing maze of tunnels to the lower concourse. Down here, directly outside the Oyster Bar, the 'Whispering Gallery' phenomenon takes effect – acoustics are so fine-tuned that murmured secrets don't stay secret for long.

E 42nd Street, Midtown ☎ 340-2583 ⬚ free ◑ 5.30–1.30am daily. Ⓜ 4•5•6•7 to Grand Central-42nd St

☆ AMERICAN MUSEUM OF NATURAL HISTORY ⏴D5

Visitors here are greeted by a soaring skeletal tableau of a three-storey-high Barosaurus protecting its frightened young from the attack of a ferocious Allosaurus. If any of this makes sense to you, then you will probably want to head up to the top floor for more prehistoric skeletons, from mammoth and sabre-toothed tiger to the Mike Tyson of the dinosaur world, the flesh-devouring Tyrannosaurus Rex. This is undeniably one of the top museums in the world; the American Museum of Natural History (abbreviated to the barely pronounceable AMNH) has been working on its presentation since 1869, and it's time that has been well spent. With a mission to study all of mankind, civilizations around the globe and the complete history of the earth – oh, and the celestial universe as well – it will come as no surprise that the museum's five sprawling floors are crammed with one fantastic, in-your-face display after another. That said, it does have its more serene corners, such as the dark but quietly dazzling Hall of Minerals, which glitters with polished rocks and crystals. A super-big-screen IMAX theatre is on the first floor, with hourly screenings of nature films all day, and 3D laser shows accompanied by rock music on Friday and Saturday nights. Even the Ocean Life Café in the basement is set amidst stuffed walruses and seals, with a 100-ft model of a blue whale suspended overhead. Just in time to welcome the new millennium, the AMNH recently unveiled the Rose Center for Earth and Space. This state-of-the-art centre, a museum in its own right, houses interactive permanent exhibits and presents absorbing space shows in a revamped Hayden Planetarium that looks like a giant dinosaur's egg trapped in a steel and glass scaffold. Lasers and sound effects speed you on your galactic journey or you can amble along the Heilbrunn Cosmic Pathway to get to grips with different orders of scale in the universe.

Central Park W, UWS ☎ 769-5000 ⊠ **$10 suggested donation; $19 combination ticket (Museum, Rose Center, Hayden Planetarium Space Show)** ◗ *10am–5.45pm daily (to 8.45pm Fri–Sat).* Ⓜ **B•C to 81st St-Museum of Natural History**

historic houses

Cooper-Hewitt, National Design Museum   ♯E4

This museum – the only one in the US devoted entirely to design – is housed within the dark, wood-panelled walls, of a mansion that was built for the super-rich and highly philanthropic steel magnate Andrew Carnegie. The opulent atmosphere provides a strange background to some of the more adventurous short-term exhibitions, such as the one of Latino culture in Los Angeles, but such juxtapositions are all part of this museum's attraction. The focus of other temporary exhibitions have ranged from Huguenot silverware to the classically modern furniture of Charles and Ray Eames. Every three years, the Cooper-Hewitt hosts the National Design Triennial, which lasts for four months and offers an overview of the issues and ideas animating design in the States. The museum's collection of over 250,000 items – including one-off and mass-produced prints, textiles and furniture – is available for personal study, but only by prior appointment.

2 E 91st Street, UES ☎ 849-8400 ⊠ **$8** ◗ *10am–5pm Tue–Sat (to 9pm Tue); 12–5pm Sun.* Ⓜ **4•5•6 to 86th St**

☆ FRICK COLLECTION   ♯E6`

If the Cooper-Hewitt has whet your appetite for leisurely strolls through echoing halls and sumptuous rooms, then head for the Frick Collection on Fifth Avenue. This mansion was the home of a steel industrialist of a more acquisitive kind, Henry Clay Frick. In the few years he spent here before his death in 1919, he covered the walls with European art, carpeted the floors in oriental rugs, and adorned the 18th-century French furniture with porcelain and other fanciful *objets d'art* to indulge his decorative whims. Today, the Frick is perhaps the most elegant small museum in the country. It features some 20 rooms filled with about 175 paintings by masters ranging from Gainsborough to Vermeer and El Greco, plus a music room for concerts and a new basement gallery for temporary exhibitions. The acutely observant may notice traces of similarity between this mansion and the NY Public Library, for the two buildings share a common architect – Thomas Hastings. His design for the indoor courtyard provides a light and serene haven in the midst of the city.

1 E 70th Street, UES ☎ 288-0700 🔄 $7 🕐 *10am–6pm Tue–Sun (from 1pm Sun)*. 🚇 4•5•6 to 68th St-Hunter College

Lower East Side Tenement Museum
♯D12

Tenement blocks are integral to the character and history of New York. These were the buildings that were thrown up all across town in the 19th century to house the swelling tides of immigrants landing upon the eastern shore of America. Often built without plumbing or running water, such expeditious and economical construction was necessary to meet the demands of this expanding city-port. The tenement at No. 97 Orchard Street was built in 1864, and its useful life was just 70 years – the building being sealed due to its unsafe condition in 1935. During its short lifespan, however, it was home to an estimated 10,000 people from 20 countries. The building stood idle for 52 years until 1987, when, with the process of gentrification transforming many of the former poor, run down and slum neighbourhoods, this tenement was selected to become a testament to the urban poor who built the multi-ethnic, tough-talking character of New York that the city still trades on today. The Tenement Museum preserves three apartments as they once were – homes to German, Italian and Lithuanian families – complete with furnishings and personal effects. The museum can be visited only by joining one of the guided tours, including a more lighthearted tour (designed for kids) where the guide plays the part of an Italian matron of 1916, welcoming relatives to the new country, while dispensing advice and admonitions in equal measure to her young charges.

90 Orchard Street, LES ☎ 431-0233 🔄 $8 🕐 *12–5pm Tue–Sun (to 11am Sat–Sun)*. 🚇 F•J•M•Z to Delancey St-Essex St; B•D•Q to Grand St.

Morris-Jumel Mansion Museum
♯off map

Said to be the oldest existing house in New York, this classical mansion's white façade now looks a little frayed, though still remains an amazing landmark. This lavishly-proportioned summer villa, built in 1765 for one Lt Col Roger Morris, stands on the island's northeast corner in a neighbourhood that has clearly seen better days. George Washington lived here during the Revolutionary War while he drew up battle plans, but the house's most infamous resident was Madame Eliza Jumel, a scandalous and wealthy widow who resided here in the 1830's (a former prostitute, apparently she allowed her rich husband to bleed to death so she could inherit his fortune). The mansion opened as a museum in 1907, and to this day you can admire the interior decor which includes period wallpaper, stained-glass roundels and many items from the time of Eliza's occupation including her mesmerizing obituary, which details her raucous life.

65 Jumel Terrace, Harlem ☎ 923-8008 💲 $3 🌓 10am–4pm Wed–Sun. Ⓜ C to 163rd St-Amsterdam Ave

Morgan Library
♭A10

This gorgeous 1902 library houses one of the finest collections of manuscripts in the world. It was built as a library and study for the financier and avid manuscript collector, JP Morgan, whose son (JP Morgan Jr) bequeathed the building and its collection to the city in 1924. Temporary exhibits change regularly: you might get a glimpse at such delights as Mozart's multicoloured music script for a horn concerto, John Tenniel's illustrations for Lewis Carroll's *Alice*, or recent acquisitions from 20th century literature (in December, an original of Dicken's *Christmas Carol* is always on show). After you've taken in the current displays in the annexed exhibition space, explore the two sumptuous rooms of the actual library and study, lavishly decorated with Italian motifs and heavy with furniture and paintings. But if the wealth of edifying visual material makes you a little weary, there is a light and airy courtyard café in which to take a breather and boost your reserves. The museum's shop has a particularly lovely selection of books and gifts.

29 E 36th Street, Midtown ☎ 685-0610 💲 $7 🌓 10.30am–5pm Tue–Sat (to 8pm Fri; 6pm Sat); 12–6pm Sun. Ⓜ 6 to 33rd St

one-offs

American Craft Museum
♭C8

The applied arts at their most exotic and imaginative are found in this museum. It has done pioneering work as a centre and clearinghouse for information on traditional crafts, and gone further to explore that strange twilight world between craft and art. There are ceramics of every shape and size, blown and cast glass, contemporary fibre art and quirky quilts, bizarre furniture, stained glass, a glittering array of jewellery and much more besides. Located in ground-level galleries in Deutsche Bank's high-rise headquarters, the museum has something of a showroom ambience, filled as it is with fancy home furnishings. But the exhibitions are consistently entrancing: In addition to theme exhibitions, which often cover historical material (art nouveau porcelain, for instance), the museum also mounts retrospective surveys of work by the leading lights of contemporary crafts. Like so many American museums in this era of dwindling government support, the museum shop fills the lobby and offers sleek high-end wares from artisans.

20 W 53rd Street, Midtown ☎ 956-3535 🎟 $5 ◑ 10am–6pm Tue–Sun (to 8pm Thu). 🚇 E•F to 5th Ave

☆ THE CLOISTERS   *off map*

If you make only one trip to a museum beyond Museum Mile make this the one. Located at the northern tip of Manhattan in Fort Tryon Park, The Cloisters is the branch of the Metropolitan Museum devoted to the art and architecture of medieval Europe. Not only is the museum itself an absolute treasure-trove of delights, but the location – within a wild and rocky 56-acre preserve – will show you an entirely different side to New York from the adrenalin-fired life of Downtown. The Cloisters is a 20th-century recreation of a medieval monastic complex that incorporates genuine architectural features pillaged from Europe, such as the secluded central cloister with its 12th-century Romanesque arcade. In fact, the whole building is a wonderful hodge-podge of sections taken from five Romanesque and Gothic cloisters that originated in France. This fabulous place was the brainchild of John D Rockefeller, who not only donated much of the money to buy the buildings in 1925, but provided the land, an endowment and the bulk of the collection, which numbers about 4000 items. There are incredible examples of polychrome sculpture, stained glass, Spanish lustreware and carved oak furniture, as well as a handful of pieces that deserve special mention: the *Belles Heures de Jean, Duc de Berry* (a staggeringly intricate and beautiful illuminated manuscript); Robert Campin's small but perfectly formed Merode Altarpiece (*Triptych of the Annunciation*); and the freshly conserved and presented *Unicorn Tapestries* from Brussels, made around 1500 AD. The Bonnefont and Trie cloisters enclose gardens containing hundreds of plants and herbs used in the Middle Ages, either medicinally or for culinary purposes. The shop offers up a pretty good selection of reproduction jewellery and other medieval-style keepsakes, as well as tapes and CDs of monks humming their ecclesiastical medleys – very relaxing.

Fort Tryon Park, Inwood ☎ 923-3700 🎟 $8 ◑ Mar–Oct: 9.30am–5.15pm Tue–Sun (Nov–Feb: to 4.45pm). 🚇 A to 190th St, then M4 bus

Jewish Museum   *E4*

It seems only appropriate that the biggest collection of Jewish artifacts outside Israel can be found in New York. In spite of a wealth of Jewish history to draw upon – 4000 years to be precise – the Jewish Museum has always been something of an avant-garde pioneer, staging exhibitions that explore the twin strands of minimal and conceptual art. Its curators consistently hazard shows on such controversial subjects as the Arab-Israeli conflict, as well as mounting retrospectives of crowd-pleasers such as Mark Chagall, Camille Pissarro and Chaim Soutine on two of the museum's four magnificent floors. In the remaining space is the permanent collection, where you can see Canaanite cult idols from 800 BC (the kind of things that got Moses' flock into such trouble), slingshot ammo (clay balls capable of slaying a Goliath) and one of the earliest surviving tax records on a 4th-century Babylonian cuneiform tablet – as now, so then, death and taxes are life's only certainties.

1105 Fifth Avenue), UES ☎ 423-3200 ⊠ $8 ◑ 11am–5.45pm Sun–Thu (to 8pm Tue). ▥ 4•5•6 to 96th St

El Museo del Barrio ⌀C4

El Museo has become the place to see frequently vibrant and life-affirming exhibitions chronicling the art that stems, either geographically or socio-politically, from the Caribbean and Latin America. It was founded in 1969 by a Puerto Rican community group as a cultural focus for East Harlem's Spanish-speaking 'el barrio', a low-rent neighbourhood that is still home to immigrants and the descendants of immigrants from Latin America and the Caribbean (particularly Puerto Rico). Some of the exhibitions explore and document the folklore and history of the Latin American peoples, but much is contemporary and tackles varied and universal issues. The museum's temporary shows are always worth a look, and recently gallery space has been given over to investigations of Afro-Caribbean Sacred Spaces and the perennial Search for Miracles. The small gift shop specializes in unusual examples of folk art, supplied locally or imported from Mexico and South America.

1230 Fifth Avenue, Spanish Harlem ☎ 831-7272 ⊠ $4 (suggested donation) ◑ 11am–5pm Wed–Sun (Jun–Sep: to 8pm Thu). ▥ 6 to 103rd St

National Museum of the American Indian ⌀F13

At the southern end of Manhattan Island, between the green tip of Battery Park and a bronze statue of a charging bull, is the Alexander Hamilton US Customs House. Built in 1890 on the site of the colonial-era Fort Amsterdam, the Customs House is a marvel of limestone and multi-coloured marble, its façade ornamented with a dozen faux Corinthian columns and four massive allegorical figure groups representing the continents. This astonishing beaux-arts structure is home to one of New York's newest museums (opened in 1994), the George Gustav Heye Center of the National Museum of the American Indian (to give it its full, illustrious title). The museum presents its wares within a rigorously educational context, complete with touch-screen video stations, dioramas and installations. Though such window-dressing is often unnecessary (and even tacky) the incredible beauty of the artefacts shines through regardless. Huron moccasins decorated with moose hair and porcupine quills, a 19th-century ledger with drawings of Lakota chiefs on horseback by Red Dog – all such items can be found in the museum's two permanent installations; All Roads Are Good: Native Voices on Life, and Culture and Creation's Journey: Masterworks of Native American Identity and Belief. Temporary exhibitions often showcase contemporary art by Native Americans living in the US as well as the traditional art and artefacts of indians from around the world. The museum shop has a wealth of books, jewellery, textiles and crafts for sale, while another is devoted to things for kids. **US Custom House, 1 Bowling Green, Lower Manhattan ☎ 514-3700 ⊠ free ◐ 10am–5pm daily. Ⓜ 1•9 to South Ferry; N•R to Whitehall St**

New-York Historical Society
$B5

Where else but in the strange world of the New-York Historical Society could you find three centuries of New York restaurant menus, some of George Washington's hair, and more Tiffany lamps than you could shake a stick at. Founded in 1804, the society – complete with the archaic hyphen in New-York – is often referred to as the city's attic, a description that suggests a musty storehouse filled with junk that no one in the family really wants. To be fair, although the Historical Society was hit by scandalous revelations in the early 1990s over mismanagement and neglect, its multifarious acquisitions could never be described as junk. Now brought back from the brink of fiscal disaster, the museum has become widely recognized as a source of artefacts in which resides the physical presence of New York (and US) history. Not only does it hold the nation's largest collection of Tiffany lamps (113 in all) and the 431 original watercolours for Audubon's Birds of America, but it is also home to the five-part series *The Course of Empire* painted by Thomas Cole, founder of the Hudson River School, and has more than 500,000 19th- and 20th-century American photographs. The society stages temporary exhibitions as well as its permanent collection on subjects such as how Manhattan was bought from the indigenous population for a mere $24 and a handful of beads. **2 W 77th Street, UWS ☎ 873-3400 ⊠ $5 ◐ 11am–5pm Tue–Sun. Ⓜ B•C to 81st St**

New York Public Library
$E8

The lions 'Patience' and 'Fortitude' sit majestically either side of the white marble-columned entrance to this stunning beaux-arts building, and the steps outside are a popular meeting place and impromptu picnic spot for both visitors and locals. Its cool rooms and ice-cold marble floors are reason enough to visit in summer, and the hushed tones throughout the building are incredibly soothing. The public reading room is a must-see, its beautiful ceiling restored to reveal a vibrantly painted blue sky with scudding clouds;

the bronze reading lamps and rows of polished tables are in immaculate condition. Around twelve million manuscripts, three million pictures, and six million books, as well as some real literary treasures are housed here. Among them are original manuscripts of TS Eliot's *The Wasteland*, Virginia Woolf's diaries, Charlotte Brontë's writing desk, and the original stuffed animals on which AA Milne based his *Winnie the Pooh* stories. The frequent, free exhibitions in the library's long corridors are always excellently re-searched if a little understated. Imaginative and varied exhibitions are held in the Gottesman Hall.

Fifth Avenue (at 42nd St), Midtown ☎ 930-0800 ⚅ free ◗ *11am–7.30pm Tue–Wed; 10am–6pm Thu–Sat.* Ⓜ B•D•F•Q to 42nd St

art museums/galleries

Brooklyn Museum of Art   ⌀off map
This is a browser's pleasure palace – the delightful epitome of a provincial museum, that brings together a miscellany of exhibits from Rodin sculptures to full-scale Dutch farmhouses of the 18th century. It was founded approximately 175 years ago as the Brooklyn Museum, and only recently added the 'of Art' to its name. The museum's encyclopedic collection, spread through a spacious five-storey building, includes assemblages of both African and Egyptian art that have few matches in the US. The first floor has a gallery dedicated to temporary shows, and a small space for contemporary art, often devoted to showing work by members of Brooklyn's burgeoning artist population. Asian art is on two – look for an elegant Chinese wine jar with a cobalt blue design of fish and waterplants on white ceramic from the Yuan dynasty – while Egyptology takes up a fair slice of the third floor. The Dutch farmhouses are on the fourth floor, which gives some indication of the size of the museum, nestled alongside 28 period rooms – Brooklyn was the first museum to present this kind of exhibit. Among the American and Euro-pean paintings on the fifth floor is a selection of 58 works by Rodin. On the first Saturday of each month, the museum organizes a series of events topped by a live dance band in the main lobby.

200 Eastern Parkway, Brooklyn ☎ 1-718-638-5000 ⚅ free ◗ *10am–5pm Wed–Fri; 11am–6pm Sat–Sun.* Ⓜ 2•3 to Eastern Parkway-Brooklyn Museum

Dia Center for the Arts   ⌀C9
Located since 1987 in a 40,000-sq-ft warehouse in Chelsea, Dia specializes in lavish, long-term exhibitions of works by contemporary artists from around the world, ranging from Francesco Clemente and Alighiero e Boetti to Jenny Holzer, Andy Warhol, and Richard Serra. Launched in the 1970s, Dia was part of a visionary scheme to provide long-term or permanent installations of major works by a select handful of primarily

Minimalist and Conceptual artists. One work by Dan Graham and two by Walter de Maria are still maintained in New York. One of Graham's trademark glass pavilions is permanently sited on the roof and is a good spot to watch the sun set over the Hudson. The Walter de Maria pieces are over in Soho and are worth a special visit: the New York Earth Room takes up a floor of a loft at 141 Wooster Street, where soil 2 ft deep has been spread throughout the gallery; viewers stand behind a perspex sheet which holds back the earth, taking in the dank smell and pointing out the occasional sprouting of grass. The second work, the Broken Kilometer at 393 West Broadway, is composed of 1066 yards of solid brass rod, divided into 500 upended lengths arranged in a formation that subtly plays with your sense of perspective.

548 W 22nd Street, Chelsea ☎ 989-5566 ⚿ $6 ◑ *16 Sep–18 Jun: 12–6pm Wed–Sun*. Ⓜ C•E to 23rd St

Guggenheim Museum Soho ♭D12
Far from Fifth Avenue's museum mile is the downtown Guggenheim – established in 1992 on the first two floors of a cavernous brick loft building on Broadway. The museum makes good use of the extensive Guggenheim collection: the temporary exhibitions tend to flit between the historical and the contemporary, and it may be that this lack of a clear agenda has contributed to the gallery's rumoured financial problems. This aside, the curators always have some interesting, and occasionally irreverent ideas up their sleeves, and the separate museum store is one of the coolest in town. Who could resist a Guggenheim snow-shaker?

575 Broadway, Soho ☎ 423-3500 ⚿ $8 ◑ *11am–6pm Wed–Sun (to 8pm Sat)*. Ⓜ N•R to Prince St; B•D•F•Q to Broadway-Lafayette St

International Center of Photography ♭E4
New York's only museum dedicated solely to photography was created in 1974 by photojournalist Cornell Capa, brother of the late war photographer Robert, and shows work with a journalistic slant. The exhibitions draw on the ICP's extensive archive and include a recent Robert Capa retrospective as well as other displays of the masters of this fascinating art form. The museum's headquarters are located Uptown on Museum Mile, where there are two floors of intimate gallery space within an imposing early 20th-century brick building. A second two-storey facility, grey-carpeted in corporate style, is located a block away from Times Square. The shop is a great resource for photo books.

1130 Fifth Avenue, UES ☎ 860-1777 ⚿ $6 ◑ *10am–5pm Tue–Sun (to 8pm Fri; 6pm Sat–Sun)*. Ⓜ 6 to 96th St-Lexington Ave
1133 Sixth Avenue, Midtown ☎ 768-4682 ⚿ $6 ◑ *10am–5pm Tue–Sun (to 8pm Fri; 6pm Sat–Sun)*. Ⓜ B•D•F•Q to 42nd St

Isamu Noguchi Garden Museum *off map*

The minimalism of high modernism meets the traditions of Zen Buddhism in this stylish, asymmetrical museum, designed by the Japanese–American sculptor Isamu Noguchi (1904–1988) and dedicated in 1985. This is one of the most serene spaces in all of the city, and it houses more than 250 of his works, spread throughout 13 galleries. Noguchi made a virtue of creating simple abstract forms that became part of the everyday environment – sculptures in stone and metal, models for public art projects, playground sculptures, and dance sets (including 20 sets for Martha Graham). The museum includes one of the artist's small, meditative gardens (closed during winter months), with weeping cherry trees, bamboo, juniper, and ivy, as well as major granite and basalt sculptures. One of the large cubes also functions as a fountain that gently bubbles its water supply. The museum shop offers a complete line of Noguchi's Akari lamps – light-sculptures inspired by classical Japanese lanterns of bamboo and pleated paper. A programme of films on Noguchi's life and work runs continuously

32–37 Vernon Boulevard, Long Island City, Queens ☎ 1-718-721-1932 ⌥ $4 (suggested donation only) ◑ 10am–5pm Wed–Fri; 11am–6pm Sat–Sun. Ⓜ N to Broadway (Queens)

☆ METROPOLITAN MUSEUM OF ART *A6*

The Met is New York's cultural behemoth. Its list of galleries and departments reads like the artistic equivalent of a Roman banquet: Assyrian sculpture, the classical art of the Greek empire, galleries packed with African, Asian and Islamic treasures, Roman sculpture, a pre-Columbian gold treasury, early Flemish and Netherlandish paintings, a succession of 19th- and 20th-century galleries and much, much more besides. Museums simply don't get any better than this, and each of the 22 curatorial departments has its own stunning highlight, whether it be the polished steel of arms and armour or the dandyish delights of Tiffany and La Farge (the latter displayed in a lovely garden setting). The Temple of Dendur stands in timeless repose on its own plinth in the Egyptian wing and, in the summertime, the huge rooftop garden provides its own attraction as a place to drink coffee, view a changing selection of sculpture and breathe in the spectacular treetop views over Central Park.

1000 Fifth Avenue, UES ☎ 570-3951 ⌥ $8 suggested donation ◑ 9.30am–5.30pm Tue–Sun (to 9pm Fri–Sat). Ⓜ 4•5•6 to 86th St

Museum for African Art *D11*

This relatively young museum, founded in an Upper East Side townhouse in 1984 and moved to Soho in 1992, occupies two cozy floors of galleries designed by Maya Lin, whose previous work includes the National Vietnam Veterans Memorial in Washington, DC. Until recently the museum has specialized in exhibitions of classical African art, whether focusing on

sights, museums & galleries

surveys of artefacts made by individual peoples, or the broader-based holdings of collectors. However, it is now widening its remit into contemporary African social and political issues. This is borne out in shows, which cover broad-ranging subjects such as political machinations of the Congo in the post-colonial era, the art emerging from South Africa since the end of apartheid and a serious look at style through the Language of Hair in African Art and Culture. A regular series of gallery talks and discussions contributes to the sense of analysis and debate. As well as a fair selection of books on African art, the museum shop, which occupies the lobby area, also sells jewellery, textiles, crafts and even furniture.

593 Broadway, Soho ☎ 966-1313 ⬚ $5 ◑ *10.30am–5.30pm Tue–Fri; 12–6pm Sat–Sun.* Ⓜ N•R to Prince St; B•D•F•Q to Broadway-Lafayette St

Museum of American Folk Art
♭E5

'We all have little obsessive concerns,' wrote Robert Penn Warren in an essay about folk art, the umbrella term for the imaginative and heartfelt artefacts and crafts produced by untutored, often rural people as a part of their everyday lives. The permanent collection includes religious art, quilts, painted trays and boxes, weathervanes, dolls and devotional figures, and paintings – a small, jewel-like selection is always on show in a special gallery. Though the facility has something of the feel of a commercial mall, its three galleries devoted to two temporary exhibitions do justice to the fascinating works of art.

2 Lincoln Square, Columbus Avenue, UES ☎ 595-9533 ⬚ $3 (suggested donation) ◑ *11.30am–7.30pm Tue–Sun.* Ⓜ 1•9 to 66th St-Lincoln Center

☆ MUSEUM OF MODERN ART (MoMA)
♭C8

The pre-eminent modern art museum in the US, if not the world, MoMA has more than 100,000 art works in its permanent collection, with only about 12% on view at any one time. This is the holy writ of modernism told the American way. Through its holdings, MoMA presents a resolutely triumphalist view of the progress of modern art, beginning in France with the Impressionists and Post-Impressionists, and opening a new chapter with Picasso, before making the giant leap across the Atlantic to Pollock, Rothko, Newman and Reinhardt. Special exhibitions of painting, sculpture, prints, drawings, photography and architecture regularly rewrite art history – or at least scribble a few important notes in the margin. High up in the fourth floor's atrium a dangling helicopter lets you know you've hit the design department. The bright enclave of the sculpture garden exemplifies the aesthetic links between the pleasures of classicism and modernism, whilst also providing a fine location for refreshments in the summertime. In the basement the museum has a movie theatre with an extensive alternative film programme, which is great if you want a rest.

11 W 53rd Street, Midtown ☎ 708-9400 ⬣ $9.50 ◑ 10.30am–5.45pm *Thu–Tue (to 8.15pm Fri).* Ⓜ E•F to Fifth Ave

New Museum of Contemporary Art ♪D11

With its recently renovated, three-storey facility and new director – former Whitney curator Lisa Phillips – the New Museum is poised to take on the art of the new millennium. The museum doesn't have a permanent collection, but can be counted on each year for a dozen or so challenging temporary exhibitions of new art from around the globe. Much of it is likely to be political, community-based and funky, as it endeavours to catch the best artists of our times on the way up. Previous exhibitions have showcased Jeff Koons and Christian Boltanski.

583 Broadway, Nolita ☎ 219-1222 ⬣ $6 ◑ 12–6pm Wed–Sun (to 8pm *Thu–Sat).* Ⓜ 6 to Spring St or Bleecker St; N•R to Prince St; B•D•F•Q to Broadway-Lafayette St

PS1 Museum of Contemporary Art ♪off map

This unique New York art institution captures the lively spirit of contemporary art. A ramshackle, four-storey, red-brick school that was converted into an art centre over 20 years ago, PS1 combines exhibition galleries with artists' studios. In 1998, with the help of an $8 million grant from the city, the museum got a new brutalist courtyard designed by architect Frederick Fischer, and spruced up its galleries considerably, though it still has a refreshing informality. What makes the place seem particularly energetic are the long-term special projects by artists all around the building, from the Robert Ryman painting bolted to the wall next to the furnace in the basement, to the picnic table on the roof decorated by Julian Schnabel (where you can also take in a dramatic view of the Manhattan skyline and the Queensboro Bridge). There's a tiny, sexy video by Pipilotti Rist embedded in the hallway floor and a perplexing neon sculpture installed by Keith Sonnier in the airshaft above the foyer. All this is in addition to the major temporary exhibitions and the artists-in-residence programme that opens up the studios for public inspections once in a while.

22–25 Jackson Avenue, Long Island City, Queens ☎ 1-718-784-2084 ⬣ $5 (suggested donation) ◑ 12–6pm Wed–Sun. Ⓜ E•F 23rd St (Ely Ave)

Schomburg Center for Research in Black Culture ♪B1

This lodestone of African American learning is the biggest resource of its kind in America. Home to a massive collection of books, artworks, artifacts and documents (5 million at the last count), the Schomburg is actually a branch of the New York Public Library and as such it continues to elucidate and inform. The centre was named after the Puerto Rican-born black scholar and bibliophile, Arturo Alfonso Schomburg, who was once told there was no such thing as black history and decided to prove otherwise. He added his personal collection to the library's Division of Negro Literature, History and Prints in 1926 and served as the collection's curator from 1932 until his death in 1938, and in 1940 it was renamed in Schomburg's honour. The collection includes publications in over 200 indigenous African and Creole languages and dialects, and more than 300,000 photographs and prints, documenting the history and culture of peoples of African descent worldwide. Schomburg's red-brick, modernist facility, located in the heart of Harlem, is also home to a lively community centre with two exhibition spaces and a theatre – there's always something going on, whether it be concerts, jazz performances or readings. There are several New York-oriented exhibition mounted in the library each year.

515 Lenox Avenue, Harlem ☎ **491-2200** ⚏ **free** ◑ **12–8pm Mon–Wed; 10am–6pm Thu–Sat; 1–5pm Sun.** Ⓜ **2•3 to 135th St**

☆ SOLOMON R GUGGENHEIM MUSEUM ♫A6

Though never quite as sharp or pristine as it appears in photographs, the spiralling rotunda of Frank Lloyd Wright's final work, the Guggenheim Museum, is one of the great architectural achievements of the 20th century; fortunately, the collection of modern and contemporary art housed here is equal to its home. Works from the permanent collection (Chagall, Picasso, Brancusi, Kandinsky, and Gauguin are all represented), are mostly hung in the tower, which was added to the back of the building in the 1990s. There's a small selection of impressionist, post-impressionist and early modernist works in the small rotunda. The rotunda is the counterbalance to the main spiral, which is the focus for all temporary exhibitions. There are two ways to view the temporary shows – by a spiralling ascent on foot or heading straight to the elevator and making your way down this cultural helter-skelter (less tiring!); whichever you choose, you are bound to spend as much time looking at the building as the art. The museum shop is packed with books and Gugg memorabilia, including ceramic mugs inspired by the building's distinctive shape.

1071 Fifth Avenue, UES ☎ **423-3500** ⚏ **$12** ◑ **9am–6pm Fri–Wed (to 8pm Fri–Sat).** Ⓜ **4•5•6 to 86th St**

Studio Museum of Harlem ♫D1

Founded in 1967 by a group that included abstract painter William T Williams, and some staffers from MOMA, the Studio Museum in Harlem grew out of the Black Art movement of the 1960s and is now the linchpin of the Upper Manhattan art scene. Its special quality comes from the constant involvement of artists – indeed, of its four or five exhibitions each year, one is always dedicated to work by the three yearly participants in the museum's artists-in-residence programme. To commemorate the museum's 30th anniversary, construction has started on new (in fact, the first ever) galleries for the permanent collection, Bearden, Elizabeth Catlett, Robert Colescott and Jacob Lawrence. Among the offerings in the museum shop are exhibition catalogues for 30 years of exhibitions at the museum, plus African jewellery, textiles and woven containers.

144 W 125th Street, Harlem ☎ 864-4500 ⊠ suggested donation
◑ 10am–5pm Wed–Fri; 1–6pm Sat–Sun. Ⓜ 2•3 to 125th Street

☆ WHITNEY MUSEUM OF AMERICAN ART ⌖C6

Founded in 1930 in the studio of Gertrude Vanderbilt Whitney, and now occupying a wonderful Bauhaus-designed building, this is *the* leading collection of American art in the world. A selection from its permanent collection (including works by Edward Hopper, Jasper Johns, Georgia O'Keeffe and Andy Warhol) is usually on show alongside temporary exhibitions, or its famed biennials of contemporary American art – US national pride writ large in paint on canvas. Anachronism or barometer? You decide. Until recently, it seemed that the Whitney loved to make trouble. The 1993 biennial, for instance, had a 40-ft-long replica of a toy firetruck parked out front, two artists dressed like natives in a cage in the basement, and the world's largest puddle of plastic vomit on the floor upstairs. Bad press and low attendance curtailed such amusing artistic tantrums, and the museum is now better-mannered, garnering praise for its retrospectives (recently of restrained abstract painters such as Mark Rothko, Richard Diebenkorn and the like) and other grand-scale exhibits.

945 Madison Avenue, UES ☎ 570-3676 ⊠ $10 ◑ 11am–6pm Tue–Wed & Fri–Sun; 1–9pm Thu. Ⓜ 6 to 77th St

commercial galleries – downtown

Ace Gallery ⌖D11

Easily New York's grandest gallery space. Look for monolithic minimalism, mural-sized painting and anything else that's massive in scale.

275 Hudson Street, Soho ☎ 255-5599 Ⓜ C•E to Spring St

American Fine Arts ⌖F11

Avant-garde gallery, specializing in 'institutional critique' by young artists.

22 Wooster Street, Soho ☎ 941-0401 Ⓜ A•C•E to Canal St

Barbara Gladstone ⌖D9

Part of the 'MGM' gallery complex, at Gladstone you can find works by Richard Prince who first made his mark with rephotographed images of the Marlboro Man.

515 W 24th Street, Chelsea ☎ 206-9300 Ⓜ C•E to 23rd St

Deitch Projects
$F11

Exhibits a wide range of hot young artists from around the world.
76 Grand Street, Soho ☎ 343-7300 Ⓜ A•C•E to Canal St

Janet Borden
$D11

For photos, visit this gallery – the wares range from the sharp-focus land-scapes of Lee Friedlander to surreal post-apocalyptic visions by Oliver Wasow.
560 Broadway, Soho ☎ 431-0166 Ⓜ B•F•Q to Broadway-Lafayette St

John Weber
$D9

Known in the 70s as the home of process-oriented art, John Weber now has a gallery on the second floor of a 10-storey building housing more than a dozen galleries large and small, and is still very strong on conceptual art.
529 W 20th Street, Chelsea ☎ 691-5711 Ⓜ C•E to 23rd St

Larry Gagosian
$D11

Alternates museum-quality shows of high moderns like Andy Warhol with the newest works of established contemporaries like Anselm Kiefer.
136 Wooster Street, Soho ☎ 228-2828 Ⓜ B•D•F•Q Broadway-Lafayette St

Matthew Marks Gallery
$D9

Part of the gallery complex known as 'MGM', this suave young newcomer has two galleries where he shows mature blue chips such as Ellsworth Kelly and Brice Marden, while also establishing a market for fashionable and collectable new artists like Gary Hume and Katharina Fritsch.
522 W 22nd Street, Chelsea ☎ 243-1650 Ⓜ C•E to 23rd St
523 W 24th Street, Chelsea ☎ 243-0200 Ⓜ C•E to 23rd St

Metro Pictures
$D9

Also located in the 'MGM' gallery complex, Metro grew famous for show-ing feminist postmodernists such as Cindy Sherman.
519 W 24th Street, Chelsea ☎ 206-7100 Ⓜ C•E to 23rd St

Pat Hearn
$D9

Specializes in poetic paintings filled with colour and light.
530 W 22nd Street, Chelsea ☎ 727-7366 Ⓜ C•E to 23rd St

Paula Cooper
$D9

This grand space brings out the most of Cooper's eclectic stable ranging from minimalist sculptor Sol LeWitt to transgressive photographer Andres Serrano.
534 W 21st Street, Chelsea ☎ 255-1105 Ⓜ C•E to 23rd St

Phyllis Kind ♯D11
The veteran Chicago dealer who specializes in Outsider art.
136 Greene Street, Soho ☎ 925-1200 Ⓜ N•R to Prince

303 Gallery ♯D9
A video gallery showing work by – among others – Doug Aitken and angry feminist painter Sue Williams.
525 W 22nd Street, Chelsea ☎ 255-1121 Ⓜ C•E to 23rd St

Tony Shafrazi Gallery ♯D11
The emphasis at this gallery is on graffiti art by Jean-Michel Basquiat, and work by Keith Haring and Kenny Scharf.
119 Wooster Street, Soho ☎ 274-9300 Ⓜ N•R to Prince St

commercial galleries – uptown

C & M Gallery ♯D6
Specializes in museum-quality exhibitions of classic moderns – sculpture by Maillol and portraits by Picasso.
45 E 78th Street, UES ☎ 861-0020 Ⓜ 6 to 77th St

Gagosian Gallery ♯D6
Houses an assortment of works from the stars of the 80s art explosion, including Eric Fischl and David Salle.
980 Madison Avenue, UES ☎ 744-2313 Ⓜ 6 to 77th St

Hirschl & Adler ♯F6
Impressionists and American Modernists are kept downstairs and the contemporary artists upstairs.
21 E 70th Street, UES ☎ 535-8810 Ⓜ 6 to 68th St-Hunter College

Kennedy Galleries ♯A8
Exhibit dozens of contemporary artists' work, as well as a huge collection of exclusively American paintings and prints dating from the 18th century.
2nd flr 730 Fifth Avenue, Midtown ☎ 541-9600 Ⓜ B•Q to 57th St

Knoedler & Co ♯F6
Specializes in sturdy Modernists such as Frank Stella and Helen Frankenthaler.
19 E 70th Street, UES ☎ 794-0550 Ⓜ 6 to 68th St-Hunter College

sights, museums & galleries

Marlborough Gallery
♯A8

An international gallery which specializes in 'pop figuration' and has recently taken on neon artist Keith Sonnier.

40 W 57th Street, Midtown ☎ 541-4900 Ⓜ B•Q to 57th St

Mary Boone
♯A8

It is a while since Mary Boone fled the boutiquification of Soho and moved Uptown – but the queen of the 80s art boom is still making new art stars.

745 Fifth Avenue, Midtown ☎ 752-2929 Ⓜ N•R to 5th Ave

PaceWildenstein
♯A8

One of the city's most successful contemporary spaces. Look for work by Photorealist Chuck Close, Minimalist Agnes Martin, feminist body artist Kiki Smith, Neoexpressionist superstar Julian Schnabel, and sculptor Henry Moore – to name just a few.

32 E 57th Street, Midtown ☎ 421-3292 Ⓜ N•R to 5th Ave

Robert Miller
♯B8

One of the galleries in the glorious art deco Fuller Building, containing an array of modernist photography, classic Modernist painters (like David Hockney) and cutting-edge Contemporaries (such as Walter Niedermayr).

41 E 57th Street, Midtown ☎ 980-5454 Ⓜ 4•5•6 to 59th St

Salander-O'Reilly
♯D6

Mixes shows of contemporary artists like Elaine de Kooning with retrospectives of work by Courbet and Ralph Albert Blakelock.

20 E 79th Street, UES ☎ 879-6606 Ⓜ 6 to 77th St

Wildenstein & Co
♯F6

This gallery, founded in Paris over 120 years ago, has assembled an inventory of old masters and impressionists which is the envy of the international art world.

19 E 64th Street, UES ☎ 879-0500 Ⓜ 6 to 68th St-Hunter College

kids

Bronx Zoo
♯off map

This is the largest urban zoo in America with a special children's zoo where kids can try out the exhilarating 'spider web' rope climb and see life underground in the 'prairie dog burrow'. The World of Darkness, full of bats, should also prove a big hit. There are camel rides – and trams, buses, and a monorail offering a narrated journey through Wild Asia make it easy to get around, but it's a big place and may become too much for kids under four.

Bronx River Parkway, Fordham Road, Bronx ☎ 1-718-367-1010 💲 $9 adults; $5 2–12 yrs (Wed free); monorail $2 ◑ *10am–5pm daily (to 5.30pm Sat–Sun).* Ⓜ 2 to East Tremont

Central Park Wildlife Center ♫E6
Children can get up close and personal with the wild things at the Petting Zoo in this, the biggest of Manhattan's parks. They can also look at, but not touch, penguins, puffins, sea lions and monkeys through eye-level Plexiglas. Divided into three zones: the Polar Circle, Temperate Territory and Tropical Zone, the centre's intimate atmosphere and convenient locale make it a great choice for some outdoor fun.
Entrance at Fifth Ave & 64th St, UES ☎ 861-6030 💲 $3.50 adults; 50¢ 3–12 yrs ◑ *10am–5pm Mon–Fri; 10.30am–5.30pm Sat–Sun & Public holidays.* Ⓜ N•R to 5th Ave; 6 to 68th St

Children's Museum of the Arts ♫C12
A true celebration of the art of play, this museum allows kids to get to grips with painting, sculpture, theatre, music and even graphic design. Sessions are tailored to match attention spans and allow children to roam from one interest to the next. There's also an additional infant playroom.
182 Lafayette Street, Nolita ☎ 941-9198 💲 $5 (under 12 months free) ◑ *12–5pm Wed–Sun (to 7pm Wed).* Ⓜ 6 to Spring St

Children's Museum of Manhattan ♫A5
Another interactive museum where children run free and explore myriad make-believe worlds. They can cook green eggs and ham in the area dedicated to Dr Seuss, shoot down an artery in the Body Odyssey or produce their own TV show in the Media Center. With the Winnie the Pooh playland, added attractions for the under fours, storytelling, face painting and theatre, it all makes for an enjoyably full schedule.
212 W 83rd Street, UWS ☎ 721-1234 💲 $5 (under 12 months free) ◑ *10am–5pm Wed–Sun.* Ⓜ 1•9 to 86th St

Intrepid Sea Air Space Museum ♫off map
A 900-ft former aircraft carrier, the Intrepid, is the centrepiece of this engrossing interactive museum, which also features a submarine, helicopters, lunar-landing modules, and simulators. It's packed with displays and models, and anecdotes from retired sea-dogs spice up your visit.
Pier 86, W 46th St and 12th Ave, Midtown ☎ 245-2533 💲 $10 adults; $7.50 12–17 yrs; $5 6–11 yrs; $1 2–5 yrs ◑ *Apr–Sep: 10am–5pm daily (to 6pm Sat–Sun); Oct–Mar: 10am–5pm Wed–Sun.* Ⓜ A•C•E to 42nd St-Port Authority Bus Terminal, then M42 bus.

Liberty Science Center
off map

Here, more than 250 scientific exhibits offer kids a chance to touch and test the physical world. Large-scale displays include a geodesic dome, a lighthouse, a solar telescope and a fully-equipped ambulance. Informative staff encourage participation. The museum also houses the largest domed IMAX cinema in the USA. The centre's observation deck offers a pleasant café and great views of Lady Liberty and the city skyline.

251 Philip Street, Jersey City ☎ 1-201-200-1000 ⊠ $9.50 adults; $7.50 2–12 yrs; IMAX cinema $2 ◑ *9.30am–5.30pm daily (Sep–Mar closed Mon).* ⬥ NY Waterway ferry (1-800-533-3779) from World Financial Center to Colgate Piers, then free shuttle bus

New York Aquarium
off map

Kids get the feel of smaller sea-life in the touch pool or marvel at sea-mammal shows held several times daily at the open-air amphitheatre. There are over 10,000 specimens, including such favourites as Beluga whales and dolphins, and interactive displays aimed at kids. The aquarium is situated near the famous Coney Island boardwalk and amusement park – a fascinating slice of Americana – which is an ideal distraction for older children and teens during summer months.

W 8th Street, Coney Island ☎ 1-718-265-3474 ⊠ $9.75 adults; $6 2–12 yrs ◑ *10am–6pm daily.* Ⓜ B•D•F•N to Stillwell Ave, Coney Island

Sony Wonder Technology Lab
C8

Four floors of hi-tech tinkering, with numerous, fun interactive gadgets from robots to ultrasound scanners. Everyone gets a card-key imprinted with their image, name and voice, which personalizes each of the exhibits when used. Printouts of the experience provide a permanent memento.

550 Madison Avenue, Midtown ☎ 833-8100 ⊠ free ◑ *10am–6pm Tue–Sat (to 8pm Thu); 12–6pm Sun.* Ⓜ E•F to 5th Ave

parks

Central Park
B3–A8

Completely man-made, Central Park is the quintessential city park. Designed in 1858 with a view to preserve a green space in the heart of Manhattan, it stretches for about 50 blocks, and contains woodland, lawns, bridle trails, plants, and ponds – all kept in impressive shape by the ever present City Parks folk. Cars are allowed on the East and West Drives (just inside the park's periphery): but not between 10am–3pm and 7–10pm Mon–Fri; 7pm Fri–6am Mon, or from 7pm the night before until 6am the day after a public holiday. Distinctive areas like The Mall, a performance mayhem of drummers, mime artists, and trick-skaters, and popular landmarks such as the Hans Christian Andersen and Alice in

Wonderland statues, are part of the park's unique appeal. Vast and fascinating to explore, it's easy to lose your bearings and so worth remembering the old New Yorker navigation-trick: the numbers on the lampposts indicate the equivalent street outside the park. Attractions within the park include Belvedere Lake and Castle, a mock medieval creation at the park's highest point, and Strawberry Fields (Yoko Ono's tribute to her late husband who was murdered nearby). The Ramble is scary after dark, but romantic by day. The paths and groves are good for bird watching, but they're also the place for a gay pick-up. In summer, hacky-sack, frisbee, and general posing are the order of the day in Sheep Meadow – some even sunbathe topless. Music, spoken word, and dance acts take place at Rumsey Playfield throughout the humid summer months.

Central Park South, Fifth Avenue, Central Park North & Central Park West ☎ 360-3444 Ⓜ A•B•C•D•1•9 to 59th St-Columbus Circle; N•R to 5th Ave; 2•3 to Central Park North (110th St); B•C to Cathedral Pkwy (110th St); B•C to 103rd St; B•C to 96th St; B•C to 81st St-Museum of Natural History

Battery Park
♯F13

Battery Park proper, in the southern tip of Manhattan, contains the Civil War-era Castle Clinton (now the ticket office for ferries to Liberty and Ellis Islands). Adjoining it, and flanking the Hudson River, is Battery Park City, a former wasteland revamped and teeming with life. It encompasses lush grassy areas, an esplanade popular for post-brunch strolls, the Museum of Jewish Heritage and, for gawpers, a dock housing millionaires' yachts, on-board helicopters and all. Great Summer events include outdoor jazz and blues performances.

Battery Place & State Street, Lower Manhattan ☎ 797-3143/3133 Ⓜ 4•5 to Bowling Green; 1•9 to South Ferry

Brooklyn Botanical Gardens
♯off map

Set back from the sprawling Prospect Park, the Botanical Gardens is a place out of time. In spring, the Cherry Orchard, with a variety of cherry trees unmatched outside of Japan, and the Herb Garden with its 300 kinds of fragrant plants, perfume the air. In the winter months the conservatory is a treat; the Tropical Pavilion includes plants from the Amazon basin while the Bonsai Museum has trees over a century in the growing. The Osbourne Garden is a kaleidoscope of colour and the Shakespeare Garden has over 80 species mentioned by the great bard.

900 Washington Avenue at E Parkway, Brooklyn ☎ 1-718-623-7200 Ⓜ D•Q to Prospect Park; 2•3 to Eastern Parkway-Brooklyn Museum

Bryant Park
♯E8

The only open space in this section of Midtown, Bryant Park is very popular with the lunchtime crowd – 'brown-bagging it' as a workers picnic is known. Its large lawn is enclosed by overflowing flowerbeds and trees; green garden chairs are scattered throughout, and two small concession stands sell over-priced beverages when the weather is good. In the summer the park hosts a boisterous, boozy singles scene at the Bryant Park Grill & Café, and the occasional classical or rock concert. Sitting in the park, surrounded by skyscrapers, it's amazing to think that less than 180 years ago the site was just a potter's field. There are free movies every Monday night in summer.

Sixth Avenue, Midtown ☎ 983-4142 Ⓜ N•R•1•2•3•7•9 to 42nd St-Times Sq

Lower East Side Gardens
♯A1

Birdsong, frog-burps, and butterflies – common sights and sounds on a summer's day in the Big Apple? The gardens of Alphabet City defy the cliché of what used to be one of the dodgiest areas in Manhattan. Proudly maintained by the local community, there's a garden on almost every block; ponds, stone chess tables, and weeping willows offer shady relief from the blaring salsa of the Puerto Rican neighbourhood and the summer heat.

East Village ☎ 439-1090 Ⓜ F to 2nd Ave; L•N•R•4•5•6 to 14th St-Union Sq

Prospect Park
♯off map

Landscaped by the architects who designed Central Park, Brooklyn' Prospect Park has some of the same features – a boating lake, an ice rink, woodland areas, and miles of pedestrian footpaths – but it also has attributes all of its own. The less manicured fields give it a much more rural feel; there's a stream that runs through a small valley; and areas that can make you feel like an explorer stumbling on uncharted territory. In summer the local neighbourhood residents pour into the park in droves – the BBQ areas are teeming with families of all ethnic diversities and kiteflying, games of soccer, and volleyball are open to anyone.

Flatbush Avenue, Brooklyn ☎ 1-718-965-8999 (events hotline)
Ⓜ 2•3 to Grand Army Plaza

beaches

Brighton Beach & Coney Island Beach
♯off map

Packed during the summer, but worth it for a juicy slice of Brooklyn life.
Coney Island/Brighton Beach Ⓜ B•D•F to Brighton Beach; Stillwell Ave-
Coney Island

Jones Beach
♁off map

When buying your train ticket, ask for the 'special', which includes the 15-min bus ride to the beach. The beach bus makes three stops; the first is best for families, the second a little more youth-oriented, and the third is less crowded and leads to the gay beach farther down.

Long Island III LIRR from Penn Station to Freeport, then bus.

Robert Moses State Park
♁off map

The extra 30 min or so on the journey is well worth it to experience the white sands and untouched dunes of Fire Island. It's always pretty mellow, even in the height of summer – and the water is cleaner too.

Long Island III LIRR from Penn Station to Babylon, then bus to the beach (again, ask for the special).

Rockaway Beach
♁off map

This seven-mile stretch of beach is not necessarily the most beautiful you'll ever see, but it's close to the city and is used mainly by locals.

Queens M A•S to any stop along the beach, from Rockaway Park Beach 116th St to Beach 25th St

body & soul

NYC is famous for a lot of things and being peaceful just ain't one of 'em. If you find yourself in need of some pampering, tranquillity, or a place to let it all sweat out, these are some of the best Gotham City has to offer.

alternative therapies

Jivamukti
$A12

Anyone hooked on yoga will dig this huge centre ($15 for any class including ashtanga and their unique jivamukti yoga). The peaceful setting is complete with a waterfall, pastel-painted rooms, each with an incense-laden altar, and a boutique dedicated to satisfying your spiritual needs – incense, books, clothes, music etc. Keep your eyes peeled – you might be contorting next to Sting.

404 Lafayette Street, 3rd fl, Noho ☎ 353-0214 Ⓜ B•D•F•Q to Broadway-Lafayette St; 6 to Astor Pl ◑ *6.45am–10pm daily.*

Open Center
$A12

This is a serene oasis in which to learn the arts of belly-dancing, yoga, tai chi, martial arts, astrology, and more at the centre's lectures, seminars and cool classes. There's also a free meditation room (donations welcome).

83 Spring Street, Nolita ☎ 219-2527 Ⓜ N•R to Prince St; 6 to Spring St ◑ *10am–10pm daily (to 6pm Sun).*

Osaka Health Center
$D1

One of the best remedies for an achy body is a shiatsu massage. The approach of this parlour is pretty intense – there are ropes above the tables for therapists to hold onto while they walk on your back and dig their toes into your pressure points – but it's worth it ($50–$100, including hot and cold tub, and sauna).

50 W 56th Street, Midtown ☎ 956-3422 Ⓜ N•R to 57th St ◑ *10am–midnight daily.*

beauty treatments

J Sisters
$B7

Famous for their pedicures (for $55 they'll even dig and get rid of in-grown toe-nails), and bikini wax service ($45), this glam venue has professionals who'll go places your partner wouldn't!

35 W 57th Street, Midtown ☎ 750-2485 Ⓜ B•Q to 57th St; N•R to 57th St ◑ *9am–5.30pm Tue–Sat (to 7.30pm Wed–Thu).*

Ling
♂E10

The shape of your brows can make or break your face. Ling's got the best eyebrow 'designers' in town. They do all the models and actors and know how to sculpt the perfect arch ($22).

12 E 16th Street, Gramercy Park ☎ 989-8833 Ⓜ N•R•L•4•5•6 to 14th St-Union Sq; F to 14th St; L to 6th Ave ◐ *10am–7pm Mon–Fri; 9.30am–5pm Sat.*

The Service Station
♂F9

The man in the street is taking better care of himself these days, and the Service Station is here to make sure it's a pleasurable experience. Kitted out like an old gas station, this is the original pampering place for men (although some women come too). They do tanning, massage ($65 per hour), manicures ($10), pedicures ($20), and hair ($35 for men; $45 for women).

137 Eighth Avenue, Chelsea ☎ 243-7770 Ⓜ A•C•E to 14th St; L to 8th Ave ◐ *10am–10pm Mon–Sat; 12–8pm Sun.*

body art

Body Adorned
♂A12

Looking to decorate your skin with some piercings or tattoos? Then head for the East Village. This neighbourhood is loaded with little haunts, but the ultra-hygienic Body Adorned is an especially friendly set-up. They have design books you can sift through for tattoo inspiration, and the professional artists (some of the most talented in town) will give you their advice before inflicting pain. Aside from tattoos (from $75), they also have mendhei painters ($20 for a hand print), and a piercing service.

47 Second Avenue, East Village ☎ 473-0007 Ⓜ F to 2nd Ave ◐ *1–8pm Sun–Thu (to 10pm Fri–Sat).*

fitness & dance

Crunch
♂A12

These gyms are known for their 'no judgements' policy, so leave your self-consciousness behind. At the Lafayette Street locale, which is by far the biggest, there are 2 floors of cardio equipment, a boxing ring, tanning facilities, and fun classes like firefighter training (a real firefighter has you lugging hoses and dragging bodies). It's $22 per day whatever you choose to do, but don't sweat at the price, they have state-of-the-art machinery to make the most of your work-out.

404 Lafayette Street, Noho ☎ 614-0120 Ⓜ 6 to Astor Pl ◐ *24 hours Mon–Fri; closes 9pm Sat; 8am–9pm Sun.*
162 W 83rd Street, UWS ☎ 875-1902 Ⓜ 1•9 to 86th St ◐ *6am–11pm Mon–Thu (to 10pm Fri); 8am–9pm Sat–Sun.*

Fred Astaire Dance Studio
♫B11

To pick up some smooth moves – swing, ballroom, Latin, waltz, tango, foxtrot, rumba, or cha-cha-cha – you'll need to take a few lessons ($25 each). Call ahead to fit into a programme of classes or, for more instant success, a private session ($88). Don't expect a grand setting – facilities are basic.

666 Broadway, Noho ☎ 475-7776 Ⓜ 6 to Bleecker St ◑ 1–10.30pm Mon–Fri; 12.30–6pm Sat.

697 E 43rd Street, Midtown ☎ 697-6535 Ⓜ 4•5•6•7 to Grand Central-42nd St ◑ 1.30–10.30pm Mon–Fri; 11am–5pm Sat.

Power Pilates
♫C10

The business of stretching the body and releasing toxins and fluids is really hot, and Pilates is one of the latest ways for the supermodels and celebs to get fit. The rigorous mat-based classes last an hour ($15). You can also have a semi-private (3 people) machine session ($40), or a one-to-one ($65–$100).

49 W 23rd St, 10th fl, Gramercy Park ☎ 627-5852 Ⓜ N•R•6 to 23rd St ◑ 7am–9pm Mon–Fri (to 8pm Thu); 9am–3pm Sat; 10am–4pm Sun.

Revolution
♫E10

Sans frills and fancy stuff, Revolution is exactly what a gym is supposed to be – a place to sweat. Classes range from spinning (static cycling), boxing, and body-conditioning to holistic self-defence, Thai kick-boxing, and strength and alignment sessions. Just pay by the class ($15). And if you're looking for some personal attention, they have some of the most educated and bodily aware trainers in the business. BYOT (towel)!

104 W 14th Street, Chelsea ☎ 206-8785 Ⓜ L•N•R•4•5•6 to 14th St-Union Sq ◑ 6am–10pm Mon–Fri; 8am–4pm Sat–Sun.

hair care

Devachan
♫D11

Having a haircut at Devachan – an airy Soho loft – is almost a spiritual experience... It all starts when they get you to lie down on a massage table, while they shampoo and give you a 10-min head massage ($60–$125 for cut; $65 and up for colour).If you have curly hair, try to see the owner Lorraine – she'll teach you how to 'cultivate your curls'.

558 Broadway, Soho ☎ 274-8686 Ⓜ N•R to Prince St; 6 to Spring St ◑ 11am–7.30pm Tue–Fri; 10am–5pm Sat.

Jerry's Men's Hair Styling Salon
♫C8

An old-school barbers, Jerry's provides shaves (with a steam towel), shoe shines, haircuts ($20), and manicures. Walk in scruffy and leave like a gentleman.

635 Fifth Avenue (in the Rockefeller Center), Midtown ☎ 246-3151
Ⓜ B•D•F•Q to 47–50th Sts; Rockefeller Ctr; 6 to 51st St
◑ 8am–6pm Mon–Fri.

Mark Garrison Salon ♯E6
This is as far away as you can get from the trad East Village hole-in-the-wall salon, where the specialty is usually crazy colour and funky cuts. One of the most chichi spots in town, this salon is beautiful, posh, and a real indulgence. They'll give you that perfect cut (approx $100) and change your hair forever. For a true splurge, see Mark for $200.
820 Madison Avenue, UES ☎ 570-2455 Ⓜ 6 to 68th St-Hunter College
◑ 9am–6pm Mon–Sat (to 8pm Tue & Thu).

spas & baths

The Avon Center ♯A8
Given that Avon is a rather old-fashioned name, this place is surprisingly chic – with make-up lessons ($85), applications ($50), and a hair salon. You can get made up for free if you buy a product or have a facial. The whole range of treatments is covered, from half leg wax ($35) to paraffin body wrap ($150).
725 Fifth Avenue, Midtown ☎ 755-2866 Ⓜ N•R to 5th Ave ◑ 9am–6pm
Mon–Sat (to 8pm Thu).

Bliss ♯D11
When Uma Thurman, Winona Ryder, and Gwyneth Paltrow crave R&R, they hit Bliss, the city's most talked-about day-spa for men and women. From the buffet of champagne and chocolates and the lavish boutique of beauty products, to the menu of ultra-luxurious treatments ($50–$225), such as a facial exfoliation with micro-crystals, a 2-hour rub down with crushed ginger and oils, and a hot almond-milk pedicure, the Bliss mantra is simple: indulge! Book anything from 2 weeks to 2 months ahead.
568 Broadway, Soho ☎ 219-8970 Ⓜ N•R to Prince St ◑ 9.30am–8.30pm
Mon–Sat (to 6.30pm Sat).

Carapan ♯E10
This is an intimate, sage-scented haven, decked out with rustic furnishings, which aims to heal the body (men's and women's) inside and out. Their specialties are massage, aromatherapy, reflexology, and cranio-sacral work ($95 per session).
5 W 16th Street, Gramercy Park ☎ 633-6220 Ⓜ L•N•R•4•5•6 to 14th St-Union Sq ◑ 10am–10pm daily.

La Casa de Vida Natural
♯C10

Shake off your world-weariness and take time out in this exotic day spa's 'rainforest' setting. On top of basic treatments – massage ($70), body wrap ($75), non-surgical face lift ($75) – you can enjoy flotation ($50 or $25 with any other treatment) or, for something more radical, *flossage*, which cleverly combines the benefits of massage and flotation ($65 per hour).

41 E 20th Street, Gramercy Park ☎ 673-2272 Ⓜ 6 to 23rd St ◑ 10am–8pm daily (to 5pm Sat–Mon).

Soho Sanctuary
♯D11

This tranquil women-only day-spa offers massages and facials (both $95 for one hour), body treatments, yoga and meditation ($20 per class), and perhaps the best steamroom in NY (mosaic tiles and delicious herbal scents).

119 Mercer Street, Soho ☎ 334-5550 Ⓜ N•R to Prince St; 6 to Spring St ◑ 10am–9pm Tue & Thu; 9am–9pm Wed & Fri; 10am–6pm Sat; 12–6pm Sun.

Tenth Street Baths & Health Club
♯F10

These old Russian baths will really flush out all those toxins and impurities. After a session in the traditional steam baths and a plunge in the cool-pool ($20), there's a choice of rigorous massages ($45 per hour), Dead Sea mud treatments, or even a spot of flagellation with genuine dried oak branches (call for prices). No pain no gain, as they say. Mixed most days or for the full monty, ladies only on Wednesdays, and men on Sundays.

268 E 10th Street, East Village ☎ 473-8806 Ⓜ L to 1st Ave ◑ 10am–10pm daily.

games & activities

You might have been there or done that, but to get the feel of the city, open wide and really get your teeth into the Big Apple by joining the locals (plus those who long to be) at play...

bowling

You can bowl your heart out all day long in the Big Apple, but for a different spin, why not 'rock 'n' bowl' at **Bowlmor Lanes** (Mon 10pm–4am) with Night Strike, NY's premier 'lights out' neon bowling party for the over-18's.

Or, at **AMS Chelsea Bowl**, try 'extreme bowling'. When the lights go out, pins and balls go day-glo and you're surrounded by a laser light show. There's also a huge video games room.

Bowlmor Lanes　　　　　　　　　　　　　　　　　　　　　　♯E10
110 University Place, East Village ☎ 255-8188 Ⓜ L•N•R•4•5•6 to 14th St-Union Sq ⌇ $4.95 per game Mon–Fri ($12 unlimited games Mon 10pm–4am); $6.45 Sat–Sun; shoe rental $3 ◐ *10–1am daily (to 4am Mon & Fri–Sat; to 2am Thu).*

AMS Chelsea Bowl　　　　　　　　　　　　　　　　　　　　　♯E9
Pier 60, Chelsea ☎ 835-2695 Ⓜ C•E to 23rd St ⌇ $7 per game; shoe rental $4 ◐ *9am–midnight (to 4am Fri–Sat).*

chess

For activity of a more cerebral kind, bring or pair up with a chess partner at **Chess Forum**. You can even brush up on your moves beforehand with a private lesson or two.

The quintessential NY chess experience, however, is to challenge one of the chess masters/hustlers who hang out in **Washington Square Park**. Should they suggest a wager, and you win the first game, quit while you're ahead; there are a lot of scam artists out there...

Chess Forum　　　　　　　　　　　　　　　　　　　　　　♯B11
219 Thompson Street, West Village ☎ 475-2369 Ⓜ A•B•C•D•E•F•Q to W 4th St-Washington Sq ⌇ $1; private lessons $25 per hour ◐ *11–3.30am daily.*

Washington Square Park　　　　　　　　　　　　　　　　　♯B11
West Village Ⓜ A•B•C•D•E•F•Q to W 4th St-Washington Sq

games & activities

The masses started coming to Coney Island in the early 1900s, and this Brooklyn outpost is still a great bet for an afternoon of amusement and some summer fun. Visit the 150ft-high Wonder Wheel (built in 1920) or the world-famous **Astroland**, home of the Cyclone (built in 1927), a 100-second, nine-hill rollercoaster ride that does its best to make you lose your cool – and your lunch.

Sideshows by the Seashore is the last remaining 10-in-1 sideshows (10 acts, one admission price) in the US; expect bearded ladies, sword-swallowers, and escape artists.

Astroland Amusement Park   *off map*
1000 Surf Avenue, Coney Island, Brooklyn ☎ 1-718-372-0275 Ⓜ B•D•N•F to Stillwell Ave-Coney Island 💲 $12.99 for unlimited major rides; single rides $1.75–$4 ◑ *Memorial Day–Labor Day: 12pm–midnight daily.*

Sideshows by the Seashore   *off map*
1208 Surf Avenue, Coney Island, Brooklyn ☎ 1-718-372-5159
Ⓜ B•D•F•N to Stillwell Ave-Coney Island 💲 $3 ◑ *May 1–Memorial Day: 1pm–midnight Sat–Sun; Memorial Day–Labor Day: 2–10pm Fri; 1pm–midnight Sat–Sun; 2–8pm public holidays.*

dance

For a full evening's entertainment, take advantage of the fact that swing is the hottest thing to hit the dance scene since *Saturday Night Fever*. At the **Supper Club**, zoot suits are prevalent and big bands blast until the small hours. Before or after an optional dinner, you can practise your footwork in the lavish ballroom setting. Beginners, relax – you can pick up lessons. On your own-eo? No sweat, there's a hopping singles scene. If you can't wait for the weekend, try the **Swing 46 Jazz & Supper Club**, where there are more live big band sounds to help you 'get hip, get hep, get right in step'.

Supper Club   *D7*
240 W 47th Street, Midtown ☎ 921-1940 Ⓜ 1•9 to 50th St 💲 $20 ($25 before 8pm) ◑ *5.30pm–4am Fri–Sat.*

Swing 46 Jazz & Supper Club   *D7*
349 W 46th Street, Midtown ☎ 262-9554 Ⓜ 1•9 to 50th St 💲 $7 Sun–Wed, $12 Thu–Sat. Price includes free class at 11pm. ◑ *12pm–4am daily.*

games & sports

A less frenetic game of pool or ping-pong might be more up your street. If so, **Fat Cat Billiards** is the real deal – a dingy hole-in-the-wall where you can kick back, shoot pool, slap a ping-pong ball around (with a net surround for minimum effort), and nurse a beer for hours. Or, with a more up-to-date take on games, **XS New York** is cyber heaven for those who dig state-of-the art virtual reality games and simulated sports. You might not want to eat lunch before you climb into the simulated airplane/spaceship 'M4' or 'Indy 500 racecar' with surround sound and slam-bam realistic movement. Lazer Tag beckons in the basement.

But if virtual thrills aren't your thing, try the awesome outdoor experience offered by **ParaSail NYC**. After a quick intro on the speedboat, you'll be strapped into a parachute harness and, before you know it, you're up and away, gliding 300 ft above the Hudson river. This exhilarating ride is the most unique way to spot the sights and take in Downtown's magnificent skyline. You can even fly with a friend to share the experience.

Fat Cat Billiards   ♭A11
75 Christopher Street, West Village ☎ 675-6056 Ⓜ 1•9 to Christopher St Ⓢ $3.75 per hour per player ◑ 2pm–2am daily.

ParaSail NYC   ♭D13
Liberty Harbor Marina, opposite the World Financial Center, Lower Manhattan ☎ 490-9375 Ⓜ C•E to World Trade Center Ⓢ $49 per person for a 10–15 min flight ◑ May–Oct: 11am–nightfall daily.

XS New York   ♭F7
1450 Broadway, Midtown ☎ 398-5467 Ⓜ N•R•1•2•3•7•9 to 42nd St-Times Sq Ⓢ video and virtual reality games $1.50–$5; internet access $4.20 for 20 min ◑ 12–10pm daily (to 2am Fri–Sat) (over 18's only after 8pm).

showtime

For a Chinese meal that's a little out of the ordinary, try **Lucky Chengs**, where their specialty is service with a song. There are three cabaret shows a night (7.30, 8.30 and 10pm). If you're (un)lucky, your waitress may put whipped cream all over you and then lick it off, dance on your table, and generally slither sexily around the room! If that's not your bag, there's Kabuki Karaoke downstairs. The service is fun, but the food... well, you don't come for the food.

Lips will also give you a good lip sync show and better than average American cuisine. The ambience is laid-back downtown – banquettes, sofas and sexy red lights. Don't get too ga-ga over your outrageously leggy waitress at either place, she's really a man in drag.

Lucky Chengs ♯C12
24 First Avenue, East Village ☎ 473-0516 Ⓜ F to 2nd Ave $ appetizers
$5–$11; entrées $12–$23 o 6pm–2am (food served 'til midnight) daily.

Lips ♯E10
4 Bank Street, West Village ☎ 675-7710 Ⓜ 1•2•3•9 to 14th St-Union Sq
⌧ average meal: $30 (with appetizers and drink) ☽ 5.30pm–midnight
Mon–Thu (to 1am Fri–Sat); 11.30am–4.30pm Sun brunch.

skate city

Ice-skating is big in NYC, and the city has several rinks. In Central Park is
the secluded **Wollman Rink**, offering the great outdoors, music, and, if
you're looking and lucky, a little romance. It's especially busy at weekends
around Christmas. The park is also prime rollerblading territory
(particularly in summer), but if you feel like taking to the streets with a
crowd, join the huge number of bladers who gather on Wednesday
evenings (summer months only) in Union Square for the weekly ritual.
Turn back the clock and head to **The Roxy**, a dance club where they turn
the floor into a roller-rink on Wednesday nights. The DJ spins 70s and 80s
disco tunes while some of the best skaters around trip the light fantastic.
Even if you're not so hot on wheels, you'll appreciate others' talents – and
it's a crazy flashback to headbands, glitter and bad hair. For 21's and over.

Union Square Mass Blade ♯E10
Meet by the parking lot on the east side of the square, Gramercy Park
Ⓜ L•N•R•4•5•6 to Union Sq-14th St ☽ 8pm Wed.

The Roxy ♯F9
515 W 18th Street, Chelsea ☎ 645-5156 Ⓜ A•C•E to 14th St ⌧ $15 plus $5
for skate hire; $10 for blade hire ☽ 8pm–2am daily.

Wollman Rink ♯A8
Park entrance at 59th St and Sixth Ave, Midtown ☎ 396-1010
Ⓜ N•R to 5th Ave ⌧ $7 (6–9.30pm Wed $3.50); $4 skate hire ☽ Nov–
Mar: 10am–3pm daily (to 9.30pm Wed; to 5pm Thu; to 11pm Fri–Sat; to
9pm Sun).

travel in style

Who wouldn't willingly part with a few extra dollars to live the life of a
celebrity? With **Smith** or **Delancey**, for a few hours you can, by cruising
Manhattan in the ultimate luxury, the stretch limo. Dress up, bring your
friends – and pretend.

Smith Limousine Service
☎ 247-0711 ⌧ $70 per hour for 6 passengers (minimum 2 hours after 6pm); $85 per hour for 8 passengers plus tips, tolls and expenses.

Delancey Car Service
☎ 228-3301 ⌧ $50 per hour (minimum 2 hours)
– bring your own booze.

tv heaven

Find yourself lamenting those missed episodes of *Baywatch* or wishing to revisit your childhood and a favourite *Lost in Space* show? Run, don't walk, to the world's most comprehensive collection of TV shows and radio clips at the **Museum of Television and Radio**. Around 100,000 programmes are available for private viewing or listening on individual consoles, and you can see everything from a classic *I Love Lucy* to a wrap up of this year's Super Bowl commercials. There are also daily screenings and seminars in the museum's two screening rooms.

Museum of Television and Radio   *C8*
25 W 52nd Street, Midtown ☎ 621-6800 Ⓜ E•F to 53rd St; N•R to 49th St; 1•9 50th St; B•D•F•Q to 47th-50th Sts at Rockefeller Center ⌧ $6
◑ 12–6pm Tue–Sun (to 8pm Thu; to 9pm Fri for screenings only).

hotels

New York has some of the trendiest, coolest hotels in the world, but there's also plenty of trad chintzy and more elegant old-world comfort too. Bedrooms tend to be larger than in European city hotels; they also tend to cost more. Find your niche in the following selections – from budget to no-expense-spared – in all areas of the Big Apple.

Key to category symbols

$ under $150 (for double room for one night, excluding taxes)
$$ $150-250 (for double room for one night, excluding taxes)
$$$ $250-350 (for double room for one night, excluding taxes)
$$$$ above $350 (for double room for one night, excluding taxes)

$

Bed & Breakfast On The Park
$off map

Staying in the fabulous period brownstone is worth the 20-minute subway ride from Manhattan. The owner, Liana Paolella, was in the antiques business and 'kept the good stuff for herself', and the best of her furniture is exquisitely arranged in every room. The Brooklyn Museum of Art and the Botanical Garden are minutes away.

113 Prospect Park West (bet. 7th & 8th Sts), Park Slope, Brooklyn, 11215 ☎ 1-718-499-6115 F 1-718-499-1385 w www.bbnyc.com ⓜ F to 7th Ave ♠ 7 ⊡ ▤ ⑨ ▭ AE/MC/V (singles & doubles from $135 shared bathroom; $195 separate bathroom)

Broadway Inn
$C7

The lobby here is full of antique charm. Bedrooms are snug and triple-glazed windows provide a soundless night's sleep in one of the city's liveliest blocks. No elevator.

264 W 46th Street (bet. Eighth & Ninth Aves), Midtown, 10036 ☎ 997-9200 F 768-2807 w www.broadwayinn.com ⓜ A•C•E to 42nd St-Port Authority Bus Terminal ♠ 41 ⊡ ▤ ↔ ▣ ▭ all (singles from $95; doubles from $135)

Carlton Arms
$D10

Perfect for art students, with cartoons in the stairwells, and 3D models in the corridors. Every room has its own theme and you may find owner John lets you pick your favourite. Bathrooms (not all are in-room) are quite basic.

160 E 25th Street (at Third Ave), Gramercy Park, 10010 ☎ 679-0680 ⓜ 6 to 23rd St ♠ 54 ▭ MC/V (singles from $57; doubles from $73)

Chelsea International Hostel ♉D9

The bedrooms are small and simply furnished; the public rooms are full of a young, beautiful, budget-challenged clientele. Making friends is easy here.

251 W 20th Street (bet. Seventh & Eighth Aves), Chelsea, 10011
☎ 647-0010 F 727-7289 W www.chelseahostel.com Ⓜ 1•9 to 18th St
✦ 255 ⌀ ⊟ AE/MC/V (singles from $25; doubles from $60)

Edison Hotel ♉D8

This large pre-war building is a tribute to the art deco era. The gargantuan lobby has lovely high ceilings and elaborate mouldings. The rooms are attractive and newly furnished. Guests are generally on the younger side.

228 W 47th Street (bet. Broadway & Eighth Ave), Midtown, 10036
☎ 840-5000 F 596-6850 e edisonnyc@aol.com Ⓜ N•R to 49th St
✦ 900 📖 ⌀° ☐ 🅿 & ⊟ all (singles from $125 doubles from $140)

Gershwin ♉D10

This place looks like a Chinese theatre run amok. Step in and the wackiness is confirmed by lots of murals and hip Euro-type travellers buzzing by. An art collector is a co-owner and you can see his booty everywhere. Private rooms have TVs and voicemail, dorms are more basic.

7 E 27th Street (bet. Fifth & Madison Aves), Midtown, 10016 ☎ 545-8000
F 684-5546 W www.gershwinhotel.com Ⓜ N•R to 28th St ✦ 106
⊟ AE/MC/V (economy $89; standard $129)

Hostelling International New York ♉D3

This Victorian Gothic building is just a couple of blocks from Central Park. The rooms are pristinely clean, large and light-filled: family rooms are great value. Public areas include a library with web-linked computers, a café, kitchen and a garden.

891 Amsterdam Avenue (bet. 103rd & 104th Sts), UWS, 10025
☎ 932-2300 F 932-2574 W www.hinewyork.org Ⓜ 1•9 to 103rd St ✦ 624
⌀ ⌀ ⌀° & ⊟ MC/V/JCB (singles from $22; family rooms from $75)

Hotel 17 ♉F10

With its eccentric decor, this 100-year-old landmark has a noir-ish glamour that draws fashionistas and savvy travellers alike. Rooms are eclectic and deco.

225 E 17th Street (bet. Second & Third Aves), Gramercy Park, 10003
☎ 475-2845 F 677-8178 W www.hotel17.citysearch.com Ⓜ L•N•R•4•5•6 to
14th St-Union Sq ✦ ☐ 📖 ㉔ ⌀ ⊟ none (singles from $86; doubles from $109)

Hudson
$A7

At 24 storey high, this is a hotel like nothing you've ever seen before. With design by Philippe Starck and the restaurant expertise of Jeffrey Chodorow, guests will be thinking that they've fallen on their feet.

356 W 58th Street (bet. Eighth and Ninth Aves), Midtown, 10019 ☎ 554-6000 F 554-6054 W www.hudsonhotel.com Ⓜ A•B•C•D•1•9 to Columbus Circle ♦ 825 ▤ ⊛ ↔ ♦ ∅ ∅ ℘ ▯ ♂ ☷ all (singles from $95; doubles from $175)

Larchmont Hotel
$E10

A pleasant, cozy brownstone hotel. Rooms are large, with pretty rattan furnishings. The shared baths and showers are sparkling clean.

27 W 11th Street (bet. Fifth & Sixth Aves), West Village, 10011 ☎ 989-9333 F 989-9496 W www.larchmonthotel.citysearch.com Ⓜ L to 6th Ave ♦ 55 ☐ ▤ ♂ ☷ all (singles from $85; doubles from $100)

Leo House
$C9

Run by a Catholic not-for-profit organization, though everyone, whatever their belief, is welcome. Bedrooms are clean and basic. The dining room offers an all-you-can-eat breakfast for $5. Non-standard facilities include a chapel and a priest on 24-hour call.

332 W 23rd Street (bet. Eighth & Ninth Aves), Chelsea, 10011 ☎ 929-1010 F 366-6801 Ⓜ C•E to 23rd St ♦ 58 ∅ ☷ MC/V (singles from $72; doubles from $78)

Malibu
$C3

A favourite with Europeans, this hotel is a great choice for the budget-conscious. The clean, good-sized rooms are in minimal black and white.

2688 Broadway (at 103rd St), UWS, 10025 ☎ 222-2954 F 678-6842 Ⓜ 1•9 to 103rd St ♦ 150 ☐ ▤ ⊛ ☷ MC/V (singles & doubles from $99)

Pickwick Arms Hotel
$D8

A modern lobby with a beautiful fireplace welcomes you. Rooms are on the small side, but they're pretty and very clean. There's a wine bar, Le Bateau Ivre, and the large roof garden is open to everyone staying.

230 E 51st Street (bet. Second & Third Aves), UWS, 10022 ☎ 355-0300 F 755-5029 Ⓜ 6 to 51st St ♦ 350 ▤ ∅ ▯ ☷ all (singles from $70; doubles from $130)

Washington Square Hotel
$B11

Smack-bang in West Village is this family-owned hotel, which pays tribute to the lovely Washington Square park outside with a lobby of beautiful antique wrought-iron garden furniture. Rooms are comfortable and decked out in pastel colours. Ask for a room with a park view.

103 Waverly Place (at MacDougal St), West Village, 10011 ☎ 777-9515
F 979-8373 Ⓜ A•B•C•E•F•Q to W 4th St-Washington Sq ✦ 170 ▭ 🗏 ↔ ☜ ℘
▯ 🗏 AE/MC/V (singles from $121; doubles from $142)

$$

Abingdon
F9

A rare city find, the Abingdon is a New England-style charmer. Each bedroom has its own distinct personality, displaying bits and pieces gathered by the owner on his global wanderings. Great for a quiet stay.

13 Eighth Avenue (at 12th St), West Village, 10014 ☎ 243-5384 F 807-7473
w www.abingdonguesthouse.com Ⓜ A•C•E to 14th St ✦ 396 ↔ ✐ ℘
▯ 🅿 ♿ 🗏 all (singles from $155; doubles from $165)

Box Tree
D8

One for romantics – the lobby, with its open fireplace, could have come
straight from Wuthering Heights. Individual bedrooms like the Fabergé
Room have hand-painted murals, French canopied beds and real fires.

250 E 49th Street (bet. Second & Third Aves), Midtown, 10019
☎ 758-8320 F 308-3899 Ⓜ 6 to 51st St ✦13 ▭ 🗏 ℘ ▯ 🗏 all
(singles & doubles from $230).

Chelsea
D9

No two rooms are alike here, but check out the pinnacle of kitsch in room 822,
where Madonna and Drew Barrymore have both staged photoshoots.
Other rooms feature crushed velvet chaises longues and leopard print curtains. The lobby is famous for its paintings by artists who've lived here.

222 W 23rd Street (bet. Seventh & Eighth Aves), Chelsea, 10011
☎ 243-3700 F 675-5531 w www.chelseahotel.com Ⓜ 1•9 to 23rd St ✦ 250
🗏 ⓧ ℘ ▯ 🅿 🗏 all (singles from $165; doubles from $185)

Country Inn The City
C5

Reserve early to stay in one of four of the homiest rooms in town, with
antique four-poster or sleigh beds, decorative fireplaces, oil paintings
and fresh roses. The owners describe the apartments as non-chaperoned
– you have your own front door key and make your own breakfast from
ingredients found in the kitchenette.

270 W 77th Street (bet. Broadway & West End Ave), UWS, 10024
☎ 874-3981 F 501-9647 w www.countryinnthecity.com Ⓜ 1•9 to 79th St
✦ 4 ▭ 🗏 🗏 none (singles & doubles from $150)

hotels

Gramercy Park Hotel ⚡D10
International and unpretentious is the order of the day. The halls and rooms have a boarding-house feel, and the doors still require old-fashioned keys. Rooms are spacious with minty green walls and dark wood furniture.
2 Lexington Avenue (at 21st St), Midtown, 10010 ☎ 475-4320 F 505-0535
Ⓜ **6 to 23rd St ✦ 509** 🖫 📶 🖵 🖃 **all (singles from $165; doubles from $180)**

Hotel Beacon ⚡C5
This lovely, privately-owned hotel is a bargain considering the high quality of the accommodation. Make the most of large, light-filled rooms with classical decor, city and Hudson River views, and pristine bathrooms. Fully equipped kitchen facilities available.
2130 Broadway (at 75th St), UWS, 10023 ☎ 787-1100 F 724-0839
w www.beaconhotel.com Ⓜ **1•2•3•9 to 72nd St ✦ 220** 🖫 📶 🅿 ♿ 🖃 **all (singles from $175; doubles from $205)**

Off Soho Suites ⚡C12
Minutes from Soho, Little Italy and Chinatown with all those ethnic food shops and restaurants. Rooms are basic motel fare with faintly Eastern decor. If you're travelling with friends, this is a good money-saving option. Suites have a separate living area with sofa bed.
11 Rivington Street (at Bowery), LES, 10002 ☎ 979-9808 F 979-9801
w www.offsoho.com Ⓜ **J•M to Bowery ✦ 35** 🖫 ↔ 📶 ♿ 🖃 **AE/MC/V (singles from $97.50; doubles from $179)**

Southgate Tower Suite Hotel ⚡B9
Ideal if you're in town for a Madison Square Garden event. Rooms are beautifully furnished, considering the reasonable price. Some suites have two double beds and sofabeds. All rooms have well-equipped kitchenettes - and even better, someone who comes in each day to wash your dishes.
371 Seventh Avenue (at 31st St), Midtown, 10001-3984 ☎ 563-1800
F 643-8028 w www.mesuite.com Ⓜ **1•2•3•9 to 34th St-Penn Station**
✦ 522 🖫 ↔ ✎ 📶 🖵 🅿 ♿ 🖃 **all (singles & doubles from $200)**

$$$

Algonquin ⚡E8
The personality of this literary landmark (where Dorothy Parker headed up the Round Table) oozes from the fabulously restored public spaces. The rooms are a decent size, in soft colours, and carry wonderful examples of old black-and-white photos of 50s New York.
59 W 44th Street (bet. Fifth & Sixth Aves), Midtown, 10036 ☎ 840-6800
F 944-1419 w www.camberleyhotels. com Ⓜ **7 to 5th Ave ✦ 165** 🖵 🖫 ↔ ✎ 📶 🖵 ♿ 🖃 **all (singles from $329; doubles from $329)**

Avalon *♭A10*
Bordering a white-hot area, this privately-owned hotel manages to feel both grand and cozy. The lobby features Veronese marble and an opulent centre rotunda - at night, snuggle up with the unique full-size body pillows.
16 E 32nd Street (bet. Fifth & Madison Aves), Midtown, 10016 ☎ 299-7000 F 299-7001 w www.theavalonny.com Ⓜ 6 to 33rd St ✦ 100 ➖ ▤ ↔ 🖉 🐾 🖵 🚻 🍴 **AE (singles from $225; doubles from $275)**

Casablanca *♭F7*
This Moroccan theme hotel provides a touch of the theatrical. Decent-sized rooms have carved headboards and prints of Moroccan villages.
147 W 43rd Street (bet. Sixth Ave & Broadway), Midtown, 10036 ☎ 869-1212 F 391-7585 e casahotel@aol.com Ⓜ N•R•1•2•3•7•9 to Times Sq-42nd St ✦ 48 ➖ ▤ 🖉 🐾 🅿 🚻 🍴 **all (singles & doubles from $295)**

Franklin *♭B6*
Diminutive in size, from the cherrywood lobby to the elegant breakfast room and café-style lounge. Compact, chic rooms in soft neutral colours are offset by black-and-white photos of contemporary NYC.
164 E 87th Street (bet. Lexington & Third Aves), UES, 10128 ☎ 369-1000 F 369-8000 Ⓜ 4•5•6 to 86th St ✦ 47 ➖ ▤ 🍴 **all (singles from $245; doubles from $269)**

Hotel Élysée *♭A8*
An impressive list of famous people have called this place home – Joe DiMaggio, Marlon Brando, Tennessee Williams to name a few. Public spaces are cheeful and the large bedrooms contain some lovely antiques.
60 E 54th Street (bet. Park & Madison Aves), UES, 10022 ☎ 753-1066 F 980-9278 e elysee99@aol.com Ⓜ E•F to Lexington Ave-3rd Ave ✦ 99 ➖ ▤ 🖉 🐾 🖵 🅿 🚻 🍴 **all (singles & doubles from $325)**

Hotel Wales *♭E4*
Recreates the NY of a bygone era. Children's book illustrations grace the public spaces, and there's a touch of whimsy in the classically European rooms.
1295 Madison Avenue (at 92nd St), UES, 10128 ☎ 876-6000 F 860-7000 e hotelwales@mindspring.com Ⓜ 6 to 96th St ✦ 87 ➖ ▤ ↔ 🖉 🐾 🚻 🍴 **all (singles & doubles from $265)**

The Inn at Irving Place *♭E10*
These adjoining 1830 townhouses have been immaculately restored: with an astonishing array of antiques and furnishings, they ooze old-world charm.
56 Irving Place (bet. 17th & 18th Sts), Gramercy Park, 10003 ☎ 533-4600 F 533-4611 w www.irvingplace.com Ⓜ L•N•R•4•5•6 to 14th St-Union Sq ✦ 12 ➖ 🖵 🍴 **all (singles & doubles from $295)**

Mansfield $E8

The lobby features hip 30s furniture; the rooms (though on the small size) have modern sleigh beds with mesh headboards, and black and white prints.
12 W 44th Street (bet. Fifth & Sixth Aves). Midtown. 10036 ☎ 944-6050
F 764-4477 W www.mansfieldhotel.com Ⓜ B•D•F•Q to 42nd St ✦ 124 ⌂ ▤
✐ Ⓟ ⊟ all (singles & doubles from $255)

Morgans $E8

Schrager's first NY hotel continues to be the place of choice for the fashion industry. Wide, low-slung beds make the smallish rooms appear larger.
237 Madison Avenue (at 37th St), Midtown, 10016 ☎ 686-0300
F 779-8352 Ⓜ 6 to 33rd St ✦ 113 ⌂ ▤ ▤ ㉔ ℘ ⛾ Ⓟ ♿ ⊟ all (singles from $295;
doubles from $320)

Paramount $D8

Billed as Schrager's 'cheap chic' hotel, there is still plenty of style and attitude in the Paramount. Though small, any feeling of claustrophobia is ruled out by ingenious room layouts and decor. The foyer encourages lobby socializing.
235 W 46th Street (bet. Eighth Ave & Broadway), Midtown, 10036
☎ 764-5500 F 354-5237 Ⓜ N•R to 49th St ✦ 600 ▤ ↔ ✐ ℘ ⛾ ♿ ⊟ all
(singles from $200; doubles from $290)

Shelburne Murray Hill $F8

Located in a 19th-century brownstone, the Shelburne has pretty, generously proportioned rooms, kitchens, laundry facilities - and a roof terrace.
303 Lexington Avenue (at 37th St), Midtown, 10016-3104 ☎ 689-5200
F 779-7068 Ⓜ 6 to 33rd St ✦ 258 ▤ ↔ ✐ ✐ ℘ ⛾ Ⓟ ♿ ⊟ all (singles from
$269; doubles from $306)

Time $D7

The lobby is designed around a sculpture by Richard Serra – known for massive pieces which challenge your sense of space. The stylish rooms have soft furnishings in a choice of primary colours - choose one to suit your mood.
224 W 49th Street (at Broadway), Midtown, 10019 ☎ 320-2925
F 320-2926 Ⓜ N•R to 49th St ✦ 192 ▤ ↔ ✐ ℘ ⛾ ♿ ⊟ all
(singles from $265; doubles from $285)

Waldorf Astoria $C8

Every President since Hoover has stayed here when in town. Public rooms exemplify tasteful American excess and even the standard bedrooms are large with classic decor. This hotel resembles a mini-city.
301 Park Avenue (bet. 49th & 50th Sts), Midtown, 10022 ☎ 355-3000
F 872-0204 W www.hilton.com Ⓜ 6 to 51st St ✦ 1385 ▤ ㉔ ↔ ✐ ℘ ⛾ Ⓟ ♿
⊟ all (singles from $210; doubles from $250)

hotels

W New York ♿D8

You can't shake the feeling that you're worshipping at the temple of a kinder, gentler chic at this hotel. Maybe it's the huge Mondrian-style stained glass windows in the lobby area. Rooms are small but beautifully designed.
541 Lexington Avenue (at 49th St), Midtown, 10022 ☎ 755-1200 F 319-8344 w www.starwoodlodging.com Ⓜ 6 to 51st St ♦ 717 ▤ ㉔ ↔ ✦ ✐ ☂ ❑ Ⓟ ♿ ⊟ all (singles & doubles from $339)

$$$$

Carlyle ♿C6

With 65 permanent residents, the Carlyle feels like a club but is glad to consider new 'members'. Many of the large rooms have baby grand pianos, are decorated in elegant yellows and greens, and are dotted with antiques.
35 E 76th Street (bet. Madison & Park Aves), UES, 10021 ☎ 744-1600 F 717-4682 Ⓜ 6 to 77th St ♦ 180 ▤ ㉔ ↔ ✦ ✐ ☂ ❑ Ⓟ ♿ ⊟ all (singles & doubles from $450)

Fitzpatrick ♿B8

This is a corner of Ireland set slap bang in the middle of New York – the lobby has peacock blue walls and a Celtic-patterned emerald green carpet. Rooms are a fair size with dark furnishings and crystal chandeliers. The towels are thick and the soaps are Irish.
687 Lexington Avenue (bet. 56th & 57th Sts), Midtown, 10022 ☎ 355-0100 F 355-1371 w www.fitzpatrickhotels.com Ⓜ 4•5•6 to 59th St ♦ 96 ▤ ✐ ☂ ❑ Ⓟ ♿ ⊟ all (singles & doubles from $335)

Four Seasons ♿A8

'Monumental' best describes the theatrical entrance and lobby of the hotel with the largest (and most expensive) rooms in town. Decor is updated art deco. Luxuriate in the sheer space, including walk-in dressing rooms and opulent marble bathrooms with deep baths that fill in 60 seconds.
57 E 57th Street (bet. Madison & Park Aves), Midtown, 10022 ☎ 758-5700 F 758-5711 w www.fourseasons.com Ⓜ N•R to 5th Ave ♦ 370 ▤ ㉔ ↔ ✦ ✐ ☂ ❑ Ⓟ ♿ ⊟ all (singles from $565; doubles from $615)

Kitano New York ♿E8

Attracts a largely Asian clientele and provides clean, minimal rooms painted in soothingly muted tones. Authentic Japanese bedroom suites offer deep soaking tubs, roll-out futon beds and a tea ceremony room. The owner's large collection of works of art appears in the halls and rooms.
66 Park Avenue (at 38th St), Midtown, 10016 ☎ 885-7000 F 885-7100 e reservations@kitano.com Ⓜ 4•5•6•7 to Grand Central-42nd St ♦ 149 ▤ ✐ ☂ ❑ ⊟ all (singles & doubles from $410)

Lowell
⟡E6

From the bijou lobby to impeccably furnished bedrooms boasting real fires, this hotel confirms good things come in small packages.

28 E 63rd Street (bet. Park & Madison Aves), UES, 10021 ☎ 838-1400 F 319-4230 e lowellhtl@aol.com M N•R to Lexington Ave ✦ 65 ▤☻ ↔ ♒ ▯ P ▤ all (singles from $345; doubles from $445)

Mercer Hotel
⟡D11

Music and entertainment industry-types love to stay and hang out here. Rooms are minimal with wonderful marble bathrooms, whose walls fold out to expose the generous tubs to the room.

147 Mercer Street (at Prince St), Soho, 10012 ☎ 966-6060 F 965-3838 w www.themercer.com M N•R to Prince St ✦ 75 ▤☻ ∅ ♒ ▯ ♿ ▤ all (singles from $375; doubles from $400)

New York Palace
⟡C8

The historical exterior of this 1882 landmark building is intact, making the hip reception area a surprising contrast. Bedrooms come in a choice of two styles; Empire furnishings or updated art deco.

455 Madison Avenue (bet. 50th & 51st Sts), Midtown, 10022 ☎ 888-7000 F 303-6000 w www.newyorkpalace.com M 6 to 51st St ✦ 897 ▤☻ ↔ ∅ ♒ ▯ P ♿ ▤ all (singles $425; doubles $465) (weekend rates are 50% less all year)

Omni Berkshire Place
⟡C8

A modern oasis of streamlined serenity. Ask for the Author's Suite, where novelists have stayed and left signed copies of their books.

21 E 52nd Street (bet. Fifth & Madison Aves), Midtown, 10022 ☎ 753-5800 F 754-5018 w www.omnihotels.com M E•F to 5th Ave ✦ 396 ▤ ↔ ∅ ♒ ▯ P ♿ ▤ all (singles from $199; doubles from $389)

Peninsula
⟡A8

Located in a beaux-arts building, this is a high-tech hotel – the stereos in the bathrooms are muted if your hands-free rings. Rooms are unfussily modern.

700 Fifth Avenue (at 55th St), Midtown, 10019 ☎ 956-2888 F 903-3949 w www.peninsula.com M E•F to 5th Ave ✦ 241 ▤☻ ≋ ↔ ∅ ♒ ▯ P ♿ ▤ all (singles & doubles from $535)

Pierre
⟡A8

Located within an upmarket apartment building, this is a social hub for the New York elite. Amazing views of Central Park, and elegant rooms help to keep the elegant clientele coming back time after time.

2 E 61st Street (at Fifth Ave), UES, 10021-5402 ☎ 838-8000 F 826-0319 w www.fourseasons.com M N•R to 5th Ave ✦ 202 ▤☻ ↔ ∅ ♒ ▯ P ♿ ▤ all (singles from $430; doubles from $480)

Plaza ♂A8

Arguably NYC's most famous hotel and the site of Truman Capote's legendary Black and White Ball. The rooms are grand and conservatively elegant – if they feel sparsely furnished, its only because of their size.

Fifth Avenue (at 59th St), Midtown, 10019 ☎ 759-3000 F 759-3167 w www.fairmont.com Ⓜ N•R to 5th Ave ♠ 808 🖩②④ ↔ ✐ 𝒮° 🔲 Ⓟ 👶 ⊟ **all (singles from $335; doubles from $425)**

Plaza Athénée ♂E6

This jewel has the look of a French château. Lovers of luxury will adore the rose-coloured marble bathrooms, flowers and Italian Frette bathrobes.

37 E 64th Street (bet. Park & Madison Aves), UES, 10021 ☎ 734-9100 F 772-0958 w www.plaza-athenee.com Ⓜ N•R to Lexington Ave ♠ 153②④ ↔ ✐ 𝒮° 🔲 Ⓟ 👶 ⊟ **all (singles from $440; doubles from $475)**

St Regis ♂A8

This doyenne of Fifth Avenue hotels harks back to a glamour-filled era. Cherubs draped in roses recline on the ceiling, while baroque gold and Louis XVI furniture fills a lobby inviting you into a gentle 'old money' existence.

2 E 55th Street (bet. Fifth & Park Aves), Midtown, 10022 ☎ 753-4500 F 787-3447 w www.luxurycollection.com Ⓜ E•F to 5th Ave ♠ 314 🖩②④ ↔ ✐ 𝒮° 🔲 Ⓟ 👶 ⊟ **all (singles & doubles from $580)**

Royalton ♂E8

Ian Schrager's cool-yet-fun tribute to modernism. A long lobby of poured concrete is softened with cartoonish wing chairs and eccentric tables. The large, minimal-decor rooms reflect the tastes of the cool, trendy clientele.

44 W 44th Street (bet. Fifth & Sixth Aves), Midtown, 10036 ☎ 869-4400 F 768-5191 Ⓜ B•D•F•Q to 42nd St ♠ 169 ⛽ 🖩②④ ✐ 𝒮° 🔲 Ⓟ 👶 ⊟ all **(singles from $365; doubles from $385)**

Soho Grand ♂F11

This hotel pays homage to the industrial buildings of the area, and its art community. The modern decor reflects an artistic theme. Pets welcome.

310 W Broadway (bet. Grand & Canal Sts), Soho, 10013 ☎ 965-3000 F 965-3200 w www.sohogrand.com Ⓜ A•C•E to Canal St ♠ 369 🖩②④ ↔ ✐ 𝒮° 🔲 Ⓟ 👶 ⊟ **all (singles from $399; doubles from $419)**

Tribeca Grand ♂F11

Though the exterior is understated, inside the decor takes a decidedly plush, modern turn. The eight-storey atrium supplies the Tribeca magic.

2 Avenue of the Americas (at White St), Tribeca, 10013 ☎ 519-6600 F 519-6700 w www.tribecagrand.com Ⓜ 1•9 to Franklin Street ♠ 209 🖩②④ ↔ ✐ 𝒮° Ⓟ 👶 ⊟ **all (singles from $399; suites from $649)**

practical information

admission charges

Charges for museums and sights vary; it's always worth checking if there are any concessions. The larger museums have one evening a week when admission is cheaper.

banks

New York's major banks are the Bank of New York, Chase Manhattan, Citibank, and Fleet. Opening hours are usually 9am–3pm on weekdays (and often 4pm Thu & Fri), with limited service at most branches on Saturday (10am–2pm). Fleet (*318 Grand St bet. Allen & Orchard Sts & 50 Bayard St at Bowery*), and Chase Manhattan (*180 Canal St at Mott St*) are open on Sundays (10am–2pm) for foreign currency exchange only. Bank rates are slightly less competitive than bureaux de change [→ bureaux de change; credit & debit cards]. To transfer money from abroad call: American Express Moneygram ☎ 1-800-543-4080 Western Union ☎ 1-800-325-6000

bars

Most bars open from around 5pm until 4am, but bartenders will close earlier when the tips aren't up to much [→ tipping]. Carry picture ID (eg passport) to prove you are of drinking age, ie over 21 years – they can 'card' anyone! If you're told not to dance in a bar, don't laugh – they're serious. Dancing licences are hard to come by and unauthorized boogying incurs fines for the bar owner. NB: it is illegal to drink a can or bottle of anything alcoholic in the street – even if it is in a brown paper bag.

bureaux de change

Rates can be slightly more competitive than the banks'.
AmEx charges $3 commission.
200 Vesey Street (at West St)
☎ 640-5998 ◑ 8.30am–5.30pm Mon–Fri; 12–8pm Sat–Sun.
Avis charges $4.50 minimum or 1% commission, whichever is higher.
1451 Broadway (bet. 41st & 42nd Sts)
☎ 944-7600 ◑ 10am–8pm Mon–Fri; 12–8pm Sat–Sun Chequepoint USA charges 9¢ on every $1.
22 59th Street (bet. Fifth & Sixth Aves)
☎ 750-2400 ◑ 8am–8pm daily.
Thomas Cook charges $5 minimum or 1% commission, whichever is higher.
1590 Broadway (at 48th St) ☎ 265-6049 ◑ 9am–7pm Mon–Sat; 9am–5pm Sun.

children

Activities: there are lots of magazines with kid-orientated listings; see also kids' sections of *New York Magazine; Time Out; Village Voice;* the Friday edition of the *New York Times;* and *NY Family Calendar and Resource Book.* Or try:
Big Apple Parents' Paper ☎ 533-2277
Parent Guide ☎ 213-8840
Babysitting: two agencies to try are:
The Babysitters' Guild ☎ 682-0227
Frances Stewart Agency ☎ 439-9222
Hotels: most allow young children to stay in their parents' room at no extra charge. Age limits vary.
Restaurants & bars: It's not illegal for kids to go into bars but they're not the best places for family outings. On the whole cheap and cheerful restaurants and cafés welcome kids but upscale places tend to be less well equipped.

practical information

consulates
Australia: *150 E 42nd Street* ☎ 351-6500;
Canada: *1251 Sixth Avenue* ☎ 596-1600;
Ireland: *345 Park Avenue* ☎ 319-2555;
New Zealand: *Suite 1904, 780 Third Avenue* ☎ 832-4038;
UK: *845 Third Avenue* ☎ 745-0200

conversion chart

Clothing	Women's				Men's			
US	6	10	14	16	36	40	44	46
British	8	12	16	18	36	40	44	46
European	36	40	44	46	46	50	54	56

Shoes	Women's				Men's			
US	5	6	7		7	8	9	10
British	4	5	6	7	6	47	8	9
European	37	38	39	40	40	42	43	44

courier services
For services within Manhattan:
Breakaway ☎ 219-8500
CD&L ☎ 337-1460 (for a pick-up or delivery); ☎ 337-1450 (for prices and administration).

National and international services:
DHL ☎ 1-800-225-5345
FedEx ☎ 1-800-247-4747
UPS ☎ 1-800-742-5877

credit & debit cards
Automated Teller Machines (ATMs) are on almost every street corner in Manhattan, in delis, supermarkets, and even some bars. Internationally recognized debit cards can be used to withdraw cash at any ATM displaying the appropriate card sign; normal bank charges apply. Or you can use your credit card if you have a PIN number. Cash advances are also available with your credit or debit card with appropriate picture ID (eg passport). Again, normal bank charges apply.

To report lost cards:
American Express ☎ 1-800-528-4800
Diners Club ☎ 1-800-234-6377
MasterCard ☎ 1-800-826-2181
Visa ☎ 1-800-336-8472

currency
The dollar is made up of 100¢. Coins are 1¢ (pennies); 5¢ (nickels); 10¢ (dimes); and 25¢ (quarters) – the most useful change for buses, vending machines, and public telephones. Occasionally you might come across a JFK half-dollar (50¢) or $1 coins, which are annoyingly oversized and often rejected in stores. Dollar bills are uniformly green and of one size and come in denominations of $1; $5; $10; $20; $50 and $100. Commemorative issues include extremely rare $2 bills.

customs
All passengers arriving in the US are given a customs declaration form to fill out on the airplane. Don't bring in any-thing from 'unfriendly' countries (Cuban cigars are a no-no) and, while we are on the subject, drugs are not only illegal but you risk being denied entry to the US ever again.

dates
Abbreviated dates are usually given as month/day/year in the USA.

dentists
Although there is no free dental care in the US, the dental schools offer the most cost-effective treatments. **The New York University Dental Center** charges a fee of $85 to cover the cost of pain relief and emergency treatment.
345 E 24th Street (at First Ave)
☎ 998-9800 ◑ *8am–9pm Mon–Thu; 9am–7.30pm Fri.*

Columbia University School of Dental Surgery has a walk-in emergency clinic; the $65 fee covers pain relief and emergency treatment.
Vanderbilt Clinic (7th floor), 622 W 168th Street (at Broadway) ☎ 305-6726
◑ *8.30am–2pm Mon–Fri.*
Private Practise offers a 24-hour call-out service *3 E 74th Street (at Fifth Ave)*
☎ 737-1212

disabled visitors

Access For All is a guide to disabled access to NYC's cultural institutions. For a copy, send $5 to *Hospital Audiences Inc, 3rd fl, 548 Broadway* (for all general enquiries call ☎ 1-888-424-4685).
I Love New York Travel Guide, available from tourist information points and some hotels, also has accessibility ratings. For information on transport.

duty free

When entering the US, the allowance on duty-free goods is: one litre of alcohol, 50 cigars, and 200 cigarettes. The duty (per extra litre) on wine is $1.07 and a pricey $13.50 on spirits (for 40% proof; the higher the alcohol content, the more you pay!). There is a $100 limit for gifts and souvenirs. Money over $10,000 must be declared. For more details call the US Duty Office at JFK ☎ 1-718-553-5470

electricity

Electrical supply is 110 volts AC with mainly two-pronged plugs, although the newest sockets and appliances are now made for three prongs. British appliances need an adaptor.

email & internet

Public libraries offer free internet access with time restrictions and inevitably long waits.
For information call ☎ 930-0800.

There are a few internet cafés. Prices are around $10/hour

emergencies

For emergency police, ambulance and fire services, dial ☎ 911.

In a medical emergency, get yourself to one of the 24-hour emergency rooms at one of these hospitals:
Bellevue Hospital,
First Avenue (at E 27th St) ☎ 562-4141;
Mount Sinai Hospital,
100 Madison Avenue (bet. 99th & 100th Sts) ☎ 241–7171;
New York Presbyterian Hospital,
510 E 70th Street (at York Ave) ☎ 746–5050;
St Vincent's Hospital, *Seventh Ave (bet. 11th & 12th Sts)* ☎ 604–7997.
More often than not (depending on the cost of treatment), you must pay the bill, then reclaim the expense from your insurance provider.

help & advice lines

AIDS Hotline ☎ 447-8200
Lesbian & Gay Community Center
☎ 620-7310
Missing Persons Bureau ☎ 374-6922
Travelers' Aid/Victim Services ☎ 577-7777

hotels

Book early, especially in December when hotels are usually full to capacity. Apart from the room price (and NY hotels don't come cheap!), you'll have to pay a sales tax (13.25%) and an occupancy tax ($2 per night). NB some hotels take a fraction of the room cost for a late cancellation (the amount varies from hotel to hotel). You could consider choosing a small B&B or an unhosted apartment (if you're staying more than seven days – you won't have to pay sales tax).

For information call the **Bed & Breakfast Network** ☎ 645-8134 or **A Hospitality Co** ☎ 965-1102 **w** www.acompanies.com

Most hotels offer discount rates, especially for weekend stays in non-peak season. There are also agencies who buy blocks of rooms and offer as much as 50% off regular rates. **Central Reservations Service**
11420 N Kendall Drive, Miami, Florida, FL 33176 ☎ 1-305-274-6832;
Accommodations Express
801 Asbury Avenue 6th floor, Ocean City, New Jersey, NJ 08226 ☎ 1-609-391-2100;
Quikbook
381 Park Avenue South, New York, NY 10016 ☎ 779-7666 **w** www.quikbook.com
For general information on room availability call the **Visitors' Bureau**
☎ 484-1200

immigration

US immigration control has become increasingly strict. If you are entering as a student or to work, make sure you have the appropriate visa and that your papers are in order. For enquiries while in the country, contact the **Immigration and Naturalization Service (INS)** *26 Federal Plaza* ☎ 264-5650; 1-800-375-5283 ◑ *7.30am–3pm Mon–Fri.* No vaccinations are needed.

insurance

It is foolhardy to travel in the US without medical insurance. Without it, you will just about be treated in an emergency, but you will spend the rest of your working days paying off the debt. It is wise to have your personal effects covered as well. Keep all receipts (including medical bills) to substantiate a claim.

left luggage

The only place to leave luggage in New York ($2 per item per day) is at Grand Central Station. ☎ 340-2555 ◑ *7am–11pm Mon–Fri; 10am–11pm Sat–Sun.*

lost property

Report the loss to the police and get an incident report for your insurance agency. The Police Property Clerk's office is where all lost articles may eventually end up. Call them only after all else fails (and not before one week). ☎ 374-5084

measurements

As a rule, imperial measures are used.

imperial : metric	metric : imperial
1 inch = 2.5 cm	1 mm = 0.04 inch
1 foot = 30 cm	1 cm = 0.4 inch
1 mile = 1.6 km	1 m = 3.3 ft
1 ounce = 28 g	1 km = 0.6 mile
1 pound = 454 g	1 g = 0.04 oz
1 pint = 0.6 l	1 l = 0.6 (US) gallon
1 (US) gallon = 3.8 l	

medical care

There is no national healthcare service. Look under 'physicians and surgeons' or 'clinics' in the *Yellow Pages*. Ask at your hotel or contact your consulate for more advice. [→ emergencies & insurance]

medicines

Most delis carry your vital pharmaceuticals, and many are open all night. The official line on filling foreign prescriptions is that it can't be done, but try any drugstore (many are open 24 hours – some even deliver), or go to a doctor's office or an emergency room [→ emergencies]. The chain drugstore **Duane Reade** (others include **Rite Aid, McKays,** and **CVS**) has three stores that are open 24 hours:

224 W 57th Street (at Broadway)
☎ 541-9708
2465 Broadway (at 91st Street)
☎ 799-3172
485 Lexington Avenue (at 47th St)
☎ 682-5338

office & business

Most upscale hotels operate 24-hour business centres, though usually for guests only. Computer terminals, fax machines, photocopiers, and printing facilities are available at **Kinko's** with 20 branches around the city (including Brooklyn) – 19 are open 24 hours. For general enquiries ☎ 1-800-254-6567 **Mail Boxes etc** ☎ 642-5000 will accept deliveries like dry-cleaning and parcels on your behalf, and have cheap mail-boxes to rent.

For stationery try **Staples** ☎ 929-6323. Mobile phones can be hired from: **AT & T Wireless** ☎ 333-3150 (charge $7.99/day and 69¢/min); **Robert's** ☎ 734-6344 (charge $5/day and $1.45/min).

opticians

A walk-in eye examination will probably set you back around $50. With a prescription, the chainstore **Lenscrafters**, open daily (including most evenings), can make glasses up in less than an hour and have contact lenses available over the counter. For locations call ☎ 967-4166 or see 'opticians' in the *Yellow Pages*.

photography

Camera Repair does just that at 37th W 47th Street (bet. Fifth & Sixth Aves) ☎ 382-0550 **CLIK** for a one-hour service. 23rd Street (bet. Fifth & Sixth Aves) ☎ 645-1971

Spectra, pricier than the average one-hour place, produces professional quality prints.
293 E 10th Street (at Avenue A)
☎ 529-3636

police

For emergencies only, call ☎ **911**. To find your nearest police precinct, dial ☎ 374-5000. **Crime Victims Hotline** ☎ 577-7777 will give you advice on making a report. For any troubles on public transport call the **Transit Police** on ☎ 1-718-330-3330. Don't antagonize the NYPD's officers in blue; jay walking, for example, incurs tickets and fines.

postal services

Post office lines at peak hours (early mornings and lunchtime) can stretch out the door; allow extra time to avoid stressing out. For any enquiries or to find your nearest branch call ☎ 1-800-725-2161.

Stamps can also be bought from most delis (although they sell domestic 33¢ stamps only). For postcards outside the US, use one 55¢ stamp. The international letter rate starts at 60¢. Letters can be posted in rail and bus terminals, post offices, and the rather scarce blue mail boxes (pull the handle to use).

To receive mail use the Post Office's Poste Restante services. Any mail should be addressed to you *c/o General Delivery, General Post Office, 421 Eighth Avenue, New York, NY 10001*.

public holidays

While banks, offices and museums close on national holidays, most convenience stores remain open for business year round.

Columbus Day: 9th Oct 2000; Veterans' Day: 10th Nov 2000; Thanksgiving: 23rd Nov 2000; Christmas Day: 25th Dec 2000; New Year's Day: 1st Jan 2001; Martin Luther King Day: 15th Jan 2001; Presidents' Day: 19th Feb 2001; Memorial Day: 28th May 2001; Independence Day: 4th Jul 2001; Labor Day: 3rd Sep 2001

religion
Avodah Jewish Services Corp ☎ 545-7759; Bah'ai Center ☎ 330-9309; Baptist ☎ 283-6517; Buddhist ☎ 406-5109; Catholic ☎ 1-516-333-6470; Evangelical ☎ 867-2066; Jehovah's Witnesses ☎ 862-0945; Mormon ☎ 928-0714; Muslim ☎ 481-5244; Quakers ☎ 682-2745

restaurants & cafés
Hours: Double-check closing times – restaurants with slow service tend to close the kitchen up to an hour earlier than stated. Call before you hail a cab. **Payment:** The majority of restaurants accept credit cards and dollar travellers' cheques with picture ID (eg passport). **Reservations:** Always book ahead: the same day is fine for neighbourhood restaurants but for upscale eateries, call as far ahead as you can.
❶ You can eat at the bar if you want to check out a great place but can't spend a lot (or just aren't that hungry).
❶ Pricey restaurants have slightly cheaper menus at lunchtime (set hours), and neighbourhood restaurants often offer special lunch deals (usually all day).
❶ Be wary of 'upselling', that is waiters subtly suggesting you choose pricier drinks and dishes.
❶ If you don't like something, send it back – but complain nicely: it pays to be friendly to NY waiters. Portions are often massive – no-one will mind if you ask for a doggie bag [→ tipping].

safety
NY is now the safest big city in the US. However, precautions should be taken: it is inadvisable for women to walk alone late at night (carrying whistles, pepper spray, and CS gas is legal and can give extra confidence); and certain areas are dodgier than others. Out of hours, wait for subway trains in the designated area on the platform, where there's video surveillance, or by the ticket booth.

sales tax
NY sales tax is 8.25% and it is added at the cash register on top of the price of goods or services purchased [→ hotels & shopping].

shopping
Export: tourists do not get a refund on sales tax when leaving the country. **Opening times:** in Manhattan, shops tend to stay open until around 7pm. Downtown shops often close at midnight. Most stores are open on Sundays. **Payment:** even small shops take the major credit cards. Dollar travellers' cheques with picture ID are widely accepted too.
Returns: keep the receipt and you will be able to return your purchase, although most stores only offer exchange or store credit. Your rights as a shopper include having the right to know the store's refund policy before you buy: if there is none displayed, then you are entitled to a full refund if you return the item within 20 days. If you feel you have been ripped off, call **Consumer Affairs** ☎ 487-4444.
Sales: twice a year (usually mid-January and mid-September), during 'no tax week' the state forgoes the sales tax on items and shopping mayhem ensues (NB sales tax on clothing and footwear

under $110 has now been eliminated). There are also summer and winter sales in May–Jun & Jan–Feb respectively.

smoking

Strictly speaking, it is illegal to smoke in hotel lobbies, banks, public restrooms, taxis, playgrounds, sports stadiums, and in restaurants with seating for over 36 people. It is permitted in bars, and restaurants with bars, if the bar is at least two yards from the nearest table.

students

STA Travel (10 Downing Street ☎ 1-800-777-0112) and Council Travel (205 E 42nd Street ☎ 1-800-226-8624) offer discounted travel. They also issue the International Student Identity Card (ISIC), which entitles full-time students to travel discounts and reduced entrance fees. In the US, the card costs $20: it could be worth getting one before you leave home (eg in the UK it's only £6).

telephoning

Calling collect (reverse charge): dial 0 then ☎ 1-800-265-5328 or 1-800-225-5288. The surcharge on Bell Atlantic payphones is $1.58.

Directory enquiries: call ☎ 411 (addresses are given too). These calls are free from payphones.

International calls: for direct calls overseas dial 011 plus the country code: Australia: 61; Ireland: 353; New Zealand: 64; UK: 44. For operator assistance dial 01 plus city code.

Local codes: Manhattan mostly uses 212. Omit the code when dialling from within Manhattan. In this guide, all telephone numbers without a code are 212 Manhattan numbers. New Manhattan numbers currently being introduced will have 646 and 917 codes, which must be dialled if you're calling from a 212 number. For Brooklyn, Bronx, and Staten Island the code is 718; for Queens it's 917. When dialling another borough put '1' in front of the area code – the same goes for a number outside the city and toll-free 800 numbers.

Operator: ☎ 0. From here you can also ask for international operator or enquiries.

Payphones: street phone booths are plentiful – stick to the Bell Atlantic ones as the rates are steadier. Payphones take 25¢, 10¢, and 5¢ coins. Local calls cost 25¢ for the first three minutes. The cheapest way to call long distance at a public phone is to buy a prepaid 'charge card', or phone card in varying denominations (dial the number on the card for instructions), widely available from delis and news stands.

Phone directories: the White Pages lists private phone numbers and businesses, the Yellow Pages details consumer-oriented businesses and services.

Phone sounds: steady 'brrrrrr' = go ahead and dial; long low-pitched tone with short gaps = ringing tone; repeated short beeps = busy tone; single high-pitched tone = unobtainable.

Private phone rates: local calls cost a flat rate of 10.6¢ no matter how long you talk, with discounts for certain times of the day and all weekend.

Toll-free numbers: all numbers preceded by 1-800 are free (standard rate applies when calling a 1-800 number from overseas).

time

The US has four different time zones – Eastern (including New York) is five hours behind GMT. Clocks go forward by one hour in spring and back one hour in the fall.

Speaking clock: ☎ 976-0001.

tipping

Tipping is a vital part of America's service-industry culture.

Bars: leave 'good' tips (around a dollar a drink) for your first two or three rounds, and the bartender will often buy you a round in return, known as a 'buy-back'.

Restaurants: a minimum of 15% is the bottom line – anything less is considered an insult. And at the finer establishments, it's more like 18–20%. For easy maths, double the sales tax at the bottom of the check.

Taxis: cab drivers expect a 15% tip and are not shy about voicing their dissatisfaction if you offer them any less.

tourist information

New York Convention and Visitors' Bureau (NYCVB)
810 Seventh Avenue (bet. 52nd & 53rd Sts)
☎ 484-1200 ◑ *8.30am–6pm Mon–Fri; 9am–5pm Sat–Sun.*
*(**London office:** 33–34 Carnaby Street, London W1* ☎ *020 7437 8300* ◑ *10am–4pm Mon–Fri)*
New York by Phone is the NYCVB's voice-activated information service ☎ 484-1222.
Times Square Visitor Information Center
1560 Broadway (bet. 46th & 47th Sts)
☎ 869-1890 ◑ *8am–8pm daily.*
on the internet: w www.nycvisit.com; **w** www.newyork.citysearch.com; **w** www.sidewalk.com; and **w** www.nyctourist.com give comprehensive listings of where to eat, stay, and shop.

travellers' cheques (US 'checks')

These are still the safest way to carry your money, with instant refunds if lost or stolen. American Express and Visa are the most widely recognized, with Thomas Cook not far behind. Buy your cheques in US dollars – it's easier than dealing with fluctuating exchange rates, and they are more versatile [→ shopping & restaurants].

If you lose your cheques call:
American Express ☎ 1-800-221-7282;
Master Card ☎ 1-800-223-9920;
Thomas Cook ☎ 1-800-287-7362;
Visa ☎ 1-800-227-6811

visas & entry requirements

For visitors from Australia, New Zealand, the UK, Ireland, and most European countries, a passport valid for at least six months after entry is all that is needed. A 'visa waiver' allows a short-stay visit of up to 90 days: the visa waiver form, to be filled out on the incoming plane, must have the address of where you will be staying on your first night in the country. All other nationals must check visa requirements at their local US embassy.

weather

Spring and fall are ideal times to visit. In the winter, the cold can be ferocious, and in summer, it's often too hot.

transport

arrivals

Two international airports serve New York: JFK is the larger, although Newark is actually busier. La Guardia, the closest to Manhattan, is used for domestic flights only.

John F Kennedy [jfk]

JFK, in the borough of Queens, covers an area equal to the lower half of Manhattan: annually, around 31 million people pass through this chaotic 'perpetual construction site', with 353,000 flights in and out out of the nine terminals.

☎ **useful numbers:**
Enquiries: 1-718-244-4444
Lost & found: 1-718-244-4225/4226
Ground Transportation:
w www.jfk-airport.com 1-800-247-7433
☞ **Ramada Plaza** 1-718-995-9000
☞ **Holiday Inn** 1-718-659 0200
General enquiries on transport to/from NYC's airports & parking:
1-800-247-7433 (Port Authority)
w www.panynj.gov

transport options

🚇 **Public Transportation**
60–75 min to/from Howard Beach on Rockaway A train.
⏱ 24 hours daily, every 10–15 min at peak times 7.30–9.30am and 4.30–7pm, every 15–30 min offpeak.
💲 $1.50
Connects with free bus service (yellow, white, and blue bus) to all terminals, every 15 min, approx 30-min ride.

✧ The cheapest option and not dependent on traffic.
✧ 1| Avoid late at night.
2| The journey can feel arduous with heavy bags.
❶ 1| Make sure you get trains going to Rockaways and not Ozone Park-Lefferts Blvd.
2| Howard Beach is not the last stop on the line.
3| Allow enough time for a) both parts of the journey and b) delays on the subway.
☎ 1-718-330-1234

🚌 **Shuttle Buses**
New York Airport Service
60–75 min to/from Grand Central Station, Port Authority, and Penn Station.
⏱ 6.05am–1pm every 30 min and 1–11.40pm every 15 min, daily.
💲 $13
✧ Set schedule and well-marked bus stops.
✧ Travel times are dependent on traffic.
❶ Formerly Carey Airport Express.
☎ 1-718-875-8200

Gray Line Airport Shuttle
60–75 min to/from any Midtown hotel.
⏱ 5am–11pm daily.
💲 $19
✧ Door-to-door service.
✧ There might be up to a 20-min wait for the shuttle bus.
❶ Allow at least an hour if booking to go to the airport.
☎ 315-3006/757-6840 or order service from Ground Transportation.

Super Shuttle
60–75 min to/from Midtown.
⏱ 24 hours daily.

⊠ $19 for the first person; $9 for each additional person in your party to east/west Manhattan (up to 110th St).
☾ Service through the night.
♈ 1| Allow a 30-min wait at the airport.
2| Buses accommodate up to seven people – drivers wait until enough people want to go to the same part of town before departing.
☎ 258-3826 or order service from Ground Transportation.

⇔ Taxis, limos & cars
Taxis
45–65 min journey
☽ 24 hours daily.
⊠ $33 flat rate, plus tolls ($3.50) and tip.
☄ Most convenient.
♈ Relatively expensive.
❶ 1| At the airport, only accept a cab from an official taxi dispatcher.
2| If you decide to share a cab to split the cost, note that after the first stop the meter starts running.

Limos & Cars
45–65 min to/from Manhattan.
☽ 24 hours daily.
⊠ $30–$35 for cars (minicabs). $70–$80 for limos. Plus tolls ($3.50) and tip.
☄ Travel in style.
♈ Most expensive option.
❶ 1| If you call a Manhattan company, ensure they already have a car at or in the vicinity of the airport.
2| It is illegal for cars to make pick-ups without being formally dispatched.
3| Make sure you know which terminal you are at when you give the pick-up details.
☎ Some companies have direct phones located at terminal exits, or call:
Town Cars Anywhere: 1-800-532-3730
Carmel: 1-800-924-9954
Classic Limousine: 1-800-666-4949
Tel Aviv: 1-800-222-9888

Newark [ewr]

Passenger traffic figures at Newark – New York's second largest international airport, based in New Jersey – now exceed JFK's, with over 32 million people using the 56 airlines flying from its three terminals each year.

☎ useful numbers
Enquiries: 1-973-961-6000
Lost & found: 1-973-961-6633
Ground transportation: 1-800-247-7433
w www.panynj.gov
☞ **Days Inn:** 1-973-242-0900

transport options

▥ Public Transportation
Airlink Bus & PATH/New Jersey Transit Trains
1| Airlink Bus: 15–30 min to/from Penn Station.
☽ 6.15–1.45am daily, every 20 min.
⊠ $4, exact fare only.
☎ 1-800-626-7433
2| Connecting with either:
a) PATH train, 15–25 min ride, via Christopher St; 9th St & Sixth Ave; 14th St & Sixth Ave; 23rd St & Sixth Ave; and 33rd St & Sixth Ave.
☽ 24 hours daily, every 15 min.
⊠ $1
☎ 1-800-234-7284
Or b) NJT train, 20 min to/from 34th St (bet. Seventh & Eighth Aves).
☽ 24 hours daily, every 15–20 min.
⊠ $2.50
☎ 1-800-626-7433
☄ Cheapest way to get to the city.
♈ Unreliable scheduling and connection times.
❶ 1| Have small bills and change for your fares.
2| Connections with the subway involve quite a walk.

3| Trains run 24 hours, but the bus link does not.

▣ Shuttle Buses
Olympia Trails Bus Company
30–40 min to/from Grand Central Station or Penn Station to Newark.
☾ 5am–11pm daily, every 20–30 min.
💷 $11/$20 return
♻ Very convenient and there are always places available.
♺ Allow a 20-min wait at the airport.
❶ For an additional $5 fare, there is a hotel connection bus (8am–9pm) to/from Grand Central Station.
☎ 964-6233 or order minibus from Ground Transportation.

Gray Line Airport Shuttle
30–60 min to/from any Midtown hotel.
☾ 6am–11pm daily.
💷 $14 ($19 return)
♺ Allow a 20-min wait at the airport.
☎ 315-3006/757-6840 or order minibus from Ground Transportation.

Super Shuttle
60–90 min to/from Midtown.
☾ 24 hours daily.
💷 $19 for the first person; $9 for each additional person in your party to east/west Manhattan (up to 110th St).
♻ Door-to-door drop off throughout the night.
♺ **1|** Allow a wait of up to 30 minutes at the airport.
2| Buses take up to seven people and drivers wait until enough people want to go to the same part of town before departing.
☎ 258-3826 or order from Ground Transportation.

🚗 Taxis, limos & cars
50–60 min to/from Midtown.
☾ 24 hours daily.

$40 and up, plus tolls ($5.70) and tip.
☎ Some cab companies have direct phones near the terminal exits, or call:
Route 22: 1-800-680-3334
Airport Express: 1-877-546-6332
Carmel: 1-800-924-9954
Tel Aviv: 1-800-222-9888
♻ The luxury way to travel.
♺ Most expensive option.
❶ **1|** Be sure you know which terminal you are at when you give the pick-up details.
2| If you take a car from the rank, check the price of your exact destination before you set out.

La Guardia [lga]

La Guardia sees 22 million people and 355,000 planes come and go each year. Twenty-three airlines, serving destinations all over the US, fly from this convenient Queens base with four terminals.

☎ **useful numbers:**
General enquiries: 1-718-533-3400
Emergencies: 1-718-533 3900
Lost & found: 1-718-533-3988
w www.panynj.gov
🔑 **Marriott:** 1-718-565-8900

transport options

▣ Public Transportation
Subway/Bus
1| To/from 74th St-Roosevelt Ave on E•F•G•R•7 trains. (approx 30-min ride to/from Midtown).
☾ 24 hours daily, every 10–15 min.
💷 $1.50
Connecting with 33 bus – a 10-min ride to/from the central terminal building.
💷 $1.50 (or free subway transfer).
2| Around 30 min to/from Astoria Blvd on N train; 125th St on A•B•C•D•2•3•

4•5•6 trains; 116th St-Columbia University on 1•9 trains.
⏱ 24 hours daily, every 10–15 min.
💲 $1.50
Connecting with M60 bus, a 20–60-min ride to/from La Guardia with bus stops outside each terminal.
⏱ approx 5–1am daily, every 15–30 min.
💲 $1.50
❶ Ask the driver for a transfer so you can hook up with another bus route.
☎ 1-718-330-1234

🚌 Shuttle Bus
New York Airport Service
Approx 50 min to/from Grand Central or the Port Authority bus terminal.
⏱ 5.10am–10pm daily, every 15–30 min.
💲 $10
👍 1| Grand Central Station is convenient for Midtown hotels.
2| Set schedule.
👎 1| Travel times depend on traffic.
2| Port Authority has lots of escalators and stairs to reach street and subway levels.
☎ 1-718-875-8200

New York Airport Express Connection
Bus (approx 30-min ride) to/from Jamaica station (Queens).
⏱ 7am–10pm daily, hourly from outside each terminal.
💲 $5
Connect with LIRR [→161] to Penn Station, approx a 20-min ride.
⏱ 24 hours daily, every 10–15 min.
💲 $5.50 (7.30–9.30am & 4.30–7pm), $3.75 (off-peak).
👍 The cheapest option.
👎 1| Making connections with luggage is difficult.
2| The LIRR is often busy.
☎ 1-718-217-5477

🚗 Taxis, limos & cars
30–45 min to/from Midtown.
⏱ 24 hours daily.
💲 approx $26 and up, plus tolls and tip. Surcharge of $1.50 per trip between 8pm–6am.
☎ Contact Ground Transportation or try
Carmel: 1-800-924-9954
Tel Aviv: 1-800-222-9888
👍 The luxury way to travel.
👎 Most expensive option.

🚢 Ferry
Delta Water Shuttle
30–45 min to/from E 62nd St pier, E 34th St pier, or Pier 11 (Wall Street).
⏱ every hour, 6.30am–5.30pm to La Guardia; 7.45am–6.45pm to Manhattan.
💲 $15 ($25 round trip).
👍 fun, quick and easy.
👎 only runs during office hours.
☎ 1-800-533-3779

suburban trains

Ⅲ Long Island Rail Road (LIRR)
The LIRR network stretches from the eastern tip of Montauk, Long Island to Penn Station (at 33rd St & Seventh Ave) nearly 120 miles away. Tickets bought on trains when ticket offices are open cost more, so buy before you board. Most stations now have ticket-vending machines. Travelling offpeak saves you about 30%; rush-hour times are 6–10am and 4–7pm. These trains are good for getting to the beaches [→85].
☎ 1-718-217-5477

Ⅲ New Jersey Transit
NJ Transit operates trains and buses throughout New Jersey. Commuter trains have two terminals: Hoboken, in northern NJ, where passengers can transfer to the PATH trains, ferries, or buses to continue to NYC; and Newark

transport

Penn Station, which has services to NY Penn Station. There is a $3 penalty for purchasing a ticket on the train when the ticket office is open.
☎ 1-973-762-5100

III PATH
PATH (Port Authority Trans-Hudson) rapid trains run between New Jersey and NYC Newark, Harrison, and Hoboken Stations 24 hours a day, seven days a week.
☎ 1-800-234-7284

III Metro-North Railroad
Serves lower New York State and SW Connecticut out of Grand Central Station (Lexington Ave at 42nd St).
☎ 532-4900

long-distance travel

III Amtrak
All long-distance rail services operate out of Penn Station.
☎ 1-800-872-7245

◻ Long distance bus travel
These services operate out of Port Authority Bus Terminal, 40th–42nd Sts (bet. Eighth & Ninth Aves).
☎ 564-8484

general info

▤ metrocards
These come in a variety of denominations. The pay-per-ride card allows you to put money on your card in whatever increment you choose ($3–$80). For refills of more than $15, there is a bonus ride – that's 11 for the price of 10. You can get cards valid for seven days ($17) or 30 days ($63). The Fun Card offers unlimited rides on buses and subways for a whole day ($4). With all MetroCards™, you can make a

free transfer within two hours subway-to-bus, bus-to-subway, and bus-to-bus (the ticket machines will display 'Xfer' for transfer). As well as in stations, $3, $6, and $15 MetroCards™ are sold in delis and supermarkets. For up-to-date information on where to buy Metro-Cards™ call ☎ 638-7622.
❶ Fun Cards are sold at Grand Central Station at the transit museum store; Times Square Visitors' Centre; some pharmacies and cheque agencies.

8 kids
Children under 44 inches high ride free on subways and buses.

♿ disabled travellers
Access for the disabled in New York is good; buses are the best option, as they are all fully equipped for wheelchairs and the drivers are good-hearted folk. For bus and subway travel enquiries
☎ 1-718-596-8585.
Accessible Travel is a free guide with a Braille subway map, available from the MTA New York City Transit.
☎ 1-718-330-1234
For private car hire, Upward Mobility Limousines have roll-in wheelchair-accessible cars. ☎ 1-718-645-7774
❶ The disabled travel at half-fare on public transportation.

going underground

• The subway is as chaotic as the city and people it serves – on average it carries 3.8 million customers a day.
• Maps are available free upon request from all stations. They are the definitive user's guide – the one drawback is that they are huge.

using the subway

• There are 25 routes, all colour-coded and identified by a number or letter. Local trains stop at all stations; express trains only stop at stations marked with a black-ringed white circle.

• On maps, two stations connected with a line shows a transfer point, ie where two or more lines serve one station.

☎ **useful numbers:**
Information: 1-718-330-1234
Transit police: 1-718-254-1990
Lost & found: 1-718-712-4500

❶ subway essentials

⏱ 24 hours daily, every 2–5 min (6.30–9.30am & 3.30–8pm Mon–Fri), every 10–15 min at other times. Reduced service after midnight – check official subway map as some stations close.
💲 $1.50 flat fare. You must buy a MetroCard™ or a token to pass through the turnstiles.
♧ 1| Cheap and handy.
2| Much cleaner and less intimidating than anything you may be expecting.
♧ 1| Not ideal for crosstown journeys.
2| If you are not used to the system, it is easy to miss your stop, get on the wrong train, or go in the wrong direction – some trains go for miles between stops.
3| The idiosyncratic service can be a nuisance if you don't know which lines and stations to avoid.
❶ Some stations have different entrances for downtown or uptown platforms – usually on opposite sides of the street. Check before going through the turnstile.

do

1| Double-check to see if you are on the local/express or uptown/downtown platform.

2| Stand in the designated area, or wait near the manned ticket booth after peak hours or at empty stations.
3| Be aware of your belongings.
4| Ask fellow passengers if you're unsure as not all subway cars have line route maps inside.

don't

1| Smoke anywhere on the subway.
2| Jump the turnstiles: police will fine you on the spot or even arrest you.

MUNY (Music Under New York)

Performing arts are making subway travel more attractive thanks to MUNY – a creative arts programme funded by the Metropolitan Transportation Authority. Call for details of performances (Cajun, bluegrass, African, South American, and jazz) scheduled in subway and commuter rail stations.
☎ 362-3830

on the buses

NYC's buses carry 1.5 million people daily – and it feels like it. Because of their plodding progress, buses carry a certain kind of New Yorker – late-night workers, families and kids going to and from school. They tend to be neighbourhood-oriented, with many passengers and drivers on first-name or at least friendly terms.
Free from all subway stations, the bus map is easy to read and doubles as a tourist guide, with major landmarks and sights clearly marked.

using the buses

• Bus stops are located every two or three blocks, marked by route signs and yellow-painted curbs. Route maps (occasionally) appear at bus stops, showing the buses that run along that avenue or street. The printed times are highly unreliable.

• The driver will stop if he sees you, but to make sure, hold out your arm and wave. After 11pm drivers will pick up and drop off between official stops.

• To indicate that you want to get off at the next stop, press any part of the 'strip' that runs in between and above the windows.

• The back doors take a bit of getting used to. Push on the yellow strip and the doors will slowly open – follow up with a firm shove. You can also get off at the front.

• There are two types of buses: regular, making all stops, and limited (an LED sign with the word 'Limited' is displayed in the front window). Limited buses stop only at major cross streets and transfer points.

❶ bus essentials

⏱ 24 hours daily, but they run less frequently after midnight.

💲 $1.50 flat fare.

Paying by MetroCard™: insert card as you get on. This entitles you to a free ride when connecting with the subway or another bus within two hours.

Paying by coins: drop into slot in front of the driver. Exact fare only, but you can also use subway tokens.

♻ 1| Buses run along all avenues and on major cross-streets; generally they are the best public transport option for cross-town travel.

2| Free sightseeing tour of the city.

♻ Don't go anywhere near a bus if you're in a hurry.

❶ Even when paying for your ride with coins or a token, you can ask for a transfer ticket, which allows you to catch another bus for free (within two hours); ie after a cross-town bus ride,

you can also hop on an uptown or downtown bus and vice versa.

do

1| Have your exact fare, token, or MetroCard™ ready.

2| Shout if the driver forgets to open the back doors.

don't

Smoke on buses.

☎ **useful numbers:**

Travel info (6am–9pm daily):
1-718-330-1234

Customer service:
1-718-330-3322

Lost & found:
1-718-625-6200

cabs

• The yellow cab is synonymous with Manhattan. Careering madly through traffic, cabs always seem able to move in even the thickest of jams; nevertheless in gridlocks the predominant colour is always yellow.

• In case you forget to 'belt up, take all of your belongings, and get a receipt', an automated celebrity voiceover will remind you. Everyone from Dr Ruth, the sex columnist, to Pavarotti has given their two-cents worth.

using yellow cabs

You can stop a cab if the middle panel only on the cab is lit. During rush hours, the competition is fierce. It is a good idea to have at least a vague notion of how to get where you want to go. 'Politely' suggest your favoured route and keep an eye open for unnecessarily long detours. Yellow cabs usually only take four people.

transport

☎ **useful numbers:**
Lost property: 302-8294
Taxi Limousine Commission: 676-1000
(for complaints)

❶ cab essentials

• Taxis are metered: the fare starts at $2 and rises 30¢/0.5 mile, or 30¢/90 seconds in slow traffic or when stationary.
• Having successfully hailed a cab, get in quickly. The driver is likely to start moving before you've even told him where you want to go.
• Tip 15–20% – or else!
• Most drivers don't like to change anything bigger than a $20 note. Pay the driver while still seated in the back of the cab.
♧ There are lots and lots!
♧ 1| Although plentiful at all other times, in bad weather conditions forgeddaboutit.
2| Get in before you ask to go to Brooklyn or the Bronx, as legally they cannot then refuse you, but most drivers have threadbare knowledge of the outer boroughs.
do
Use them – taking a cab is not considered a luxury in NY.
don't
1| Argue with the driver: in yellow cabs the customer is never right.
2| Smoke – the driver could lose his licence.

car services

Generally referred to as 'cars', not 'minicabs', and suitable for longer journeys. The company should supply a driver who is familiar with the neighbourhood you are going to.
♧ 1| Convenient if you are not near a busy main street, or if it is late or raining.

2| You can specify what kind of car (eg 'station wagon' if there are more than four of you).
♧ Poor language skills, bad driving and no sense of direction... only the worst-case scenario.
❶ 1| When they say they'll be there in '5 minutes', they mean it!
2| You must look out for them – drivers never ring the bell.
3| Check the price of the ride before you set off or, better still, with the controller when you order the car.

do
Only call when you are ready to leave.
don't
Get in a gypsy cab (unlicensed, unmarked cars) – they will rip you off.

☎ **useful numbers:**
Downtown Delancey Car Service: 228-3301
Brooklyn Evelyn Car Service: 1-718-230-7800/8244
Random Carmel: 1-800-924-9954/666-6666
Tel Aviv: 1-800-222-9888/777-7777

cars

Since New York's public transport system is both relatively efficient and inexpensive, the only reason to rent a car is to get out of town. Driving and parking in the city gives new meaning to the word nightmare, and only the most foolhardy would want to share the road with New York's army of yellow cab maniacs.

rules of the road in NYC

• Drive on the right.
• You cannot make a right turn on a

red light.
• Seatbelts are compulsory in front and rear seats.
• School buses are sacred and the fines for passing one which has stopped are huge.
• Do not park within 50 ft of a fire hydrant.
• Speed limit is 30 mph.
• Vandalism and car theft are rife.

car hire

Nowhere do the rules of supply and demand apply more than in New York's car rental business – prices rocket on a holiday weekend. If you call one of the major rental agencies, be prepared: know from what location you want to rent, how long for, and the exact dates – all of these factors affect cost and availability (average $50–60 per day). You must have a major credit card, a passport, and a valid driver's licence (foreign licences are accepted). Large companies have a minimum age of 25, but for an extra $10–30 per day, they'll bend the rules.

❶ 1| You should always get the most comprehensive insurance.
2| It's cheaper to rent from outside the city. Ask the big companies for their regional office locations.

☎ **useful numbers:**
A-1 Value: 348-5151
Avis: 1-800-831-2847
Budget: 1-800-527-0700
Enterprise: 1-800-325-8007
Hertz: 1-800-654-3131
Rent-a-Wreck: 1-718-784-3302
They will pick you up at the station (based in Long Island City).
Gas
Gas stations in Manhattan are few and

far between. These two are reliable and open 24 hours:
Uptown: Atlas Garage, 303 W 96th St (bet. West End Drive & Riverside Drive).
Downtown: Amoco, 610 Broadway (at Houston Street).

Parking meters and lots
Meters: depending on the neighbourhood and the time of day, it will cost you anything from 25¢ (for 20 min) to 25¢ (for 1 hr). If you are towed, call the helpline (Mon–Fri) and expect a fine of around $150.
☎ 1-718-422-7800
Lots: private parking lots are more expensive but at least you are guaranteed to find your car in one piece.

do
Note signs on the side of streets indicating which days the street cleaners come.
don't
Park anywhere a sign says 'no stopping' or 'no standing'; in a bus stop; or by a fire hydrant.

bicycles

• Most cycle routes are in city parks, but if you've got the guts, cycling is an excellent way to see the city. Though not illegal, it would be unwise to ride without a helmet or lights.
• Cyclists must follow the same road rules as car drivers and fines for running red lights or riding without a bell (!) in Midtown are commonplace.

Bike rental: A security deposit of $150 held on a credit card is usually required.

Bike hire:
Bikes in the Park

Loeb Boathouse, Central Park
(summer only). ☎ 861-4137
⊠ $8–$10 per hr (5- or 10-speed bikes)

Bicycles Plus
Second Avenue (bet. 87th & 88th Sts)
☎ 722-2201
⊠ $7.50/hr or $25/day

Metro Bike
14th Street (bet. First & Second Aves)
☎ 228-4344
1311 Lexington Avenue (at 88th Street)
☎ 427-4450
Sixth Avenue (at 15th Street) ☎ 255-5100
417 Canal Street ☎ 334-8000
⊠ $7/hr or $45/day.

roller blades

So, you really want to get around in a
hurry, while looking cool. Try blading it.
Only for the very proficient.

☎ **Roller Blade hire**
Blades East & West
160 E 86th Street (bet. Lexington &
Third Aves) ☎ 996-1644
105 W 72nd Street (bet. Columbus Ave
& Broadway) ☎ 787-3911
Second Avenue (at 74th St) ☎ 249-3178
⊠ $16 per day Mon–Fri; $27 per day
Sat–Sun
❶ hire includes free protective gear.

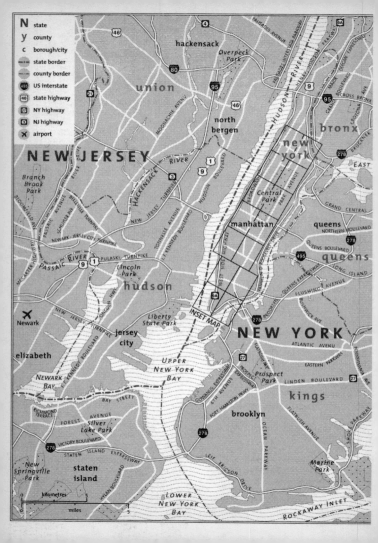

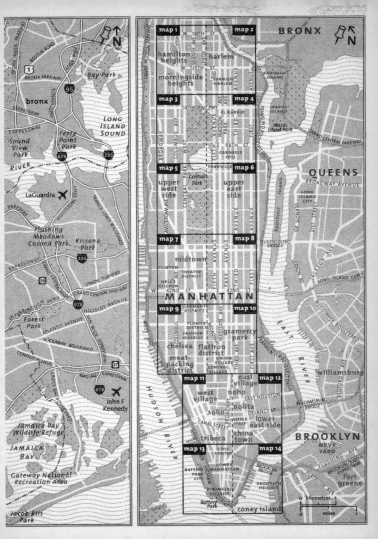

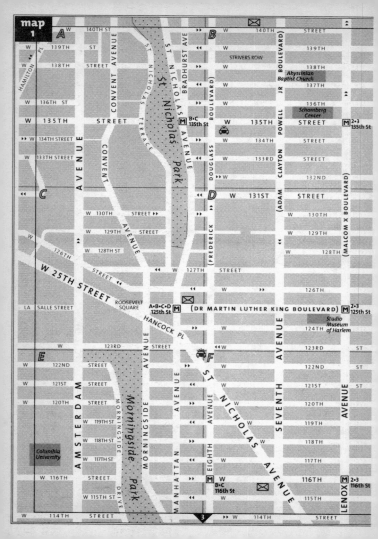

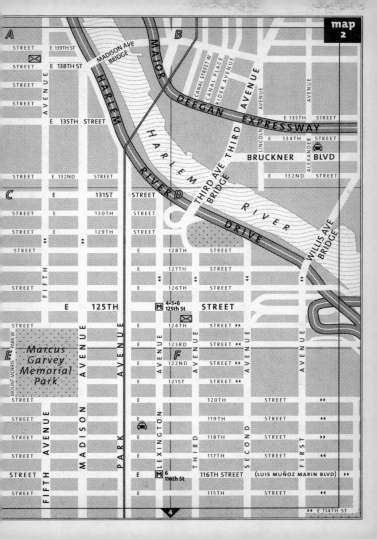

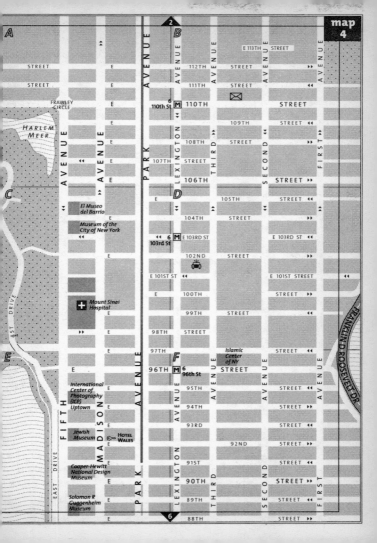

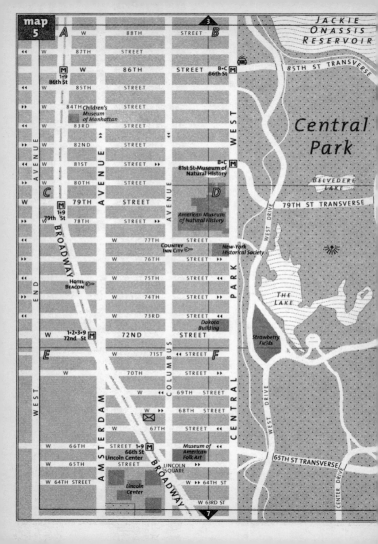

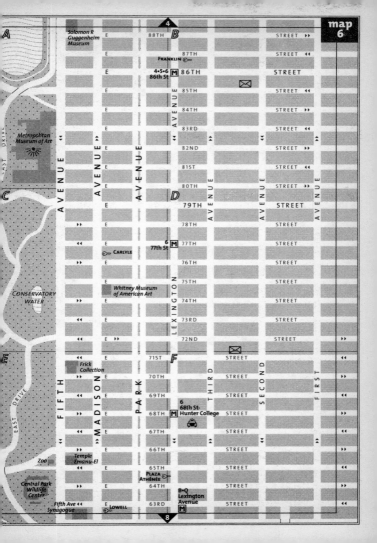

map
7

Lincoln Center

5

Central Park

A W 62ND STREET

◄◄ W 61ST STREET

►► W 60TH STREET ◄◄

W 59TH STREET

BROADWAY

B

COLUMBUS CIRCLE

A•B•C•D•1•9
59th St-
Columbus Circle M

CENTRAL PARK

W 58TH STREET ►►
HUDSON

N•R
57th St M

B•Q
57th St M

W 57TH STREET
Carnegie Hall

W 56TH STREET ►►

W 55TH STREET

C
W 54TH STREET

D
W 53RD STREET
NYCVB ℹ
B•D•F
7th Ave M

W 52ND STREET

W 51ST STREET
✉

C•E
50th St M
W 50TH STREET
1•9
50th St M

Canadian Consulate

B•D•F•Q
47th-50th Sts-
Rockefeller Center M

W 49TH STREET
TIME
N•R
49th St M

Hell's Kitchen Park
W 48TH STREET

BROADWAY

W 47TH STREET
EDISON HOTEL
PARAMOUNT

W 46TH STREET
BROADWAY INN

E
W 45TH STREET

F

Virgin Megastore

W 44TH STREET

W 43RD STREET
CASABLANCA

Times Square

ICP Midtow

W 42ND STREET
A•C•E
42nd St-
Port Authority
Bus Terminal M
N•R•1•
2•3•7•9
Times Square-
42nd St M
Times Square
Visitor Information Center ℹ

B•D•F•Q
42nd St M

W 41ST STREET ◄◄
✉

**Port Authority
Bus Terminal**

W 40TH STREET

BROADWAY

W 39TH STREET

W 38TH STREET
✉

W 37TH STREET

9

W 36TH STREET

AMSTERDAM AVENUE

NINTH AVENUE

EIGHTH AVENUE

SEVENTH AVENUE (FASHION AVE)

AVENUE OF THE AMERICAS (AVENUE)

SIXTH AVENUE

ELEVENTH AVENUE

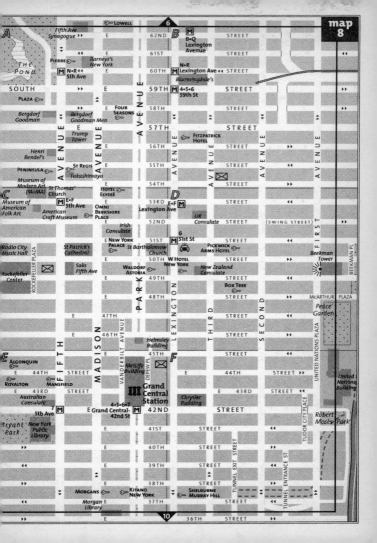

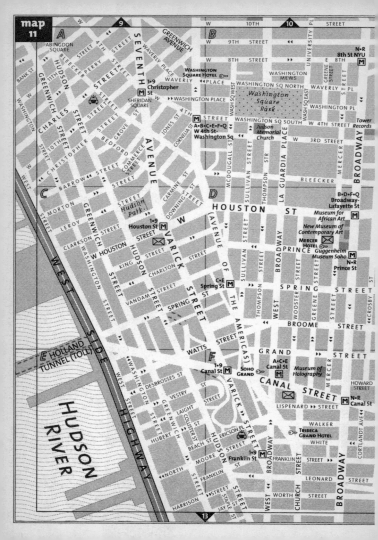

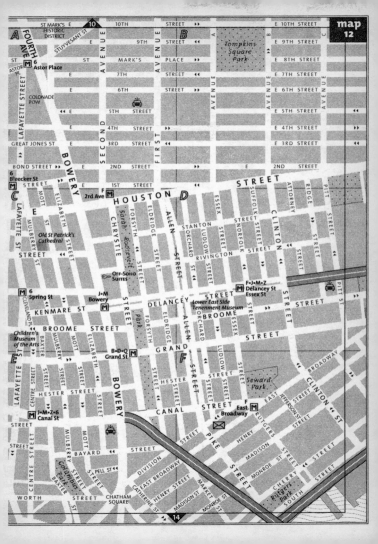

ST MARK'S E 10TH STREET ▶▶ E 10TH STREET
HISTORIC
DISTRICT
A STUYVESANT ST 9TH STREET ◀◀ E 9TH STREET B
ST MARK'S PLACE ▶▶ E 8TH STREET
M 6 Astor Place
COLONADE 7TH STREET ◀◀ E 7TH STREET
ROW 6TH STREET ▶▶ E 6TH STREET
5TH STREET ◀◀ E 5TH STREET ◀◀
4TH STREET ▶▶ E 4TH STREET ▶▶
GREAT JONES ST 3RD STREET ◀◀ E 3RD STREET
BOND STREET ▶▶ E 2ND STREET E 2ND STREET

6 Bleecker St
M STREET
C 2nd Ave F M HOUSTON D
Old St Patrick's
Cathedral
STREET ◀◀
Off-Soho
Suites
M 6 Spring St J·M
Bowery M DELANCEY STREET F·J·M·Z
Delancey St
KENMARE ST Lower East Side Essex St
Tenement Museum
BROOME STREET BROOME STREET
Children's
Museum
of the Arts
E B·D·Q F
Grand St M GRAND
STREET
Seward
HESTER STREET Park
J·M·Z·6 CANAL
M Canal St STREET East M
Broadway
STREET
STREET
BAYARD STREET
PELL ST ◀◀
COLUMBUS
PARK
WORTH STREET CHATHAM
SQUARE

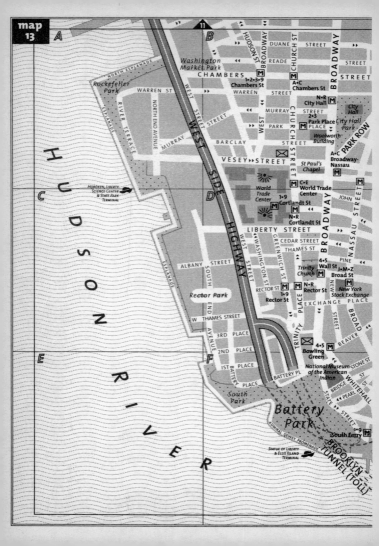

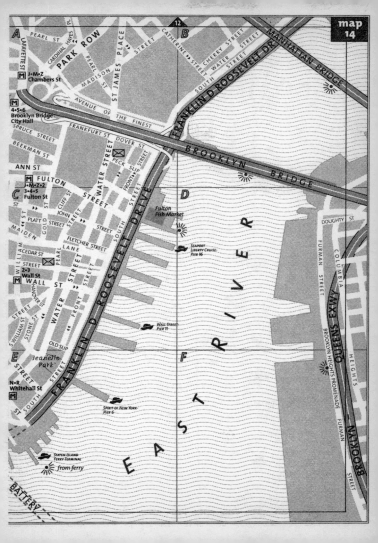

key to symbols

☎ telephone number
▣ recorded information line
F fax
e email
w worldwide web
❶ hot tips
◑ opening times
♿ wheelchair access
☞ hotel
⏲ frequency/times
♯ map reference
▤ credit cards
  AE = American Express
  DC = Diners Club
  MC = Mastercard
  V = Visa
  all = AE/DC/MC/V
  are accepted

☆ recommended (featured in listings section)

restaurants
$ cheap (main courses under $10 excluding taxes)
$$ moderate (main courses $10–$20 excluding taxes)
$$$ expensive (main courses over $20 excluding taxes)

entertainment
♗ capacity
👑 dress code

transport
👍 good points
👎 bad points
Ⓜ subway
▢ city bus/coach
▣ shuttle bus
🚗 cabs
Ⅲ trains
✈ airport
🚢 ferry/cruise boat pier

hotels
♠ number of beds
🍽 breakfast included
▤ air conditioning
⏰ 24-hour room service
↔ fitness facilities
✎ business facilities
✿ outdoor area/garden
☕ restaurant/café
🍺 bar/pub
🅿 parking

key to map symbols

⬤ sight/museum/gallery/landmark/notable building/shop
◌ park/garden/square
🚉 train station
Ⓜ subway station
ℹ tourist information
🚌 bus terminal
⚓ ferry

⚜ view point
➤ one-way street
🚓 police station
✉ post office
⌂ hotel
➕ hospital casualty unit
A1 map reference

acknowledgements

Conceived, edited & designed by
Virgin Publishing Ltd
London w6 9ha

Editorial assistance: Tim Brown, Jessica Hughes
Index: Hilary Bird
Cartographic editor: Dominic Beddow
Cartographer: Simonetta Giori
Draughtsman Ltd, London
020 8960 1602 | Email: mail@magneticnorth.net

Printed by Omnia Books Ltd, Scotland

Based on information from the Virgin Guide to New York written and researched by:
Transport: Katya Rogers | **Getting Your Bearings (areas):** Katya Rogers | **Area intros:** Eve Claxton | **Shopping:** Julie Besonen, Eve Claxton, Michael Dolan, C Leggett, Denise Maher, Karen Robinovitz | **Restaurants:** Julie Besonen, Karen Robinovitz, Kate Sekules | **Bars:** Diana Shafter, Angela Tribelli | **Brooklyn:** Alfred Gingold, Helen Rogan | **Landmarks:** Katya Rogers | **Sights, Museums and Galleries:** Karen Robinovitz, Walter Robinson, Katya Rogers | **Sport and Kids:** Anngel Delaney | **Parks & Beaches:** Katya Rogers | **Body & Soul and Game for a Laugh:** Karen Robinovitz | **Entertainment:** Michael Atkinson (cinema), Dan Bova (comedy), Lorie Caval (clubs), Viven Goldman (music & poetry), Scott Jolley (cabaret), Ann Midgette (dance, opera & classical music, theatre), Katya Rogers (media and events) | **Hotels:** Brekke Fletcher, Monica Forrestall | **Practical:** Katya Rogers.

Acknowledgements and credits:
New York subway and bus maps were reproduced with the permission of MTA New York City Transit.

Great care has been taken with this guide to be as accurate and up-to-date as possible, but details such as addresses, telephone numbers, opening hours, prices and travel information are liable to change.
The publishers cannot accept responsibility for any consequences arising from the use of this book. We would be delighted to receive any corrections and suggestions for inclusion in the next edition.

Please write to or email:
Virgin Travel Guides
Virgin Publishing Ltd
Thames Wharf Studios
Rainville Road
London w6 9ha
Fax: 020 7386 3360
Email: travel@virgin-pub.co.uk

notes